THE
COOK'S
COMPANION

THE
COOK'S
COMPANION

The definitive cook's guide

First published in 2011

LOVE FOOD is an imprint of Parragon Books Ltd

Parragon
Queen Street House
4 Queen Street
Bath BA1 1HE, UK

www.parragon.com

ISBN: 978-1-4454-4689-9

Printed in China

Seasonal Food Chart by Christine McFadden

Cover illustration by Georgina Luck, www.georginaluck.com

This book uses imperial, metric, and US cup measurements. Follow the same units of measurement throughout; do not mix imperial and metric. All spoon measurements are level: teaspoons are assumed to be 5 ml, and tablespoons are assumed to be 15 ml. Unless otherwise stated, milk is assumed to be whole, eggs and individual vegetables, such as potatoes, are medium, and pepper is freshly ground black pepper.

The times given are an approximate guide only. Preparation times differ according to the techniques used by different people and the cooking times may also vary from those given as a result of the type of oven used. Optional ingredients, variations, or serving suggestions have not been included in the calculations.

Recipes using raw or very lightly cooked eggs should be avoided by infants, the elderly, pregnant women, convalescents, and anyone with a chronic condition. Pregnant and breast-feeding women are advised to avoid eating peanuts and peanut products. People with nut allergies should be aware that some of the prepared ingredients used in the recipes in this book may contain nuts. Always check the package before use.

Picture Acknowledgements
The publisher would like to thank the following for permission to reproduce copyright material on the following pages:

Getty images: 2, 4-5, 8-9, 10, 11, 12, 48-49, 74-75, 100-101, 126-127, 152-153, 178-179, 204-205, 230-231, 256-257, 261

Introduction

Seasonal Food Chart

	Spring			Summer			Fall			Winter		
FISH & SEAFOOD	Early	Mid	Late	Early	Mid	Late	Early	Mid	Late	Early	Mid	Late
Clam (California)	•	•							•	•	•	•
Clam (East Coast/Pacific)	•	•	•	•	•	•	•	•	•	•	•	•
Cod	•	•	•	•	•	•	•	•	•	•	•	•
Crab, soft-shell		•	•	•	•	•	•					
Haddock				•	•	•	•	•				
Halibut	•	•	•	•	•	•	•	•				
Lobster	•	•	•	•	•	•	•	•	•	•	•	•
Mussel (West Coast)	•	•							•	•	•	•
Salmon (Atlantic)				•						•		
Salmon (Pacific)	•	•	•	•	•	•	•	•	•			
Sardines				•	•							
Scallop, bay (East Coast)							•	•	•			
Scallop, sea	•	•							•	•	•	•
Swordfish			•	•	•	•	•					
Tuna			•	•	•	•	•					
MEAT												
Beef	•	•	•	•	•	•	•	•	•	•	•	•
Lamb	•	•	•	•	•	•	•	•	•	•	•	•
Pork	•	•	•	•	•	•	•	•	•	•	•	•
POULTRY												
Chicken	•	•	•	•	•	•	•	•	•	•	•	•
Duck	•	•	•	•	•	•	•	•	•	•	•	•
Goose				•	•	•	•	•	•	•	•	•
Pheasant	•	•	•	•	•	•	•	•	•	•	•	•
Quail	•	•	•	•	•	•	•	•	•	•	•	•
Turkey	•	•	•	•	•	•	•	•	•	•	•	•
VEGETABLES												
Arugula	•	•	•	•								
Asparagus	•	•	•	•	•		•					•
Bean, fava				•	•					•	•	•
Bean, green				•	•	•	•	•				
Bean, lima				•	•	•	•	•	•			
Bean, runner					•	•	•	•				
Beet	•				•	•	•	•	•	•	•	•
Broccoli	•	•	•				•	•	•			
Brussel sprouts (North)							•	•	•	•	•	•
Cabbage	•	•	•	•		•	•	•	•	•		
Cabbage, Chinese							•	•	•			
Carrot				•	•		•	•	•	•	•	
Cauliflower	•	•	•				•	•	•	•	•	•
Celery				•	•	•				•	•	•
Chile				•	•	•	•					
Corn			•	•	•	•	•					
Cucumber			•	•	•	•						
Eggplant						•	•					
Fennel	•	•	•				•	•	•			

Many fresh produce is now available year round; however, choosing products when they are at their peak will provide the best flavor and nutrients. Because growing seasons vary from region to region, this is only an approximate guide to peak seasons when vegetables, fruit, and herbs are at there best. The seasons for fish and shellfish apply to wild, not farmed, food.

	Spring			Summer			Fall			Winter		
	Early	Mid	Late	Early	Mid	Late	Early	Mid	Late	Early	Mid	Late
Garlic (fresh)			•	•	•	•	•	•				
Globe artichoke	•	•	•									
Jerusalem artichoke	•							•	•	•	•	•
Leek	•							•	•	•	•	•
Lettuce	•	•	•				•	•	•	•	•	•
Mushroom, button							•	•	•	•	•	•
Onion	•	•	•	•	•	•	•	•	•	•	•	•
Parsnip	•						•	•	•	•	•	•
Pea		•	•	•								
Pepper, sweet					•	•	•	•				
Potato	•	•	•	•	•	•	•	•	•	•	•	•
Pumpkin							•	•	•	•	•	•
Radish	•	•	•				•	•	•			
Rutabaga							•	•	•	•		•
Scallion	•	•	•	•	•	•						
Shallot	•	•	•									
Spinach	•	•	•				•	•	•			
Squash, winter (e.g. butternut)	•						•	•	•	•	•	•
Sweet potato										•	•	•
Tomato					•	•	•	•				
Turnip	•							•	•	•	•	•
Watercress	•	•	•	•	•	•	•	•	•	•	•	•
Zucchini and summer squash				•	•							
HERBS												
Basil			•	•	•	•	•					
Chives	•	•	•	•	•	•	•	•	•	•	•	•
Cilantro		•	•	•	•	•	•	•	•			
Dill			•	•	•	•	•					
Mint			•	•	•	•	•					
Oregano		•	•	•	•	•	•	•	•	•	•	•
Parsley, curly	•	•	•	•	•	•	•	•	•	•	•	•
Parsley, flat-leaf		•	•	•	•	•	•	•	•			
Rosemary	•	•	•	•	•	•	•	•	•			
Sage	•	•	•	•	•	•	•	•				
Tarragon				•	•	•	•	•				
Thyme	•	•	•	•	•	•	•	•	•	•	•	•
FRUIT												
Apple	•						•	•	•	•	•	•
Blackberry			•	•	•	•						
Blueberry				•	•	•	•					
Cherry			•	•	•	•						
Cranberry								•	•	•		
Grape						•	•	•				
Melon					•	•	•	•				
Orange and other citrus	•	•	•	•	•	•	•	•	•	•		
Peach and nectarine			•	•	•	•	•	•				
Pear	•						•	•	•	•	•	•
Plum			•	•	•	•	•	•				
Raspberry			•	•	•	•	•	•	•			
Strawberry		•	•	•								

Healthy Eating

The American writer Marjorie Rawlings once said that food imaginatively and lovingly prepared, eaten in good company, warms the soul with something more than mere calories. While this is true, it is also true that the human body needs a regular and balanced intake of over 70 nutrients, such as vitamins and minerals, in order to keep it working properly and protect it from disease.

Dietary needs

A healthy and balanced diet that includes food from all of the food groups will provide adequate amounts of your dietary needs for protein, carbohydrates, fat, minerals, and vitamins.

Protein

Protein provides the building blocks for the body. Everyone's requirement differs, depending on health, age, and size, but as a rough guide, the average minimum requirement is around 1¾ oz/50 g per day. There are two types of protein: complete protein, found in foods of animal origin, such as meat, poultry, fish, eggs, milk, and cheese, and in certain plants, such as buckwheat and quinoa; and incomplete protein, found in foods of nonanimal origin, such as nuts, seeds, grains, beans, and other legumes. Complete proteins provide the proper balance of amino acids necessary to build body tissues; incomplete proteins need to be mixed with other types of protein in order to provide adequate nutrition.

Carbohydrates

The main source of the body's energy is carbohydrates. No official daily requirement exists, but a minimum of 1¾ oz/50 g daily is recommended to avoid an acid condition of the blood called "ketosis." This condition occurs when your body has to use fat instead of carbohydrates to provide its energy.

Carbohydrates are, therefore, an essential part of a healthy human diet. They can be found in starchy and sugary foods. There are two types of carbohydrate: complex carbohydrates, which can be found in bread, pasta, rice, cereals, beans and other legumes, fruit, and vegetables; and simple carbohydrates, which can be found in many desserts, cakes, chocolate, candies, and soft drinks.

Complex carbohydrates take longer to be broken down in the body, which means they release energy into the body more slowly and gradually. These are the best carbohydrates to eat. The sugary, simple type of carbohydrate will provide a quick boost of energy, but this surge of energy is quickly used up; such "highs and lows" of energy are not good for maintaining good health and vitality.

Fats

These days we are encouraged to eat a low-fat diet, but to cut fat out completely would be unhealthy. What we should be doing is eating the types of fat that are good for us, and reducing our intake of the potentially harmful kinds. Saturated fat is potentially harmful in excessive amounts: it can raise our blood cholesterol levels and blood pressure.

A good way to remember which foods are high in saturated fat is to think of those fats that stay solid at room temperature, such as lard and butter. It is these kinds of solid fats that clog our arteries and can lead to heart disease. The healthier kinds of fat are polyunsaturated fats, such as sunflower oil and soybean oil, and mono-unsaturated fats, such as olive oil and peanut oil. We also need a regular intake of essential fatty acids (EFAs): these actually help the body to burn off excess fat. Good sources of EFAs include oily fish, sunflower seeds, pumpkin seeds, and avocados. So it is not true to say that all fat is bad for you. Restrict saturated fat in your diet by all means, but not the other kinds. Remember also that a low-fat diet is unsuitable for children under five years of age.

Minerals

There are 18 minerals required for healthy body function, and the 6 best-known minerals are: calcium (found in milk, cheese, and beans), iodine (found in seafood, kelp, and onions), iron (found in red meat, egg yolks, oysters, nuts, and beans), magnesium (found in figs, lemons, nuts, seeds, and apples), phosphorus (found in meat, poultry, fish, whole grains, eggs, nuts, and seeds), and zinc (found in steak, wheat germ, brewer's yeast, eggs, and pumpkin seeds). Minerals are essential for maintaining good health. For example, a deficiency of calcium can lead to rickets or osteoporosis, and a deficiency of iron can cause anemia.

Vitamins

This food group comprises organic substances that can be found within the foods we eat. We need only minuscule amounts of these substances in order to be healthy, but a deficiency of even one type of vitamin can cause us to be unhealthy. Vitamins range from the "fat-soluble" kind, such as A (found in green leafy vegetables, liver, and dairy products), D (found in fish liver oils, sardines, tuna, and dairy products), and E (found in soybeans, whole wheat and grains, and eggs), to the "water-soluble" kind, such as C (found in citrus fruit, green leafy vegetables, and tomatoes). Some people think that it is possible to live on only vitamin pills, but this concept is a myth: vitamins are only one of the main nutrients necessary for a healthy body. It is always preferable to get your vitamins naturally from the foods you eat instead of from synthetic materials such as pills, because synthetic vitamins can sometimes cause toxic reactions. Natural vitamins are much safer.

Making the right choices

It is vital to make good food choices and eat sensibly. Did you know, for example, that a diet high in salt and saturated fat can increase the risk of heart disease, while eating other foods, such as beans, can help to reduce cholesterol and prevent heart disease? The message here is that what you absorb into your body plays a crucial role in your health and overall well-being, Eating more of the right foods, and reducing your intake of the potentially harmful ones, can contribute greatly to how well you feel and the state of your physical health.

So which are the right foods to eat and which are the wrong ones? It is not always easy to decide. For example, too much salt can lead to higher blood pressure and depleted adrenal glands, but to cut it out completely would be very unwise because we need a certain amount each day in order to stay healthy. Salt actually helps to keep our fluid levels in balance and our muscles healthy. The amount we need, however, is very low—less than 5 g/1 teaspoon per day. Because many foods we buy have salt added already—for example, cheese or prepared foods, such as pizzas, cookies, or sauces—we can usually get the amount we need without having to add extra salt to our meals. It is the habit of adding extra salt to our food that tends to push us over the healthy limit. Basically, a balanced diet should consist of plenty of fruit, vegetables, whole grains and cereals, dairy products, and smaller quantities of protein foods from animal sources (such as meat, fish, eggs, or dairy products) as well as from nonanimal sources (such as beans, peas, nuts, and seeds). A vegetarian diet is also perfectly healthy as long as it is balanced and contains all the essential nutrients.

DOS AND DON'TS FOR A HEALTHY DIET

Here are some tips to help keep your diet healthy and your body in peak physical condition:

DO eat regular meals—never skip them, especially breakfast. Skipping meals will encourage your body to go into "starvation mode," which causes it to store more fat.

DO eat at least five portions of fruit and vegetables each day. They can be fresh, frozen, or canned, but vary them as much as possible. Not all fruit and vegetables contain the same amount of health-giving nutrients, but when you are in any doubt, you can estimate that one portion is equal to about 3 oz/85 g. Any of the following foods equal a portion:

• one ⅔ cup of fruit juice
• one orange, apple, nectarine, peach, or banana
• half a grapefruit
• two plums
• one-quarter of a cucumber
• one bell pepper or tomato
• ½ cup of cauliflower or broccoli
• three heaping tablespoons of any vegetable, for example, peas, carrots, beans, or diced carrots or bell peppers.

DO eat more whole grains, such as oats, barley, rye, and corn. Choose whole wheat bread and pasta instead of white types, and brown rice instead of polished white rice.

DO eat oily fish regularly, at least three times a week if possible.

DO choose organic produce wherever possible: organic foods are free from artificial additives and pesticides, and are a much healthier choice.

DO drink at least eight 8 fl oz/ 225 ml glasses of water a day. This means consumption of at least 2 quarts/1.7 liters daily. You need a regular and adequate intake of water to flush toxins from the body and replace water lost through urine and sweat. Inadequate water consumption leads to dehydration with symptoms, such as headaches, tiredness, and loss of concentration. Prolonged dehydration can lead to constipation and kidney stones.

DON'T eat too much saturated fat. Reduce your intake of greasy fried foods and fatty red meat.

DON'T eat too many sugary foods, such as candies, chocolate, cakes and other desserts, and soft drinks.

DON'T buy processed foods. Processed foods are often full of artificial additives, such as preservatives, colors, and sweeteners—even packaged salad greens have undergone chemical processing before they reach the retailers' shelves. Instead, choose foods that are fresh and in their natural state. The benefits in terms of better flavor and more health-giving nutrients far outweigh the convenience of prepared, packaged foods.

DON'T drink too much caffeine. It is a powerful stimulant and can make you feel lively, but in excess it can lead to health problems. Too much caffeine can lead to irritability, insomnia, and feverish symptoms. Very high doses can cause more serious problems. It has been reported that people who drink five or more cups of coffee a day have a 50 percent higher risk of a heart attack than people who do not drink coffee. The main sources of caffeine are coffee, tea, cola drinks, and cocoa, so avoid these drinks as much as possible. Switch to herbal teas and fruit juices instead. Some medicines also contain caffeine, so check the ingredients before you take them, and use an alternative if possible.

DON'T consume too much alcohol. Women should drink no more than 1 drink a day, and men should drink no more than 2 drinks a day. A standard drink is 12 fl oz/350 ml of beer, 5 fl oz/150 ml of wine, or 1½ fl oz/45 ml or a shot of liquor. Try to keep at least two days a week alcohol free, and don't save up your weekly unit allowance for consumption on a single occasion.

DON'T add salt to your food. Alternatively, taste the food before you add salt, then keep the added salt to a minimum.

Health & Safety

The kitchen is often the focal point of the home. However, it is also the riskiest area: fires are much more likely to break out in the kitchen than in any other part of the home, and there is a risk of infestation by pests or potentially harmful bacteria. Adopting good hygiene habits and taking sensible precautions will protect your household from unnecessary accidents and illnesses.

Kitchen hygiene

Cleanliness is essential in the kitchen. Keep all kitchen surfaces scrupulously clean, and wash your hands thoroughly with soap and water before preparing food. Use a separate towel to dry your hands, not a dish towel. Whenever you leave the kitchen or touch a surface, such as a door handle or a curtain, even if it is only for a few moments, remember that your hands will quickly pick up bacteria, even if you think your home is scrupulously clean, so always wash your hands again before resuming any food preparation.

Make sure you use different cutting boards and utensils for cooked and raw foods to prevent cross-contamination of bacteria, especially when you are preparing meat or poultry. If you can afford it and have the room to store them, it is a good idea to have several cutting boards in different colors for different purposes. You can keep one for raw meat, one for cooked meat, one for vegetables, one for a pet's food, and so on. Wash cutting boards and utensils well in hot, soapy water before and after each use. Glass and plastic cutting boards can be washed at relatively high temperatures in the dishwasher.

Change and wash dish cloths and towels regularly. Use a covered trash can and disinfect it frequently.

Food preparation

Make sure that you thoroughly wash any foods that need cleaning, such as soil-covered vegetables, and pat dry with paper towels. You should also thoroughly defrost any frozen food that requires it, especially meat and poultry, and do not refreeze once it has thawed. The best place to defrost food is in the refrigerator. However, if you are short of time, you can defrost it in a cool room as long as it is well covered to prevent any potentially harmful bacteria from contaminating it.

Throw away any thawed juices from meat and poultry— do not use them in your dishes. And remember never to reuse a marinade, especially if it has been used for meat or poultry.

When reheating cooked meat dishes, remember that they may be reheated only once, and must reach a temperature of at least 167°F/75°C.

Do not leave cooked rice uncovered at room temperature for any length of time. Potentially harmful bacteria can multiply quickly on cooked rice, so if you have to store it, let it cool, cover it with plastic wrap as soon as possible, and keep it in the refrigerator. Use it within two days. The same goes for any cooked meats or poultry.

Safe storage

Always buy food as fresh as possible, and from a reputable supplier. Check any expiration dates, because sometimes out-of-date items languish on retailers' shelves and are bought by the unwary. Cover all exposed foods with plastic wrap before refrigerating. If you buy a whole bird, remove any giblets from the cavity, cover with plastic wrap, and refrigerate separately from the bird. Store raw and cooked meat and poultry separately in different parts of your refrigerator. Store raw meat on the bottom shelf to prevent it from dripping into other foods.

Store your potatoes in a dark place, away from sunlight, or they will turn green—even fluorescent lighting can make them turn green. Green patches in potatoes contain a chemical called solanine. Solanine is bitter, and in large concentrations it can give you stomachache. Do not buy potatoes with green patches. If, however, a potato you have bought or grown does develop a small green patch, cut the patch out, then use the rest of the potato. If the green covers a large area, discard the whole potato.

Kitchen first aid

Every kitchen should have a basic first-aid kit. Your standard kit should include rubber gloves, antiseptic wipes, burn cream, eye pads, safety pins, dressings in different sizes, and triangular bandages. Catering establishments use blue bandages in order to make them easier to see if they fall off. Although you don't have to use this type at home, their deep blue coloring makes them ideal for home use, too.

A fire blanket is also a good precaution in a kitchen. It can be a very useful item to have on hand in case a fire breaks out, and it can also be used to help keep a shock victim comfortable until help arrives.

FIRE SAFETY

As an absolute minimum, fit a battery-operated smoke alarm outside your kitchen, and check the battery regularly. Do not position it in the kitchen itself or over a direct source of smoke or heat, or it may be set off accidentally. Even better, ask a qualified electrician to install smoke and heat detectors throughout your home—for reliability, they should be connected to your main electricity supply.

It is also a good idea to keep a fire extinguisher in the kitchen. Here are some other tips for kitchen fire safety:
• Keep electrical cords, oven mitts, and dish towels away from the oven.
• Keep your oven clean, especially the broiler. A buildup of fat can catch fire.
• Do not let your sleeves or other loose clothing hang over the stove while you are cooking.
• Never leave pans on the stove unattended. If you have to leave them, even for a few seconds, perhaps to answer the telephone, remove them from the heat.
• When you've finished cooking, make sure the stove or oven is turned off.
• If a pan catches fire and you can't put it out easily and quickly, don't take any risks with your safety. Leave the house at once (making sure that you close all doors behind you as you go), and call the fire department immediately. If the fire is small and you are confident you can handle it, put a fire blanket over it, or alternatively run a cloth under the faucet, wring it out, and then cover the pan with it. Do not throw water into the pan because this action could exacerbate the problem. Turn off the heat as soon as you can get to it safely.

Equipment

A selection of carefully chosen tools is essential in the kitchen. If you are a beginner, you can make do with a few multipurpose utensils, then add to them as your confidence grows. If you are an experienced cook, you may want to add some more sophisticated items, such as a pasta machine, to your range of tools.

Bread knife

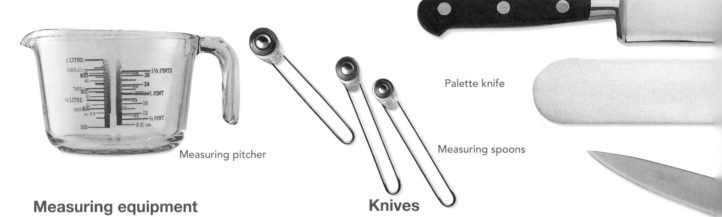

Carving knife

Palette knife

Measuring pitcher

Measuring spoons

Measuring equipment

The items listed here are useful for measuring liquids and solid foods. If you have a measuring pitcher, spoons, or scales with both imperial and metric measurements, use only one type of measurement.

Measuring pitcher
Usually available in a 2-cup size, a measuring pitcher has marks down the side that are useful for measuring liquid ingredients. For accurate measuring, bend down so the marks are at eye level.

Measuring spoons
These spoons are ideal for measuring both liquid and dry ingredients accurately. Unless otherwise indicated in a recipe, level off the ingredient with the straight edge of a knife.

Measuring cups
A nesting set of measuring cups usually comes in four different sizes: ¼, ⅓, ½, and 1 cup. They are available in stainless steel or plastic. Unless otherwise indicated in a recipe, level off the ingredient with the straight edge of a knife.

Kitchen scales
Professional cooks, particularly bakers, sometimes use scales for measuring dry ingredients, because these are more accurate than using measuring cups.

Knives

Buy the best-quality knives you can afford because they will last longer, and keep them sharp. The first three listed here are the essential knives; the rest can be added later.

Small paring knife
A paring knife is invaluable for cutting vegetables, fruit, meat, and cheese. It is 2½–3½ inches/6–9 cm in length.

Cook's knife
This good multipurpose knife is 6–12 inches/15–30 cm long, and is essential for slicing and chopping.

Bread knife
This long, serrated knife is ideal for slicing bread.

Small serrated knife
This knife is most often used for cutting vegetables and fruit. It is usually about 5 inches/13 cm long.

Cleaver
Its flat, rectangular blade is ideal for cutting meat pieces.

Filleting knife
This knife has a flexible blade of about 8 inches/20 cm in length, and is used for fruit, vegetables, and raw fish.

Carving knife
This knife has a blade about 12 inches/30 cm long, with a point for easy carving around the bones of roasts. It usually comes with a carving fork, which has two long prongs, and sometimes a guard to protect against accidents.

Cook's knife

Small paring knife

Grater

Other cutting tools and equipment

In addition to a basic set of knives, you will need some other cutting tools. Some of these tools are very specific, such as the zester, while others are for more general use.

Mezzaluna
The mezzaluna has two handles and a curved blade, and is used for chopping herbs and vegetables.

Palette knife
This knife is used for spreading instead of cutting, and it has many uses in the kitchen. It is ideal for frosting cakes.

Knife sharpener
Although this has a handle like a knife, instead of a blade it has a long rod of roughened steel. When the edge of a knife is run along the rod at a 45-degree angle, it sharpens the blade.

Can opener
This everyday tool comes in many varieties, from hand-operated ones to wall-mounted automatic devices.

Zester
A citrus zester has a rectangular metal head with holes along the top edge. The holes are there to help remove fine shavings of zest from citrus fruit without picking up the white pith.

Vegetable peeler
You can buy a swivel-blade version or one that has a slicing blade in the middle and a sharp tip for coring.

Grater
There are different graters for different purposes, but a good, multipurpose version to buy is a hollow, box-shape grater with a handle at the top and different cutting holes on each side.

Apple corer
This hollow, cylindrical tool is essential for removing cores from apples and pears quickly and easily.

Cookie cutters
These round circles are available in metal or plastic and are useful for shaping cookies. They are also ideal for cutting pastry shapes.

Kitchen scissors
Choose stainless steel, all-purpose scissors and keep them especially for use in the kitchen.

Zester

Vegetable peeler

Pots and pans

When you are buying pots and pans, choose the best quality you can afford. If cared for properly, they will more than repay the extra cost because they will last for many years.

Saucepans

You will need a small, preferably nonstick, milk pan for making sauces and scrambled eggs, and at least three other saucepans of different sizes: small, medium, and large. Choose saucepans that have secure lids. A large casserole dish with a lid is useful for casseroles, stews, and whole birds.

Skillets and frying pans

You will need a small omelet pan, and a larger skillet for more substantial foods. Nonstick types are ideal for cooking low-fat meals, but are not essential. A ridged grill pan imparts a wonderful striped effect to food and is ideal for charbroiling beef and tuna steaks.

Steamer

Steamers come in different varieties. For example, you can buy a folding metal steamer that adjusts to any size of saucepan. You can also buy metal and bamboo steamers that are placed on top of the saucepan—some have more than one tier so that you can steam more than one food at a time. In addition, there are electric steamers, which are useful if you want to save space on the stove.

Wok

A wok is a deep, round, bowl-shape pan with either one or two handles. It is ideal for cooking stir-fries.

Ovenware and bakeware

Nonstick baking equipment will help you to slide out your culinary creations with ease. Take care not to scour it, however, or you will scratch the nonstick coating. Silicone bakeware needs little or no greasing or oiling.

Baking and cookie sheets

Most of these rectangular and square metal sheets have a lip around the edges, but a cookie sheet is flat. They are essential for baking a variety of foods, from oven-roasted vegetables and pizzas to meringues and cookies.

Cake pans

To start with, a couple of round 8-inch/20-cm diameter shallow pans will come in handy for making yellow cakes, and a deeper 9-inch/23-cm diameter springform cake pan will be useful for making larger cakes. A large square pan with removable section dividers will enable you to make square and rectangular cakes of several different sizes.

Tart pans

Metal tart pans are usually round, and often have a fluted edge. They are ideal for baking quiches, flans, and tarts, and come in a variety of sizes. The loose-bottom, stainless steel type conducts heat better than ceramic types and enables food to be lifted out easily.

Pie plates and dishes

These have sloping sides, come in different shapes and sizes, and are usually deep with a protruding rim for pastry edging.

Roasting pans

These metal pans are deeper than baking sheets, and are ideal for roasting meat and poultry.

Muffin pans

These rectangular pans usually come with 12 large, round indentations, which are ideal for making savory or sweet muffins, individual fruit pies, or cupcakes.

Loaf pans

These rectangular pans have deep sides and come in different sizes. They are useful for baking bread or savory nut roasts.

Ramekins

These small, round dishes have many uses in the kitchen. They are very handy for making individual soufflés and crème caramels. They also double up conveniently as serving dishes for butter, olives, and nuts.

Large saucepan with lid

Saucepan

Skillet

Ramekins

Sieves and strainers

The following items are useful in any kitchen. In particular, a sieve is essential for sifting dry ingredients such as flour, while a colander will make light work of draining a variety of foods.

Bowls and basins

You can buy bowls and basins in a variety of different materials and sizes, but metal will react with acid ingredients such as lime juice, so do not use metal bowls for acid-based marinades.

Strainer
This comes in metal or nylon, and is useful for straining liquid ingredients. Always use the nylon type for acidic ingredients, such as berries.

Colander
A colander is a metal or plastic perforated bowl that is used for draining liquid from foods. They are available in different sizes and may have one or two handles and a flat bottom so that they can sit steadily on a work counter.

Egg separator
Although this small, round, slotted spoon is not essential, new cooks, in particular, will find it helpful for separating egg yolks from whites.

Sifter
A container with small holes and a trigger handle, is especially useful for sifting flour or sprinkling confectioners' sugar or cocoa onto cakes and desserts.

Mixing bowls
Mixing bowls are available in a variety of materials, including ceramic, glass, plastic, and stainless steel. At least one large mixing bowl is essential, although several bowls of different sizes are even better. For example, you will need a smaller bowl to whip cream. You can also buy bowls that are sufficiently decorative to double up as serving bowls at the table.

Ovenproof bowls and casseroles
These come in different sizes and materials, including metal, ceramic, plastic, and glass. A large ovenproof bowl is ideal for making a Christmas pudding, while a set of smaller bowls is useful for making individual chilled or steamed puddings. Also invest in a casserole dish. A flameproof casserole can also be used on the stove.

Strainer

Colander

Ovenproof bowl

Large mixing bowl

Spoons and spatulas

Spoons and spatulas are very helpful for lifting, turning, shaping, draining, and serving a variety of foods. Here are some of the utensils you will find most useful.

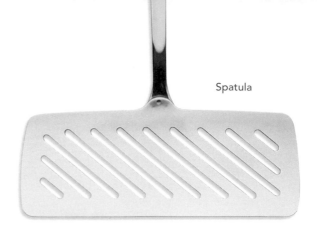

Spatula

Spatula

This slotted lifting tool is essential when lifting floppy food, such as omelets, fried eggs, or fish fillets, from skillets and other pans. A second type of spatula is available in wood, rubber, or silicone, and is used for folding mixtures, such as egg whites. The rubber and silicone types are also ideal for scraping down the sides of mixing bowls to get all the mixture out.

Wooden spoon

This type of spoon is available in different sizes and is handy for mixing ingredients evenly, without scratching the delicate surfaces of pans and bowls.

Draining spoon

This large, slotted spoon is ideal for lifting solid foods out of liquids so that the liquid drains away, and for skimming foam from the surface of simmering liquids, such as stock, and from preserves and marmalade.

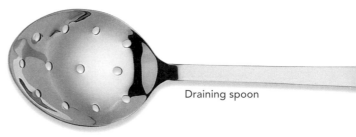

Draining spoon

Serving/basting spoon

This large spoon is useful for serving food onto plates. It often has a groove on one side to direct the flow of juices and sauces.

Serving/basting spoon

Ladle

This is helpful for ladling soups into bowls or punch into glasses.

Tongs

A set of tongs is handy for turning hot food on a grill or broiler pan or a barbecue.

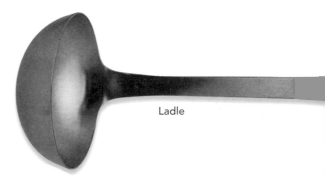

Ladle

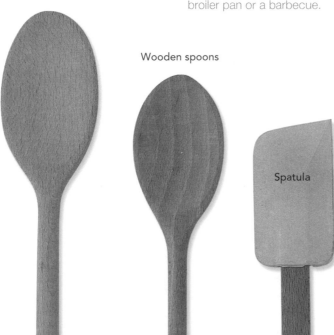

Wooden spoons

Spatula

HOT HANDLES

Do not leave spoons and spatulas with metal handles to stand in the pan while cooking on a hot stove. Metal handles can get very hot, and are likely to cause burns.

Other useful utensils

You can add to your cooking utensils as and when you need them. Here are some of the items you are likely to find most useful and will want to buy sooner rather than later.

Citrus squeezer

These usually come in plastic or glass. They have a strainer to catch any seeds, and a bowl underneath to catch the juice.

Corkscrew and bottle opener

You can buy these either individually or combined into one utensil. The lever-action corkscrew is the easiest kind to use.

Pastry brush

Brushes are useful for sealing pies with water as well as for glazing.

Garlic press

A garlic press is not essential but is handy for crushing garlic cloves cleanly and efficiently. Some have a detachable grille for easy cleaning.

Hand whisks

Whisks are available in a variety of shapes and sizes. The most common is the balloon whisk, used for whisking egg whites and cream. Whisks with silicone-coated wires can be used in conjunction with nonstick saucepans.

Rolling pin

This long, cylindrical utensil comes in wood, glass, or ceramic, and is essential for rolling out pastry.

Potato masher

This utensil is essential for mashing potatoes and other vegetables, such as rutabaga.

Mortar and pestle

These two utensils come as a pair in a variety of sizes and materials, such as marble and porcelain. They are used for crushing herbs and spices.

Cutting boards

Buy several boards in different colors so that you can keep one for raw meat and poultry, one for cooked meats, one for vegetables, and so on.

Wire cooling racks

These metal racks can be round or rectangular, and are ideal for cooling cakes, cookies, and bread. It is often useful to have two racks to accommodate larger batches.

Skewers

Long, stainless steel skewers are a good choice, although other materials, such as wood, are also available. Skewers are essential for cooking kebabs. They are also useful for inserting into cakes and pieces of meat to test if they are cooked all the way through.

Pie funnel

This is available in a variety of shapes and materials, and is used to hold up the pastry in pies. It prevents pastry from becoming soggy by letting the steam escape.

Ice-cream scoop

This tool is useful for scooping neat domes of ice cream or mashed potatoes onto plates.

Decorative molds

These molds are available in many shapes and sizes, and in plastic, metal, or silicone. They can be used for shaping mousses, ice creams, gelatins, and creamy desserts.

Pastry bags and tips

These decorating tools come in various sizes and shapes and are useful for piping decorations in frosting or cream on cakes and desserts.

Thermometers

Use a thermometer to test the temperature of your refrigerator and oven, in the preparation of meat and sugar, and when deep-frying.

Kitchen timers

Timers are available in different designs and sizes, and are useful for monitoring the cooking times of dishes.

Citrus
squeezer

Garlic press

Potato masher

Hand balloon
whisks

Pastry brushes

Machines and electric utensils

There is a wide variety of machines and electrical devices for the kitchen, and these make quick and easy work of preparing food, which is especially useful when catering for families or parties.

Pasta machine

Freestanding mixer

Food processor
This multipurpose machine has metal blades that chop, shred, and grate foods. Usually, it also comes with a selection of other attachments that mix and knead ingredients, such as yellow cake mixes and pie dough.

Mini chopper
This compact machine is handy for chopping small quantities of nuts, garlic, and herbs.

Blender
A blender is useful for pureeing foods, such as soups, batters, milk shakes, and smoothies. It is also known as a liquidizer. The handheld type lets you puree food in a saucepan while it is cooking on the stove.

Pasta machine
If you prefer to make your own fresh pasta, you will find this machine indispensable for rolling and cutting pasta into noodles, ribbons, and various decorative shapes.

Grinder
This very useful machine is essential for grinding nuts and coffee beans. It is also ideal for making fresh breadcrumbs, as are food processors and blenders.

Freestanding mixer
This machine, which is also called a food mixer, has a large bowl and a selection of mixing tools, such as a whisk and a dough kneader. It enables you to beat and whisk foods much faster than you can by hand.

Handheld mixer
This tool, which you can hold over a bowl or saucepan, is more portable than a freestanding mixer. It is suitable for light mixtures, such as eggs and cream, but for more substantial mixtures you will find a freestanding mixer easier to use.

Deep-fat fryer
This heavy machine usually comes with a wire basket that can be hooked onto the side of the machine for easy draining of the cooking oil.

Pressure cooker
This deep, heavy electric saucepan is not essential, but it is useful for steaming food, such as rice, in about half of the normal cooking time.

Slow cooker
This small appliance is very useful for cooking stews and casseroles slowly, and saves you having to use the oven. It also uses less electricity than an oven does. Simply add the food, cover, plug it in, and wait for the lovely aromas to emerge.

CONVERSION CHARTS

OVEN TEMPERATURES

Fahrenheit	Celsius	Gas mark	Oven heat
225°	110°	¼	very cool
250°	120°	½	very cool
275°	140°	1	cool
300°	150°	2	cool
325°	160°	3	moderate
350°	180°	4	moderate
375°	190°	5	moderately hot
400°	200°	6	moderately hot
425°	220°	7	hot
450°	230°	8	very hot
475°	240°	9	very hot

SPOON MEASUREMENTS

1 teaspoon of liquid = 5 ml

1 tablespoon of liquid = 15 ml

OTHER MEASUREMENTS

Liquid volume		Weight		Linear	
US Standard	Metric	US Standard	Metric	US standard	Metric
1 fl oz/2 tbsp	30 ml	⅛ oz	5 g	¹⁄₁₆ inch	2 mm
2 fl oz/¼ cup	60 ml	¼ oz	10 g	⅛ inch	3 mm
2¾ fl oz/⅓ cup	80 ml	1 oz	25 g	¼ inch	5 mm
4 fl oz/½ cup	120 ml	1¾ oz	50 g	⅜ inch	8 mm
5 fl oz/⅔ cup	150 ml	2¾ oz	75 g	½ inch	1 cm
6 fl oz/¾ cup	175 ml	3 oz	85 g	¾ inch	2 cm
8 fl oz/1 cup	240 ml	3½ oz	100 g	1 inch	2.5 cm
10 fl oz/1¼ cups	300 ml	5½ oz	150 g	2 inches	5 cm
12 fl oz/1½ cups	350 ml	8 oz	225 g	3 inches	7.5 cm
16 fl oz/2 cups	475 ml	10½ oz	300 g	4 inches	10 cm
24 fl oz/3 cups	700 mlr	1 lb	450 g	8 inches	20 cm
4 cups/1 quart	950 ml	1 lb 2 oz	500 g	12 inches/1 foot	30 cm
1.06 quarts	1 liter	2 lb 4 oz	1 kg	18 inches/1½ feet	46 cm
4 quarts/1 gallon	3.8 liters	3 lb 5 oz	1.5 kg	20 inches/1⅔ feet	50 cm

Preparation Techniques

You will find this section a valuable source of reference for all the basic preparation techniques you are likely to need in everyday cooking. There are also some advanced techniques for the more experienced cook.

> Grind > Crush > Fold

Grind

To crush food, such as nuts or coffee beans, to a powder or into very small pieces. For this job, you can use a coffee grinder, food processor, or a mortar and pestle for a coarser result.

Infuse

To steep flavorful ingredients, such as herbs or spices, in a liquid in order to flavor it.

Bard

This means to wrap pieces of fat, such as bacon, around lean cuts of meat and poultry to keep them moist and impart more flavor. For example, you can wrap chicken or turkey breasts with strips of bacon before baking. You can also wrap a meat loaf with bacon strips to keep it moist during baking.

Crush

This technique is useful for bringing out the flavor of garlic and herbs, and can be done by pressing the flat side of a knife blade down onto the garlic or herbs. You can also adapt this technique to make cookie crumbs for cheesecakes. Simply place the cookies in a plastic bag, tie the end securely, then use a rolling pin to crush the cookies inside the bag.

Baste

When you spoon juices or fat over food during cooking, this is known as "basting." It helps to keep the food moist and seal in the flavor.

Fold

This technique involves mixing a light mixture into a heavier one using a spoon or spatula in a figure-eight movement. This is done to keep the air within the mixture.

Marinate

This term means to soak food in a marinade for a few hours or days to tenderize it and give it more flavor. You can marinate meat, poultry, fish, and vegetables. Marinades usually consist of oil and vinegar, and are flavored with different mixtures of herbs and spices.

> Beat　　　> Rub in　　　> Shred

Beat

This technique involves using a fork, spoon, or electric mixer in a vigorous stirring motion to remove any lumps from sauces and incorporate air into omelets and cake batters.

Deglaze

This technique is used after sautéeing food (normally meat). After the food and excess fat have been removed from the pan, a small amount of liquid, such as stock or wine, is stirred in to loosen browned food sediment stuck to the pan. This mixture often forms the base for a sauce to accompany the food.

Punch down

This entails knocking the air out of bread dough after it has risen by punching it down.

Rub in

This technique is mainly used when making pastry. Using the fingertips, rub the fat into the flour, lifting it high over the bowl in order to trap air in the mixture, making it lighter and giving a better result.

Marble

This technique is used to combine two ingredients of different colors in order to create a marbled effect. For example, you can lightly mix melted white chocolate into melted dark chocolate to create a marbled pattern.

Clarify

You can clarify butter or a liquid. To clarify butter, heat it slowly to separate the milk solids, which sink to the bottom of the pan, skimming any foam off the top. Clarified butter, such as Indian ghee, has a higher smoke point than ordinary butter, so you can cook with it at higher temperatures. To clarify a liquid, such as a stock, add egg whites and/or egg shells to it and simmer for 10 minutes, then cool and strain it. The egg whites or shells draw out the impurities.

Shred

This technique involves using a small, sharp knife or grater to cut food into very thin lengths.

Line

To line a pan with something to prevent food from sticking to it during cooking. The most common method is to rub butter or oil over the surface of the pan, then cover with parchment paper before adding the food. You can also use bacon strips as a lining for savory nonvegetarian dishes.

> Butterfly   > Whisk   > Chiffonade

Butterfly

To butterfly a leg of lamb, insert the knife into the cavity of the leg bone and cut to one side to open out the meat, then make a shallow surface cut down the center to keep the meat open flat. You can also butterfly other foods, such as chicken breasts or large shrimp.

To butterfly a small bird, such as a game hen, remove the backbone from the bird and secure it so that it can be cooked flat and, therefore, more rapidly. To remove the backbone, first tuck under the wings and remove the wishbone. Then turn the bird over and cut along each side of the backbone to remove it. Use your hands to push down on the bird's breast and flatten it. Finally, push a metal skewer through the thighs and another through the wings and breast to secure the bird.

Whisk

Whisking involves beating a light mixture, such as cream and eggs, vigorously with a whisk to incorporate more air. You can use a balloon whisk (but it takes a lot of effort), an electric handheld mixer, a freestanding mixer, or a food processor with a whisk attachment.

Knead

This technique uses the heel of the hand to pull and stretch bread dough in order to develop the gluten in the flour, so that the bread will keep its shape when it has risen. You can also knead dough in a food processor or food mixer that has a dough hook attachment.

Chiffonade

A French term meaning "made of rags," it refers to the effect you get when you roll leafy vegetables together, then slice them widthwise into ribbons with a sharp knife.

Glaze

This involves brushing water, beaten egg, or sugar and water onto pastry before baking to give it a glossy shine (and make it crunchy if sugar is added). To glaze a ham, remove the skin from the partially cooked meat, then coat the outer surface with some sugar and mustard and continue cooking. You can also glaze sweet dishes with melted jelly or chocolate.

> Emulsify

> Tenderize

> Mash

Emulsify
Emulsification happens when one liquid is slowly added to another in a gradual stream while stirring or blending rapidly. For example, mayonnaise is made by adding oil in a slow stream to a beaten egg mixture while beating or blending vigorously.

Skim
This term means to remove foam or fat from the surface of a simmering liquid with a large slotted spoon or a ladle.

Julienne
This technique involves cutting food, such as carrots and celery, into fine batons or strips.

Tenderize
This involves pounding meat, such as steak, with a mallet in order to break down the tough fibers. You can also tenderize meat by marinating it.

Grease or oil
This is to rub a little butter or oil over the surface of a pan to prevent food from sticking to it during cooking.

Steep
Steeping means to soak an ingredient in hot liquid in order to release its flavor into the liquid.

Cut
This method means to use a sharp knife to make an incision or separate a food into smaller pieces.

Mash
Mashing means to reduce food, usually cooked potatoes and other root vegetables, such as rutabaga, to a pulp using a potato masher or a freestanding mixer.

Chop
To cut food into small pieces using a sharp knife. For example, to chop a herb, hold the tip of the knife blade down with one hand, then use your other hand to raise the handle of the knife up and down as you chop the herb. You can chop food coarsely or finely, depending on your requirements. Coarsely chopped food will be left in larger pieces than when finely chopped.

Dress
This can mean to add a dressing to a salad, to decorate a dish before serving, or to pluck and truss poultry.

> Truss

> Puree

> Crimp

Truss

This means to pull a poultry or game bird into shape, then to secure it with string or skewers before cooking. This technique is particularly useful for preventing stuffing from falling out of a bird.

Cream

Creaming is similar to beating, in that you use a fork, spoon, or electric mixer to beat ingredients together until they are smooth. This technique is usually associated with something rich and creamy, such as butter.

Puree

This describes reducing food to a smooth pulp. You can do this by pushing food through a strainer or using a blender.

Macerate

To macerate means to soak a food in a liquid, often alcohol, to soften it.

Open freeze

This technique means to freeze foods, uncovered, in a single layer. For example, you can cut fruit, such as mango, into small pieces, spread them out on a baking sheet, and freeze them uncovered. Then transfer the pieces individually to a freezer bag and use as required. This technique is also useful for freezing small individual fruit, such as berries.

Crimp

For this technique, use the finger and thumb of one hand and the index finger of the other hand to "pinch" pastry together around the edge of a pie or pastry. This gives it a decorative effect.

Cure

Curing means to preserve a food by salting or smoking it.

Degorge

This is soaking meat, poultry, or fish in a solution of cold water and salt to remove impurities. It also means salting eggplants to remove their bitter juices.

Dredge

Dredging means to sprinkle flour onto a surface when rolling out pastry, or confectioners' sugar or unsweetened cocoa over desserts.

> Sift   > Crosshatch   > Strain

Sift
This technique involves moving dry ingredients, such as flour, through a sifter to remove lumps and introduce more air into the mixture.

Grind
This is to grind food, such as meat, into small pieces, using a knife or grinder.

Peel
Peeling involves removing the outer skin or rind from foods, such as oranges, avocados, or potatoes. Depending on the food, you can use your hands, a sharp knife, or a vegetable peeler

Lard
To lard means to insert strips of pork fat into a lean cut of meat to flavor it and keep it moist.

Crosshatch
To crosshatch means to score crisscross patterns on the surface of foods to let them absorb marinades or be removed from their skins. You can crosshatch the outer layer of fat on a pork roast before cooking to let the fat drain and create a decorative effect.

Grate
This means to shred food into small pieces. You can use a box-shape grater or food processor.

Shuck
This is how we remove the husks from corn and the shells from peas.

Strain
This involves pushing food through a strainer in order to create a puree.

Zest
This means to remove the outer layer of citrus fruit. A zester shaves off the zest without picking up the bitter white pith underneath.

Enrich
This means adding a rich ingredient to a dish in order to create a richer texture or flavor. For example, you could add butter to a dough, or cream to a sauce.

Snip
This means using kitchen scissors to cut green, leafy vegetables or herbs into very small pieces.

Cooking Methods

In this section you will find all the traditional cooking techniques, from boiling to roasting, as well as the popular health-conscious methods, such as steaming and stir-frying.

> Fry   > Deep-fry   > Dry-fry

Fry

This method involves cooking food in hot fat, usually oil, in a skillet. Frying food gives it a delicious flavor. You can shallow-fry or deep-fry food. Deep-frying needs a lot more oil and can be dangerous, so it is always better to shallow-fry food, if possible. However, for some foods, such as tempura (a Japanese dish of batter-coated pieces of fish and vegetables), deep-frying is unavoidable. You can also stir-fry food; this method needs only a little oil and is a very healthy way to cook.

Deep-fry

This technique involves immersing food completely in very hot oil and cooking it at a very high temperature. It is important to choose the correct oil: peanut and soybean oil have the highest smoke points (the temperature at which the oil begins to emit smoke) and are, therefore, the most suitable for deep-frying. Canola and corn oil have the next highest, and are also suitable. Sunflower oil has a lower smoke point and should not be used for deep-frying. Deep-frying food can be dangerous because it is possible to spill the hot oil or the pan can catch fire, so you must be careful and the pan should never be left unattended. A thermostatically controlled deep-fat fryer is a safer and easier option, but still needs care and attention during use. The oil should be heated to a high temperature in order to achieve rapid cooking; the high

temperature will also help to seal the food and prevent it from absorbing too much oil. Add the food to be cooked in small quantities—adding too much at the same time will reduce the temperature of the oil and the cooked food will be soggy instead of crisp. When the food is cooked, lift it out carefully using a spatula or slotted spoon, or the wire basket if using a deep-fat fryer. Let any excess oil drain away from the food onto paper towels.

Dry-fry

This method involves cooking food or spices in a skillet without using fat or oil. For example, you can cook Indian spices, flat breads, or Mexican tortillas in a dry frying pan. You can also dry-fry pumpkin seeds or pine nuts until they are golden and lightly toasted, but watch these carefully while cooking, because they can burn easily.

> Pan-fry   > Shallow-fry   > Stir-fry

Pan-fry

This is another quick and healthy way of cooking food. It involves cooking food quickly in a skillet with either no fat at all (as in dry-frying) or with the absolute minimum amount of fat necessary. Some foods, such as bacon strips, have enough fat content of their own and, therefore, do not need any added fat. In fact, the fat they emit during cooking can be enough to pan-fry other foods at the same time—in this way, the dish has a minimum amount of fat and maximum flavor.

Shallow-fry

This method of cooking is suitable for foods that will not burn easily—for example, foods that are protected in some way, such as foods coated with flour, breadcrumbs, or batter. You will need to add enough oil so that the food will not stick to the pan or burn. Be careful to heat the oil to a high temperature because this will help to seal the food when it is added and prevent it from absorbing too much oil. (Food cooked in oil that has not reached the right temperature will be soggy and laden with oil.) Cook the food in the oil for the required time, then turn it over and cook on the other side. Use a spatula to lift out the food, and let any excess oil drain away from the hot food onto paper towels. Where this method differs from sautéing is that the food is not moved around the pan, and generally a little more oil is used.

Stir-fry

This method comes from Asia and is another healthy way to cook because of the small amount of oil needed. Foods, such as meat, poultry, and vegetables, are cut into small, even pieces and cooked rapidly, while being tossed continuously, in a wok. You can also use a large skillet for stir-frying, but a wok is better because the food cooks more rapidly as it comes into contact with the hot sides of the wok. There are several Chinese methods of stir-frying, but two are the most common. The first is a rapid technique, where the food is fried in a little oil at the highest heat while being tossed continuously. Foods cooked in this way are often marinated first. The other technique is less vigorous and more moist; the food is cooked in a little liquid, such as a stock, and continuously turned and moved around the pan. Noodles and sauce are often added near the end of the cooking time. It is important not to overfill the wok, or the food will steam instead of fry.

> Boil   > Simmer   > Reduce

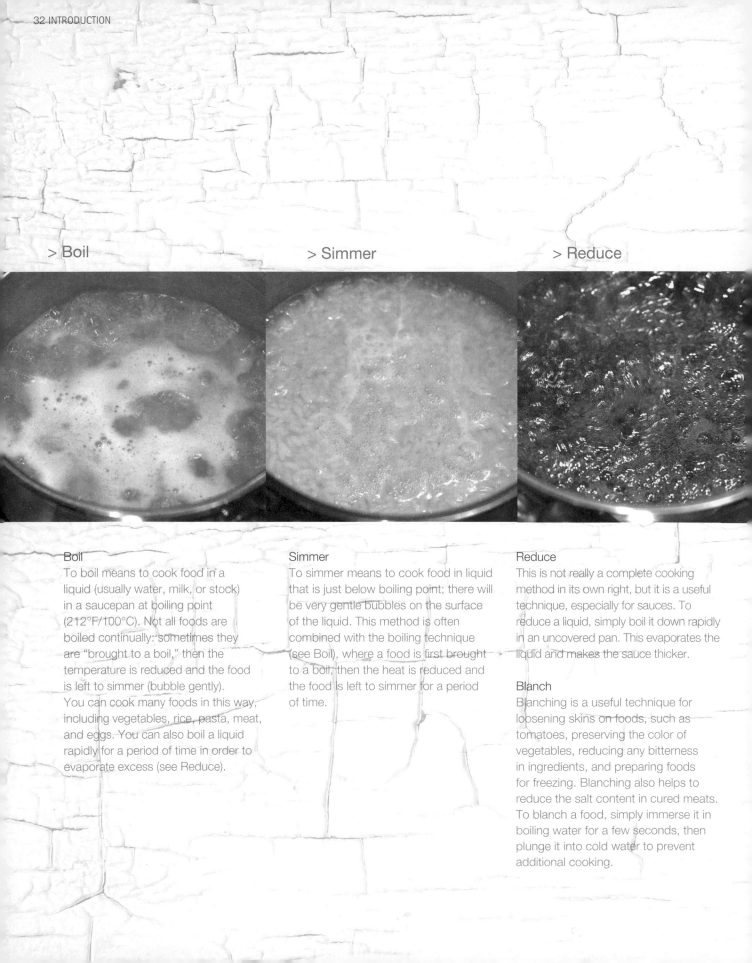

Boil

To boil means to cook food in a liquid (usually water, milk, or stock) in a saucepan at boiling point (212°F/100°C). Not all foods are boiled continually: sometimes they are "brought to a boil," then the temperature is reduced and the food is left to simmer (bubble gently). You can cook many foods in this way, including vegetables, rice, pasta, meat, and eggs. You can also boil a liquid rapidly for a period of time in order to evaporate excess (see Reduce).

Simmer

To simmer means to cook food in liquid that is just below boiling point; there will be very gentle bubbles on the surface of the liquid. This method is often combined with the boiling technique (see Boil), where a food is first brought to a boil, then the heat is reduced and the food is left to simmer for a period of time.

Reduce

This is not really a complete cooking method in its own right, but it is a useful technique, especially for sauces. To reduce a liquid, simply boil it down rapidly in an uncovered pan. This evaporates the liquid and makes the sauce thicker.

Blanch

Blanching is a useful technique for loosening skins on foods, such as tomatoes, preserving the color of vegetables, reducing any bitterness in ingredients, and preparing foods for freezing. Blanching also helps to reduce the salt content in cured meats. To blanch a food, simply immerse it in boiling water for a few seconds, then plunge it into cold water to prevent additional cooking.

> Steam

> Sauté

> Caramelize

Steam

Steaming is a healthy way to cook because the food does not come into direct contact with the liquid and, therefore, more of the nutrients are preserved. Steaming is suitable for a wide range of foods, from poultry and fish to vegetables and puddings. If you use a folding metal steamer, simply bring a small amount of water to a boil in the bottom of a pan, place the steamer inside, add the food, cover the pan, and steam until cooked to your taste. Bamboo steamers are used in a similar way. You can also steam puddings: bring enough water to a boil to come halfway up the side of the ovenproof dish, then place the dish inside the pan and steam the pudding for the recommended time (being careful to top off with boiling water, if necessary, during cooking).

Sauté

This is similar to frying, but involves moving the food around the pan to prevent it from browning too rapidly. Usually a small amount of oil or butter is used to oil or grease the pan and prevent the food from burning.

Caramelize

This term most often refers to the method of caramelizing sugar or onions. To caramelize sugar, heat it until it melts into a syrup. The color varies from light golden to dark brown, depending on the cooking time. A sugar thermometer is useful here, to get the sugar to the required temperature. When the sugar is removed from the heat, it quickly sets and becomes brittle, but retains its caramelized appearance. You can also sprinkle sugar over a food and caramelize it under a preheated hot broiler or by heating its surface with a kitchen blow torch. To caramelize onions, cook them gently in butter for 30 minutes, or until they turn a rich golden brown.

> Sear

> Poach

> Sweat

Sear

To sear means to brown meat, poultry, and fish rapidly over high heat. This process helps to seal in the juices and keeps the center of the food moist.

Braise

This is a long, slow way to cook food. It is especially useful for tough cuts of meat, and for poultry and vegetables. To braise foods, first brown them in oil, then cook them slowly in a small amount of flavored liquid, such as stock or wine, in a dish with a tight-fitting lid. You can cook them on a stove or in an oven.

Poach

To poach means to cook food in a liquid at just below boiling point; it is a gentle method of cooking. The liquids commonly used for poaching are water and alcohol. You can poach poultry, fish, eggs (as long as they are very fresh), and fruit.

Poaching fruit

Pour enough wine or sugar syrup into a pan to cover the fruit. Bring to a simmer, add the pitted fruit, and simmer for 15 minutes, or until tender. Lift out the fruit, reduce the liquid by boiling it down, then pour it over the fruit.

Sweat

This means to cook food (often vegetables, such as onions) gently in water or fat until they are softened but not brown.

Toast

This process uses dry heat to cook foods. For example, you can toast nuts by baking them dry in the oven or cooking them under a preheated hot broiler. You can also toast bread under the broiler, or you can spear marshmallows on forks and toast them over a fire.

> Flambé   > Bake blind   > Roast

Flambé

Strictly speaking, to flambé is more to do with food presentation than it is a cooking method, but because it involves warming an ingredient it is included here. Flambé is a French word meaning "flamed." It involves sprinkling liqueur over a food, such as a Christmas pudding, then setting the alcohol alight just before serving. It makes a dramatic spectacle at the table, and also burns off the alcohol content.

Bake

To bake means to cook food in an oven using dry heat. For example, you can bake potatoes, cakes, cookies, breads, and custards.

Bake blind

This means to bake a pastry shell without a filling. To bake blind, first line a greased pie plate or tart pan with rolled-out pastry, prick it with a fork, place a layer of parchment paper over the pastry, and weigh it down with pie weights. Then place it in a preheated oven and bake it. Remove from the oven and let cool slightly before removing the weights and paper (if you remove them too soon, the pastry will stick to the paper). If you don't have any pie weights, you can use dried beans or rice instead. Baking blind helps to ensure that the pastry stays crisp after the filling is added, and is especially necessary if the filling does not need to be cooked, or needs only a very short cooking time.

Roast

Roasting is similar to baking in that food is cooked in the oven using dry heat. In this case, however, the process is often used for meat, poultry, and vegetables. It is usually necessary to add a little fat when roasting foods to keep them moist. Roasting can really bring out the flavor of a food; for example, bell peppers that have been roasted are extra sweet and flavorful. You can roast a wide variety of vegetables—potatoes and parsnips, garlic, onions, carrots, fennel, sweet potatoes, eggplants, and rutabaga.

> Stew   > Pot roast   > Griddle

Stew

Stewing is a very slow method of cooking. It is similar to braising, except that the food is cut into smaller pieces and more liquid is used. This technique is suitable for meat (especially tough cuts because the long cooking process helps to tenderize the meat), poultry, fish, vegetables, grains, such as barley, and certain fruit, such as apples, pears, peaches, and nectarines.

Casserole

This method is similar to braising; use a large, heavy-bottom casserole dish with a tight-fitting lid. First brown the food in oil, then add a small amount of flavored liquid, cover with the lid, and cook slowly in the oven. Sometimes a casserole is likened to a stew (see Stew), where the food is cut into smaller pieces and more cooking liquid is added. After cooking, you can serve the food directly from the casserole dish.

Pot roast

This technique is very similar to braising in that it involves cooking food (usually meat, especially beef) very slowly in a covered pot in the oven. Very little liquid is used.

Blowtorch

One of the cook's best-kept secrets is blowtorching food. This method of cooking is simple, quick, and effective. You can buy a kitchen blowtorch from any reputable kitchen equipment store, and you will find it inexpensive and convenient. It has a variety of uses. For example, to make a crunchy, caramelized topping for crème brûlées, simply sprinkle them generously with white sugar until the surfaces are completely covered, then heat with the blowtorch.

Griddle

Traditionally, a griddle is a flat, usually rimless, heavy metal device used over one or more burners on a stove; it is used to cook pancakes with the least amount of oil. Griddle pans usually have a long handle and are often made of a heavy metal that conducts heat well, such as cast iron. The term "griddle" is often confused with chargrill (see following page).

> Chargrill   > Barbecue   > Broil

Chargrill

Chargrilling enables you to cook food in the minimum amount of fat and it gives the food attractive charred stripes. You can cook meat, poultry, fish, and vegetables in this way. Simply heat a ridged grill pan on the stove, brush the food with a little oil (never brush the oil on to the pan directly), then place the food on the heated pan. Cook according to the recipe, turning the food over once to cook on the other side. You can also chargrill food on a metal grill set over hot coals.

Barbecue

With this method the food is usually cooked on a rack over hot coals. The barbecue apparatus can range from a simple portable tray consisting of a mesh with flammable, slow-burning paper underneath, to an elaborate electric barbecue. Foods are often marinated first in order to give them more flavor and to aid the cooking process. To prevent burns, you should use long-handled utensils to lift and turn the food.

Broil

Broiling is a quick and healthy way to cook food. Modern ovens usually have an integral broiler; they also come with a broil pan with a wire rack to let excess fat to drain away. A broiler should always be preheated before use. Broiling is a versatile method of cooking: you can cook meat, poultry, fish, and vegetables under a broiler, and toast other foods, such as bread and cheese. Broiling food involves cooking it directly under the heat source, which ensures that the outside of the food is browned quickly, while the inside stays moist.

Pantry Ingredients

A good stock of nonperishable foodstuffs is an essential part of every cook's kitchen. Well-stocked kitchen cupboards, and perhaps a freezer, ensure that you always have a good selection of staple items on hand for every occasion. Make sure you check the use-by dates of your stored items regularly, and discard any that are out of date.

Olive oil

Extra virgin olive oil

Sunflower oil

Nut oil

Corn oil

Oils

There are many different varieties of oil available these days, but it is not necessary to buy them all. You simply need oil that is suitable for drizzling and for cooking at high temperatures.

Olive oil
This mildly fruity oil is ideal for drizzling over salads. It can range from a champagne color to bright green. The best oils are cold-pressed, a chemical-free process that uses only pressure and produces a low level of acidity. You can also flavor it with different ingredients. For example, try adding some herbs, such as basil leaves, or some garlic to it—after a day or two the oil will be infused with their flavor. Its smoke point (the temperature at which it begins to smoke) is 410°F/210°C.

Extra virgin olive oil
Produced from the first cold-pressing of the olives, this oil has a low acid level. It is the most expensive type of olive oil, and has a peppery, fruity flavor. You can use it for drizzling over salads and hot dishes, such as pizzas. Its smoke point is 410°F/210°C.

Corn oil
This oil is economical to buy, and is a good choice for cooking. However, it has a strong flavor that makes it unsuitable for dressings and drizzling over dishes. Its smoke point is 410°F/210°C.

Sunflower oil
This is a good multipurpose oil that can be used for most cooking purposes. However, it is not recommended for deep-frying because this method needs an oil with a higher smoke point. The smoke point of sunflower oil is 390°F/199°C. Sunflower oil has a very light flavor and is, therefore, ideal in dressings.

Sesame oil
This oil comes in two varieties: one has a light color and a nutty flavor, the other is darker and has a stronger flavor. The darker one is most often used in Asian dishes. This oil is excellent for frying and stir-frying. Its smoke point is 410°F/210°C.

Vegetable oil
A blend of various oils, mainly canola, soybean, coconut, and palm. It is best used for frying instead of in salads because it is greasy.

Soybean oil
This economical oil is extracted from soybeans and has a light yellow color. Like canola oil, its popularity is growing because it is low in saturated fat. Its smoke point is 450°F/232°C, which makes it ideal for all types of cooking, including deep-frying. However, it has a strong taste and is, therefore, not suitable for dressings or for drizzling over finished dishes.

| Vegetable oil | Basil-flavored olive oil | Malt vinegar | Red wine vinegar | Balsamic vinegar |

Canola oil

This oil is gaining in popularity because it is lower in saturated fat than other oils. It also contains the omega-3 essential fatty acid, which is now widely believed to help reduce cholesterol levels. It has a mild flavor and so is suitable for salad dressings as well as for cooking. Its smoke point is 444°F/229°C.

Peanut oil

A combination of a very mild flavor and a high smoke point of 450°F/232°C makes peanut oil extremely versatile. It is, therefore, suitable for dressings and mayonnaise, and for drizzling over dishes, as well as for all forms of cooking, including deep-frying.

Vinegars

Vinegar adds a wonderful, pungent kick to dressings, marinades, sauces, and a wide range of dishes. It is available in different types, and here are some of the most popular ones.

Wine vinegars

These are available in different varieties, mainly red, white, and sherry. They can be used in dressings, marinades, and sauces, and can be sprinkled over food.

Cider vinegar

This vinegar is made from apples and has a strong, sharp taste. It is best used with meats and in condiments and pickles.

Balsamic vinegar

This delicious vinegar is thick, dark, and slightly sweet. It is made from grape juice that is aged in barrels over a period of years.

Rice vinegar

Made from fermented rice, this mild, sweet vinegar is often used in Asian cooking.

Malt vinegar

This is made from malted barley and is used for making condiments.

White vinegar

Also referred to as distilled white vinegar, this harsh, sour vinegar is best reserved for pickling.

Specialty vinegars

Some vinegars are infused with fruits, such as berries, nuts, or a wide variety of herbs. Other popular favorites are cane vinegar, which has a rich, slightly sweet taste.

Flour

Keep your flour fresh by storing it in an airtight container with a tight-fitting lid in a cool, dry place. You can store white flours for 6–8 months, and whole wheat flours for up to 2 months.

Cornstarch
This powdery flour is made from corn kernels and is used for thickening sauces, soups, and desserts. It is usually mixed with a small quantity of cold liquid to make a smooth paste before being added to hot dishes.

All-purpose flour
This flour is used for thickening sauces as well as for making batters and pastry.

Self-rising flour
All-purpose flour that has had baking powder and salt added is known as self-rising flour. It is used for making cakes and cookies. If you don't have self-rising flour, substitute the same amount of all-purpose flour and add 1½ teaspoons of baking powder plus ½ teaspoon of salt for each 1 cup of flour.

Rice flour
This powdery flour is made from white rice, and is used mainly in baked foods and to make Asian rice-flour noodles.

Bread flour
This flour is used for making bread. It contains a high level of gluten, which helps to give the bread dough its elasticity. If you are using a whole-wheat type, keep it in an airtight container in the refrigerator.

Whole wheat flour
This flour has a stronger flavor than white flour and contains wheat germ, so it has a higher fiber, fat, and nutrient content. However, since it has a higher fat content, it should be stored in the refrigerator to prevent it from turning rancid.

Rye flour
A heavy, dark flour, rye flour has less gluten than all-purpose flour and whole wheat flour.

Pasta, noodles, and grains

All these different dried pasta shapes, noodles, and grains keep well in the pantry. They are ideal for cooking quick, satisfying meals at short notice.

Long pasta

There are different varieties of dried pastas with long shapes, including spaghetti, fettuccine (narrow ribbons), tagliatelle (slightly wider ribbons), and vermicelli (very fine, hairlike lengths). These pastas are usually made with durum wheat or whole wheat flour, and may be colored using such ingredients as spinach (green), beet juice (red), tomatoes (orange-red), or even squid ink (black).

Short pasta

Dried pasta in short shapes include conchiglie (shells), fusilli (spirals), farfalle (bows), and tubular types, such as penne and macaroni. These shapes are particularly good for holding chunky sauces.

Other shapes of dried pasta

Other favorite shapes to keep in your pantry include lasagna (rectangular noodles) and cannelloni (large tubes).

Dried noodles

Most noodles are associated with Asian cooking. The main difference between noodles and long pasta is that noodles usually have egg added, such as Chinese egg noodles. Alternatively, sometimes they are made from rice flour. Noodles are popular in stir-fries and soups. Many types need no cooking—you simply soak them in hot water for a few minutes before adding them to the dish of your choice.

Long-grain rice

You can buy white and brown types of long-grain rice. When cooked, the grains stay dry and separate and do not clump together. This rice is used in savory dishes.

Medium-grain rice

These grains are a little shorter than long-grain rice, and more moist. They tend to clump together when cooked. This rice is used in savory dishes, such as Spanish paella and Japanese sushi.

Short-grain rice

This rice has short grains that are more starchy and moist than medium- and long-grain rice. There are different types, including glutenous rice (used in Asian cooking) and Italian Arborio and carnaroli rice (used in risottos).

Instant rice

The grains in instant rice are polished and partially boiled so that they are quick and easy to cook and stay fluffy and separate. Instant rice is a convenient alternative to white or brown rice, but does not have as much flavor.

Wild rice

This is a marsh grass that is cultivated in the United States and Canada. The grains are long and black and have a nutty flavor. Wild rice is expensive, so for economy reasons it is often mixed with less-expensive brown long-grain rice.

Bulgur wheat

This comprises wheat kernels that have had the bran removed. They are then steamed, dried, and ground into different degrees of coarseness. The result is a golden brown grain that has a nutty flavor. It can be cooked like rice and is also excellent in salads.

Couscous

This is not a true grain, but pieces of semolina dough that have been rolled, dampened, and coated with a fine wheat flour. It makes a fine accompaniment to savory dishes.

Cornmeal

Ground from dried corn kernels, cornmeal is available in fine, medium, and coarse textures and is white, yellow, or blue. The Italian polenta is a coarsely ground version sold in some supermarkets.

Spaghetti

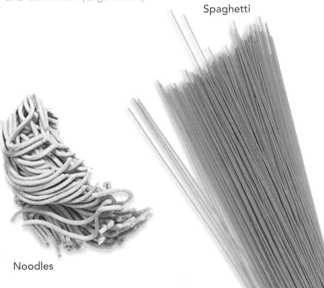

Noodles

Long-grain brown rice

Assorted dried pasta shapes

Beans and other legumes

All legumes except lentils and split peas need soaking for at least 8 hours, then boiling rapidly for 10 minutes before cooking for around 45 minutes. Soybeans need even longer cooking.

Cannellini beans

Red kidney beans

Red lentils

Chickpeas

Aduki beans

Cannellini beans
A type of haricot bean, these long, creamy white beans are excellent in soups and salads.

Red kidney beans
These red, kidney-shape beans can be added to soups, salads, stews, and other savory dishes, such as chili con carne. They can cause food poisoning if not boiled rapidly for at least 10 minutes.

Aduki beans
These small red beans are popular in Japanese cooking, especially coated with sugar. They are also good in soups and salads.

Lima beans
These white, kidney-shape beans are excellent in soups and salads.

Soybeans
Although most soybeans are yellow, they can also be black, brown, or green. They are much richer in nutrients than the other beans, and are particularly full of protein as well as iron and calcium. Soybeans are used to make cooking oils and margarine, flour, soy milk and cheeses, soy sauce, tofu, miso, and textured vegetable protein. They are good in soups and other savory dishes, particularly curries. They should be soaked for at least 12 hours, drained, and rinsed, then covered with fresh water and brought to a boil. Boil them for the first hour of cooking, then simmer them for the remaining 2–3 hours that it takes to cook them.

Chickpeas
These round, beige legumes have a nutty flavor and are excellent in soups, stews, and salads, as well as ground up in dips such as hummus. Like soybeans, they need a longer soaking and cooking time than many legumes, so it is good to keep some canned chickpeas on hand for when you have little time.

Lentils
These tiny, disk-shaped legumes are available in different varieties and colors. Red and orange lentils become mushy when cooked, so are ideal pureed and used in soups and sauces. The green and European brown types (Puy lentils) keep their shape when cooked and are ideal in warm winter salads, sauces, stews, and other savory dishes.

Split peas
These small peas are disk shaped and split along a natural seam. They can be yellow or green, and are excellent cooked and pureed. They are also good in soups, casseroles, and other savory dishes.

Black-eyed peas
These small beige beans have a circular black "eye." They are commonly found in Chinese cooking, and are very popular in sauces, stir-fries, and soups.

Borlotti beans
These oval-shape beans have pale pink to maroon streaked skin. They are creamy when cooked and are excellent in soups, dips, and other savory dishes.

Nuts and seeds

Nuts and seeds have a high oil content, and can quickly turn rancid. If they have shells, store them in a cool, dry place. If they do not have shells, refrigerate them in airtight containers.

Peanuts

Pistachio nuts

Almonds

Pine nuts

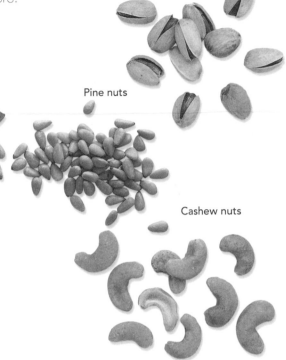

Cashew nuts

Hazelnuts

Walnuts

Almonds
These lozenge-shape nuts have a thin brown covering and a cream center. They come in two types—sweet and bitter—but it is the sweet variety that is normally used. Available whole, blanched, chopped, and candied, they are excellent in both savory and sweet dishes, from salads and savory casseroles to cakes, cookies, and marzipan.

Hazelnuts
These small, round nuts have a brown covering and a cream interior, and a rich, sweet flavor. They are especially popular in granola and cereals, savory dishes, and baked dishes, such as nut loaf, as well as sweet dishes including cakes and cookies.

Walnuts
These nuts have a large, round, wrinkled shell and two double lobes inside. The nuts have a delicious creamy taste and are good in salads and savory dishes, as well as sweet dishes and cakes. They also make a very flavorful oil.

Pecans
These nuts are golden brown with a beige interior. They have a very high fat content. They are used in a variety of savory dishes and desserts, such as pecan pie.

Cashew nuts
These creamy, butter-flavored kidney-shape nuts have a high fat content and are delicious roasted and added to stir-fries and baked dishes.

Pistachio nuts
These pale green nuts have a delicate flavor. They are often used in stuffings and also to decorate desserts.

Pine nuts
These small, oval nuts are creamy in color and in flavor. They are excellent toasted or dry-fried, and are used in salads and rice dishes, sauces, such as pesto, and a variety of savory and sweet dishes.

Peanuts
Despite their name, peanuts are not actually nuts; they are legumes and very versatile. They are used to make oil and also peanut butter, which in turn makes a delicious satay sauce. They are also good in salads, side dishes, and stir-fries.

Seeds
A selection of seeds can be very useful in your pantry. Sunflower seeds, for example, are rich in essential fatty acids and are delicious sprinkled into granola and salads. Pumpkin seeds are also nutritious and make a good snack. Sesame seeds are popular in Asian cooking and are delicious toasted and in stir-fries. Dill seeds have an anise seed flavor and are good with fish and vegetables. Caraway seeds have a pungent flavor and are used in soups, stews, vegetable dishes, and in bread. Poppy seeds are slightly sweet and make an attractive decoration sprinkled over salads and bread rolls.

Spices and seasonings

A selection of spices in your pantry is extremely useful for enhancing the flavor of dishes. Some spices, such as ginger and turmeric, are also said to aid digestion.

Cumin

Paprika

Cloves

Peppercorns

Ground ginger

Turmeric

Ginger
This hot, pungent spice has a lemony flavor when fresh, but a sweeter flavor when dried. It is popular in Indian cooking, as well as in chutneys, desserts, and baked items, such as cakes, notably gingerbread, and cookies.

Turmeric
A peppery spice with a distinctive yellow color. Turmeric is often used instead of the more expensive saffron. It is especially good in curries and in rice dishes, such as paella.

Saffron
This yellow spice has a slightly bitter flavor and a pungent aroma. It is sold in strands and is used in dishes to color and flavor them.

Allspice
This small berry comes from the West Indies and South America and has a sweet flavor of nutmeg, cinnamon, and cloves. You can buy it whole or ground. It is used with meat, onions, and fruit desserts, as well as in cakes and bread.

Coriander
The aromatic flavor of this spice is excellent with meat, poultry, and vegetables.

Cumin
This spice has a strong, slightly bitter flavor, and is particularly good with poultry and vegetables.

Cloves
A sweet spice with a strong flavor. Use whole cloves to stud hams and fruit, and ground cloves to add flavor to desserts.

Nutmeg
This sweet-flavored spice is used in savory and sweet dishes.

Mace
This spice has a sweet flavor and is excellent in soups and sauces.

Cinnamon
A very popular spice. Cinnamon is sweet and fragrant and is used in desserts and baked foods, such as cakes, sweet pies, and cookies.

Curry powder
This is a blend of spices, and the flavor varies from mild to hot. It adds a distinctive flavor to sauces and savory dishes.

Apple pie spice
A mixture of sweet spices, such as cinnamon, nutmeg, and cardamom. It gives a delicious flavor to desserts, cakes, cookies, and drinks.

Chili powder
This is a blend of dried chiles. It adds a kick to sauces and savory dishes.

Five spice
This blend of five spices usually contains cinnamon, cloves, fennel seeds, Sichuan peppercorns, and star anise. It is very popular in Chinese cooking, and gives a wonderful flavor to stir-fries.

Paprika
This has a hot flavor and an attractive red color. It is ideal as a garnish.

Dried herbs

It is always worthwhile having a collection of dried herbs on hand. They are especially useful for dishes that require a long cooking time, such as casseroles. Use half the recommended fresh quantity.

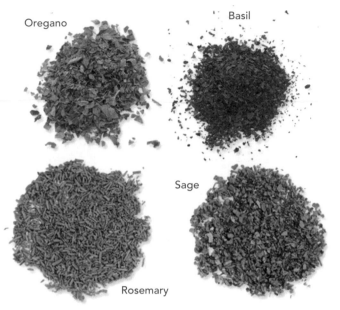

Oregano

Basil

Sage

Rosemary

Sugars and syrups

Store your sugar in a dry place at room temperature. Syrups should be kept in tightly sealed containers at room temperature or in the refrigerator.

Confectioners' sugar

Brown sugar

Superfine sugar

Raw brown sugar

Granulated sugar

Peppercorns
These come in different varieties. Ground black or white peppercorns are an extremely popular seasoning for a wide variety of savory foods and also some sweet dishes, such as balsamic strawberries. You can also buy green peppercorns.

Salt
This is a great favorite as a seasoning, but care must be taken not to overuse it or it will overpower the food, and it can be bad for health.

Oregano
This herb has a strong flavor and is perfect sprinkled on pizzas and in pasta sauces.

Basil
This popular herb is delicious in sauces and is particularly good with tomatoes.

Sage
This herb is good in egg, cheese, poultry, and meat dishes.

Dill
Also called dill weed, the leaves make an excellent herb to use with vegetables and fish.

Rosemary
A pungent herb that goes well with poultry and meat, and also root vegetables, especially potatoes.

Mixed herbs
This combination usually consists of oregano, rosemary, and thyme, plus one or two other herbs. Mixed herbs can be used in a variety of savory dishes, including sauces and Italian dishes, such as pizza and pasta.

Granulated sugar
This basic, cheap sugar is essential in your pantry. Use it to sweeten drinks and cereals and to sprinkle on desserts. This coarse sugar is also essential in preserves.

Superfine sugar
This sugar is finer than granulated sugar and dissolves quickly, so it is ideal for meringues and cakes. To make your own, process granulated sugar in a food processor for a minute.

Confectioners' sugar
Also called powdered sugar, this fine sugar is ideal for making frostings and icings and for dusting on desserts.

Brown sugar
This stronger-flavored sugar comes in various shades from light to dark and is used in making cakes and cookies.

Raw brown sugar
This crunchy brown sugar is delicious sprinkled over desserts and cakes before broiling or baking.

Honey
This comes in many flavors, usually in a clear, liquid form. It has many uses, from glazing ham and flavoring vegetables to sweetening desserts and drinks.

Corn syrup
This clear, golden syrup is made from corn. Dark corn syrup has a stronger flavor than light corn syrup, which is often used in baking.

Maple syrup
This delicious, sweet syrup is used in a wide variety of savory and sweet dishes, including pancakes.

Sauces, pastes, and condiments

A good selection of sauces and condiments is invaluable in the kitchen, and will ensure you always have the right ingredients on hand to add exciting and interesting flavors to your dishes.

Ketchup
This sauce is popular in Western cooking and is eaten with cooked foods, such as fries and hamburgers. It is also good as an ingredient in dressings and relishes.

Steak sauce
This brown sauce, whether a sweet or tart version, is often used to flavor beef.

Soy sauce
This popular sauce is essential for stir-fries and other Asian dishes. You can buy the Chinese version, which is salty, or the Japanese type, which is slightly sweeter.

Hoisin sauce
This sweet soybean-based sauce with a sticky texture is very popular in Chinese cooking. It is known by various names, such as Peking sauce.

Worcestershire sauce
This strongly flavored sauce is made with onions, molasses, and anchovies, and is used to season meats, gravies, and soups, and occasionally cocktails. A vegetarian version is available.

Pesto sauce
Made from basil, garlic, pine nuts, Parmesan cheese, and olive oil, pesto is good with pasta.

Tabasco sauce
This very hot chili sauce is used in dishes to give them a kick, such as Mexican salsas. It is also used to season certain cocktails.

Thai fish sauce (nam pla)
This salty sauce is made from fermented fish and has a very strong taste and smell. It is used to flavor Thai dishes and as a table condiment.

Horseradish sauce
Horseradish is a root with a very hot flavor. It makes an excellent creamy white sauce, which is very good with meat, poultry, fish, and egg dishes.

Plum sauce
This fruity sauce is popular in Chinese cooking and is traditionally served with spring rolls and also Peking duck.

Harissa
This North African condiment is made from oil, garlic, herbs, and spices, and is served with soups and couscous.

Tahini
A thick paste made from finely ground sesame seeds. It is used to flavor Middle Eastern dishes.

Thai curry paste
This is available in different varieties: green is the hottest, yellow is the mildest, and red varies in the amount of heat. It is a popular ingredient in Thai dishes.

Miso
A paste made from fermented soybeans. It is used in Japanese cooking to thicken and flavor soups and other dishes.

Tomato paste
This is a tomato puree that is useful in sauces and soups because of its intense flavor.

Tomato puree
This is simply strained tomatoes. It is ideal for soups and sauces, and for spreading over pizzas.

Mustards
You can buy different types of mustard, from coarse grain types such as Dijon mustard, which has a strong flavor and is used in dips and dressings. English mustard, is very hot and useful in dips and dressings. The popular American-style mustard is usually milder, and is good with a variety of savory dishes, especially meats.

Soy sauce

Thai fish sauce

Mustard

Pesto sauce

Tabasco sauce

Horseradish sauce

Canned and bottled foods

Keep your pantry stocked with a selection of canned and bottled foods, such as legumes, fish, vegetables, and pickled items, and you will never be short of ingredients for delicious meals at short notice.

Canned beans
You can buy a wide variety of canned beans, such as red kidney beans and chickpeas, which will save you time because you do not have to soak them or cook them. Cans of baked beans in tomato sauce are also indispensable for quick meals.

Canned fish
Canned fish, such as tuna, salmon, crab, anchovies, sardines, and pilchards, are versatile items to have in the pantry. They are particularly useful when added to pastas and salads.

Canned tomatoes
Canned tomatoes can be used in a wide variety of dishes, from sauces and soups to stews and casseroles.

Coconut milk
Canned coconut milk is very useful for cooking Thai dishes, particularly creamy curries and desserts.

Corn
Canned corn kernels are deliciously sweet and ideal in salads, soups, and casseroles.

Water chestnuts
These are popular in Chinese cooking, and are particularly good in stir-fries.

Olives
It is always useful to keep a can or bottle of olives on hand. They make ideal tapas for unexpected guests and are delicious in salads and pastas and on pizzas.

Sun-dried tomatoes
These are very good in Italian recipes, particularly salads, pastas, and bread.

Pickled foods
Onions, pickles, and capers make perfect accompaniments and garnishes for meat and vegetable dishes.

Dried fruits and berries

A selection of dried fruits and berries is very useful to keep on hand. They make ideal snacks and can be used in a wide variety of savory and sweet dishes, from muesli, vegetable curries, and meat dishes to desserts and sweet pies. Dried fruits and berries include currants, raisins, golden raisins, apricots, prunes, figs, dates, mangoes, pears, apples, bananas, cranberries, and blueberries.

Other items

Here is a selection of other items you will find useful to keep in your pantry.

Bouillon cubes
These are very convenient for soups, casseroles, and other dishes, particularly if you do not have enough time to make fresh stock.

Gelatin
You will need gelatin to set mousses and gelatin-based desserts. You can also buy a vegetarian equivalent, such as agar agar.

Chocolate and unsweetened cocoa
These are useful for desserts and baked goods, and also for some savory dishes.

Vanilla
You can buy vanilla in bean or liquid form (extract) as a flavoring. It is particularly delicious in desserts.

Alcohol
White wine, red wine, sherry, and Marsala are handy for a variety of savory and sweet dishes. Although not essential, flavored liqueurs are also useful, such as orange, coffee, and almond.

Refrigerator and freezer essentials

Your chilled essentials should include eggs, milk, yogurt, and cream. You should also keep some butter, including an unsalted type, for baking and desserts. Bread is another essential, not just as an accompaniment, but for making breadcrumbs and recipes such as crostini. Cheeses should include an all-purpose firm variety, such as cheddar, and also Parmesan, as well as cream cheese. You may find bacon strips useful. Tofu is full of protein: it is good in stir-fries and is useful for vegetarian meals. In the freezer, you might like to keep frozen shrimp and fish fillets, vegetables, and ice cream.

Chapter 1
Eggs & Dairy

Introduction

Nowadays we can buy a wide range of delicious eggs, from white and brown, organic and free-range, to more exotic types, such as the distinctive blue eggs from the Oakham Blue hen. Likewise, more dairy products are available than before, and we can choose from an ever-increasing array of milk, yogurt, cream, butter, and cheese, which are full of protein and very easy to prepare and cook.

| Brown duck egg | Goose egg | Quail egg | Brown hen egg | Medium duck egg | Large duck egg |

Buying and storing eggs

Always buy your eggs from a reputable supplier, and do not buy any with cracked shells. Be sure the eggs are as fresh as possible by checking the expiration date on the carton. You can also check an egg's freshness by floating it in water: if it sinks to the bottom of the bowl horizontally, it is very fresh; if it stays vertical with its tip on the bottom, it is less fresh; if it floats to the top, it is old and should be discarded.

Store your eggs, pointed ends down, in their carton at the back of a low shelf in the refrigerator. They should not be stored in the refrigerator door, where they will be subject to fluctuations in temperature each time the door is opened. Separated egg whites will keep in the refrigerator in a lidded container for a week, and in the freezer for up to 6 months. (You can freeze egg whites in ice cube trays, then remove and store them in freezer-proof bags.) Egg yolks or whole beaten eggs will keep in the refrigerator for up to 2 days, or in the freezer for up to 3 months (add a little salt to them before freezing). Always label the container with the date of freezing and what it contains. Eggs are best cooked at room temperature, so remember to take them out of the refrigerator about an hour before they are needed. Pasteurized liquid eggs are also available in cartons.

Whisking egg whites

Eggs that are 3–5 days old are best for whisking. Make sure that everything is clean and that your bowl is free of grease. Put the egg whites in a large bowl. If whisking by hand, use a large balloon whisk in an upward, circular movement. Alternatively, use a handheld electric mixer or freestanding food mixer. If the recipe calls for a "soft peaks" consistency, the mixture should form peaks that are soft and will flop over when the whisk is removed. If you need "firm peaks," the peaks should stand rigid.

Scrambling eggs

Plan 2 eggs and 1 tablespoon of milk per person. Whisk together the eggs and milk in a bowl, then season with salt and pepper. Melt 1 tablespoon of butter in a nonstick pan, then pour in the egg mixture. Stir continuously over low heat for 5–7 minutes, until almost set, then remove from the heat. Stir for 1 more minute, then serve.

Separating eggs

There are some clever devices available for separating yolks from egg whites, but if you don't have a separating gadget, you can use the shell method; using cold eggs makes this method easier. 1.) Crack the egg shell gently on the edge of a bowl. 2.) Open the shell slowly, letting the white drip into the bowl. 3.) Being careful not to break the yolk, pass it from one shell half to the other. 4.) Repeat until the yolk and white are fully separated. Alternatively, open the egg into your hand, cradling the yolk gently, and let the white drip through your fingers to separate.

Boiling eggs

To boil eggs, bring a small saucepan of water to a boil. Reduce the heat to a simmer, add a pinch of salt, then carefully add the eggs. Simmer gently for 4–5 minutes for soft-cooked, and 9–10 minutes for hard-cooked (no longer, or a dark ring will appear around the yolk). Remove with a slotted spoon and plunge into cold water to prevent additional cooking. Serve as required.

Frying eggs

Heat 1–2 tablespoons of oil in a skillet until hot (but not smoking). Break the eggs carefully into the pan so the yolks remain intact. Cook over medium heat for 3–4 minutes, until the white has set. Use a spatula to lift out the eggs for sunny-side up; alternatively, for easy-over, flip over and cook for another 1–2 minutes. Serve immediately.

Poaching eggs

Eggs need to be very fresh for poaching or they will break up in the water. You can use a nonstick egg poacher or silicone poaching pods for this, or alternatively you can use the following method.

Fill a small pan with enough water to cover an egg. Bring to a boil, then reduce the heat to a simmer. Break the egg carefully into a cup, then pour it gently into the boiling water so that the yolk does not break. Cook for 3–4 minutes; you can baste the egg with a little of the cooking liquid to ensure it is cooked. Lift it out with a slotted spoon and serve.

Coddling eggs

An egg coddler is a porcelain cup with a lid. Grease the cup with butter, break an egg into it, season wth salt and pepper, and loosely screw on the lid. Bring a pan of water to a boil, stand the coddler in the water up to its lid, and simmer for 7–8 minutes. Eat straight from the coddler.

SAFETY

Eggs can carry harmful bacteria and may cause food poisoning if not thoroughly cooked, so do not give dishes with raw or lightly cooked eggs to people who may be particularly vulnerable, such as pregnant or breast-feeding women, babies and toddlers, the elderly, people who are ill, or those with a chronic illness.

Fresh
milk

Clotted cream

Yogurt

Butter

Buying and storing milk

Milk is a good source of protein and calcium. The most commonly available is fresh cow's milk, which comes in whole (3½% fat), low-fat (the two types have less than 2% or 1% fat), and nonfat or skim (less than ½% fat). Most milk has been homogenized, which means that the fat has been spread throughout the milk so that there is no creamy layer on top. Buttermilk tastes a little like yogurt or thickened low-fat milk. Dry milk is a powdered form of milk with the moisture content removed; you can reconstitute it with water and use in place of fresh milk. Long-life milk has been heated quickly to about 300°F/149°C, then cooled and vacuum-packed to ensure a shelf-life without refrigeration of 6 months. You can also buy condensed milk, which is very thick and sweet, and evaporated milk, which is sterilized in cans. If you are sensitive to cow's milk, you can buy goat's milk or sheep's milk, or milk made from soybean or rice instead.

Most fresh milk has been pasteurized (heated then quickly cooled) to kill off any harmful bacteria, although some unpasteurized milk is available (see Safety box, opposite). Always check the expiration date on milk before you buy it, and store fresh milk, covered, in the refrigerator. Leaving milk out at room temperature for as little as 30 minutes is long enough to substantially effect it's storage life.

Buying and storing yogurt

Yogurt is made by fermenting milk with healthy bacteria. It has a slightly tangy taste and is a healthy choice because it is thick and creamy yet low in fat. Greek yogurt is the thickest and has the creamiest consistency. You can also freeze yogurt for a healthy low-fat alternative to ice cream. Check the expiration date before buying, and store it in the refrigerator. Keep it covered when not in use.

Buying and storing butter

Butter is made by churning cream until it separates into semisolids. It comprises at least 80% fat and the other 20% is made up of milk solids and water. Sometimes it is colored with annatto (a natural color made from the paste of seeds). Butter is available in salted and unsalted types: unsalted is essential for sweet dishes. You can also buy "spreadable" butter; this has been blended with oil so that it will stay soft and can be spread more easily. Make sure your butter is always tightly wrapped to prevent it from absorbing odors. Check the expiration date on the packaging. Butter also freezes well, for up to 6 months in the freezer.

Cheddar

Parmesan

Curd cheese

Stilton

Buying and storing cream

Cream is made from the fattiest part of milk. It, therefore, has a higher fat content than milk, and a milder flavor. Half-and-half is a mixture of milk and cream and has the lowest fat content (10–12 percent); it is ideal for sauces and soups. Light cream is preferred for pouring into drinks, such as coffee, but has a higher fat content (18–30% fat). Heavy cream, also known as heavy whipping cream, has a high fat content (36–40%) that is ideal for whipping and piping into decorative shapes. It is a delicious luxury for special occasions, perhaps to enrich a sauce or accompany a dessert. Sour cream (18–20% fat) has a slightly tangy taste and is ideal in savory dishes, as is the higher fat specialty crème fraîche (up to 50% fat). Other speciality creams include clotted cream (look for at a specialty British food supplier), which is very thick. It is ideal on scones (sweet biscuits) or served with special desserts. All cream should be kept covered, stored in the refrigerator, and used by the expiration date on the carton. Heavy cream can be frozen up to 3 weeks.

Buying and storing cheese

Cheese is made from milk that is allowed to thicken and then separate into curds (semisolids) and whey (a liquid). Fresh cheeses are rindless and vary in consistency. Typical cheeses in this category are cream cheese and cottage cheese. Soft and semihard cheeses are firmer, and range from creamy soft cheeses with rinds, such as Brie, to firmer cheeses, such as Port Salut. Generally, the harder the cheese, the higher the fat content, and hard cheeses have the highest fat of all. They are often easy to grate, and range from cheddar cheese to Parmesan. Blue cheeses are also available: these have blue veins running through them and a strong flavor and aroma (the veins are made by a friendly bacteria). Blue cheese types include Gorgonzola and Stilton. You can also buy cheese made from goat's milk and sheep's milk.

Keep your cheese tightly wrapped. Store fresh cheese in the coldest part of the refrigerator, and the other cheeses in the warmest part. Hard cheeses can be grated ready for use and kept in the refrigerator for up to 1 week. Use cheeses by the expiration date. You can freeze hard cheeses, but they will have a crumblier texture when defrosted. Grated cheese also freezes well but is only suitable for cooking, not for adding to salads.

SAFETY

Unpasteurized milk is available from specialty suppliers, but there is still a risk of disease and, therefore, this milk should not be given to vulnerable people, especially pregnant or breast-feeding women, babies and toddlers, the elderly, and people with a chronic illness.

Spinach & Mozzarella Omelet

Serves 4

ingredients

- 1 tbsp butter
- 4 eggs, beaten lightly
- 1½ oz/40 g mozzarella cheese, thinly sliced and cut into bite-size pieces
- small handful baby spinach, stems removed
- salt and pepper
- 1 oil-cured red bell pepper, sliced into strips, to garnish

1 Heat a 10-inch/25-cm nonstick pan over medium–high heat. Add the butter and when it sizzles, pour in the eggs. Season with salt and pepper, then stir gently with the back of a fork until large flakes form. Let cook for a few seconds, then tilt the pan and lift the edges of the mixture with a spatula, so that uncooked egg flows underneath to cook evenly.

2 Scatter the cheese and spinach over the top and let cook for a few seconds. Once the surface starts to solidify, carefully fold the omelet in half. Cook for a few seconds, pressing the surface with a spatula. Turn the omelet over and cook for another few seconds, until the cheese is soft and the spinach wilted.

3 Slide the omelet onto a warm serving dish and slice into segments. Garnish with strips of red bell pepper before serving.

Asparagus with Poached Eggs & Parmesan

Serves 4

ingredients
- 10½ oz/300 g asparagus, trimmed
- 4 extra-large eggs
- 3 oz/85 g Parmesan cheese
- pepper

1 Bring 2 saucepans of water to a boil. Add the asparagus to 1 saucepan, return to a simmer, and cook for 5 minutes, or until just tender.

2 Meanwhile, reduce the heat of the second saucepan to a simmer and carefully crack the eggs into a cup, then slide them gently into the water, one at a time. Poach for 3 minutes, or until the whites are just set but the yolks are still soft. Remove with a slotted spoon.

3 Drain the asparagus and divide among 4 warm plates. Top each plate of asparagus with an egg and shave over the cheese. Season to taste with pepper and serve immediately.

Quiche Lorraine

Makes one 9-inch/23-cm quiche

ingredients

for the pie dough
- heaping 1⅓ cup all-purpose flour, plus extra for dusting
- pinch of salt
- ½ cup butter, diced
- ¼ cup grated pecorino cheese
- 4–6 tbsp iced water

for the filling
- 4 oz/115 g Gruyère cheese, thinly sliced
- ½ cup crumbled Roquefort cheese
- 6 oz/175 g rindless lean bacon, broiled until crisp
- 3 eggs
- ⅔ cup heavy cream
- salt and pepper

1 To make the pie dough, sift the flour with the salt into a bowl. Add the butter and rub it in with your fingertips until the mixture resembles breadcrumbs. Stir in the grated cheese, then stir in enough of the water to bind. Shape the dough into a ball, wrap in plastic wrap, and chill in the refrigerator for 15 minutes.

2 Preheat the oven to 375°F/190°C. Unwrap and roll out the dough on a lightly floured work surface. Use to line a 9-inch/23-cm tart pan. Place the pan on a baking sheet. Prick the bottom of the pastry shell all over with a fork, line with foil or parchment paper, and fill with pie weights or dried beans. Bake in the preheated oven for 15 minutes, until the edges are set and dry. Remove the lining and weights and bake the pastry shell for another 5–7 minutes, or until golden. Let cool slightly.

3 For the filling, arrange the cheeses over the bottom of the pastry shell, then crumble the bacon evenly on top. Place the eggs and cream in a bowl and beat together until thoroughly combined. Add salt and pepper to taste. Pour the mixture into the pastry shell and return to the oven for 20 minutes, or until the filling is golden and set.

4 Remove from the oven and let quiche cool in the pan for 10 minutes. Transfer to a wire rack to cool completely. Cover and store in the refrigerator, but return to room temperature before serving.

Chive Scrambled
Eggs with Brioche

Serves 2

ingredients
- 4 eggs
- scant ½ cup light cream
- 2 tbsp snipped fresh chives, plus
  4 whole fresh chives to garnish
- 2 tbsp butter
- 4 slices brioche loaf, lightly
  toasted
- salt and pepper

1 Break the eggs into a medium bowl and whisk gently with the cream. Season to taste with salt and pepper and add the snipped chives.

2 Melt the butter in a sauté pan and pour in the egg mixture. Let stand to set slightly, then move the mixture toward the center of the pan, using a wooden spoon, as the eggs begin to cook. Continue in this way until the eggs are cooked but still creamy.

3 Place the toasted brioche slices in the center of 2 plates and spoon over the scrambled eggs. Serve immediately, garnished with whole chives.

Deep-Fried Mozzarella

Serves 4

ingredients

- 8 slices bread, preferably slightly stale, crusts removed
- 3½ oz/100 g mozzarella, thickly sliced
- 1¾ oz/50 g black olives, chopped
- 8 canned anchovy fillets, drained and chopped
- 16 fresh basil leaves, plus extra to garnish
- 4 eggs, beaten
- ⅔ cup milk
- oil, for deep-frying
- salt and pepper

1 Cut each slice of bread into 2 triangles. Top 8 of the bread triangles with equal amounts of the mozzarella slices, olives, and anchovies.

2 Place the basil leaves on top and season with salt and pepper to taste. Lay the other 8 triangles of bread over the top and press down around the edges to seal.

3 Mix the eggs and milk together and pour into a dish. Add the sandwiches and let soak for about 5 minutes.

4 Heat the oil in a large saucepan to 350–375°F/180–190°C, or until a cube of bread browns in 30 seconds.

5 Before cooking the sandwiches, squeeze the edges together again.

6 Carefully place the sandwiches in the oil and deep-fry for 2 minutes, or until golden, turning once. (You will have to cook them in batches.) Remove the sandwiches with a slotted spoon and drain on paper towels. Serve immediately while still hot, garnished wth basil leaves.

Double Cheese Soufflés

Makes 6

ingredients
- 2 tbsp butter, plus extra for greasing
- 2 tbsp finely grated Parmesan cheese
- ¾ cup milk
- 3 tbsp self-rising flour
- whole nutmeg, for grating
- 3½ oz/100 g soft goat cheese
- scant ⅔ cup grated sharp cheddar cheese
- 2 extra-large eggs, separated
- salt and pepper

1 Preheat the oven to 400°F/200°C. Put a baking sheet in the oven to warm. Generously grease the inside of 6 small ramekins with butter, add half of the Parmesan cheese, and shake to coat the butter.

2 Warm the milk in a small saucepan. Melt the remaining butter in a separate saucepan over medium heat. Add the flour, stir well to combine, and cook, stirring, for 2 minutes, until smooth. Add a little of the warmed milk and stir until absorbed. Continue to add the milk a little at a time, stirring continuously, until you have a rich, smooth sauce. Season to taste with salt and pepper, and grate in a little nutmeg. Add the cheeses to the sauce and stir until well combined and melted.

3 Remove from the heat and let the sauce cool a little, then add the egg yolks and stir to combine. In a separate bowl, whisk the egg whites until stiff. Fold a tablespoonful of the egg whites into the cheese sauce, then gradually fold in the remaining egg whites. Spoon into the prepared ramekins and scatter with the remaining Parmesan cheese.

4 Place the ramekins on the hot baking sheet and bake in the preheated oven for 15 minutes, until puffed up and brown. Remove from the oven and serve immediately. The soufflés will collapse quickly when taken from the oven, so have your serving plates ready to take the soufflés to the table.

Zucchini, Goat Cheese & Red Onion Pizza

Serves 4–6

ingredients

- 4 tbsp butter, plus extra for greasing
- 14 oz/400 g canned chopped tomatoes with chopped herbs
- 1 tbsp olive oil
- 1 small red onion, sliced
- 2 small zucchini (about 8 oz/ 225 g), sliced
- heaping 1¾ cups all-purpose white flour
- 2 tsp baking powder
- about ½ cup milk
- ½ cup grated mozzarella cheese
- 1 large vine-ripened tomato, thinly sliced
- 3½ oz/100 g soft goat cheese, crumbled
- salt and pepper

1 Preheat the oven to 425°F/220°C. Grease a baking sheet and set aside. Pour the tomatoes and their juices into a strainer placed over a bowl. Set aside, stirring occasionally, until most of the juice has drained away to create a thick tomato pulp. Reserve the tomato pulp and discard the juice.

2 Heat the olive oil in a saucepan, add the onion and zucchini, and cook for about 5 minutes, or until softened, stirring occasionally. Remove from the heat and set aside.

3 Sift the flour and baking powder into a bowl, add a pinch of salt, then lightly rub in the butter until the mixture resembles breadcrumbs. Stir in enough milk to form a fairly soft dough. Knead lightly.

4 Lightly roll out the dough on a lightly floured surface to form a 10-inch/25-cm round and place it on the prepared baking sheet. Spread the strained tomato pulp evenly over the dough, season with salt and pepper, then sprinkle over the mozzarella. Top with the zucchini mixture. Arrange the tomato slices on top, then scatter the goat cheese over the tomatoes.

5 Bake in the oven for about 25 minutes, or until cooked and deep golden brown around the edges. Remove from the oven and serve.

Spaghetti alla Carbonara

Serves 4

ingredients
- 1 lb/450 g dried spaghetti
- 1 tbsp olive oil
- 8 oz/225 g rindless pancetta or bacon, chopped
- 4 eggs
- 5 tbsp light cream
- 2 tbsp freshly grated Parmesan cheese
- salt and pepper

1 Bring a large heavy-bottom saucepan of lightly salted water to a boil. Add the pasta, return to a boil, and cook for 8–10 minutes, or according to the package directions, until tender but still firm to the bite.

2 Meanwhile, heat the oil in a heavy-bottom skillet. Add the pancetta and cook over medium heat, stirring frequently, for 8–10 minutes.

3 Beat the eggs with the cream in a small bowl and season to taste with salt and pepper. Drain the pasta and return it to the saucepan.

4 Add the contents of the skillet, then add the egg mixture and half of the Parmesan cheese. Stir well, then transfer to a warm serving dish. Serve immediately, sprinkled with the remaining cheese.

Ricotta Cheesecake

Serves 6–8

ingredients

for the pie dough
- heaping 1⅓ cups all-purpose flour, plus extra for dusting
- 3 tbsp superfine sugar
- pinch of salt
- ½ cup unsalted butter, diced and chilled
- 1 egg yolk

for the filling
- 1¾ cups ricotta cheese
- ½ cup heavy cream
- 2 eggs, plus 1 egg yolk
- scant ½ cup superfine sugar
- finely grated rind of 1 lemon
- finely grated rind of 1 orange, plus extra to garnish

1 To make the pie dough, sift the flour, sugar, and salt onto a work surface and make a well in the center. Add the butter and egg yolk to the well. Using your fingertips, gradually work in the flour mixture until completely incorporated.

2 Gather up the dough and knead very lightly. Cut off about one-quarter, wrap in plastic wrap, and chill in the refrigerator. Press the remaining dough into the bottom of a 9-inch/23-cm loose-bottom tart pan. Chill in the refrigerator for 30 minutes.

3 To make the filling, beat all the ingredients together in a bowl. Cover with plastic wrap and chill in the refrigerator until required.

4 Preheat the oven to 375°F/190°C. Prick the bottom of the pastry shell all over with a fork. Line with parchment paper, fill with pie weights or dried beans, and bake in the preheated oven for 15 minutes.

5 Remove the lining paper and weights and let cool in the pan on a wire rack.

6 Spoon the ricotta mixture into the pastry shell and smooth the surface. Roll out the reserved dough on a lightly dusted work surface and cut into strips. Arrange the strips over the filling in a lattice pattern, brushing the overlapping ends with water so that they stick.

7 Bake in the oven for 30–35 minutes, until the top of the cheesecake is golden and the filling has set. Let cool on a wire rack before removing the side of the pan. Cut into wedges and serve garnished with grated orange rind.

Lemon Meringue Pie

Serves 4

ingredients

for the pie dough

- scant 1⅔ cups all-purpose flour, plus extra for dusting
- scant ½ cup butter, diced, plus extra for greasing
- heaping ⅓ cup confectioners' sugar, sifted
- finely grated rind of 1 lemon
- 1 egg yolk, beaten
- 3 tbsp milk

for the filling

- 3 tbsp cornstarch
- 1¼ cups cold water
- juice and grated rind of 2 lemons
- heaping ¾ cup superfine sugar
- 2 eggs, separated
- light cream, to serve

1 To make the pie dough, sift the flour into a large bowl. Add the butter and rub it in until the mixture resembles breadcrumbs. Mix in the remaining ingredients. Knead briefly on a lightly floured work surface. Let rest for 30 minutes.

2 Preheat the oven to 350°F/180°C. Grease an 8-inch/20-cm ovenproof pie plate with butter.

3 Roll out the dough to a thickness of ¼ inch/5 mm and line the plate with it. Prick with a fork, then line with parchment paper and fill with pie weights or dried beans. Bake in the preheated oven for 15 minutes. Remove the lining paper and weights and let the dish cool on a wire rack. Reduce the oven temperature to 300°F/150°C.

4 To make the filling, mix the cornstarch with a little water to form a paste. Pour the remaining water into a saucepan. Stir in the lemon juice and rind and the cornstarch paste. Bring to a boil, while stirring, and cook for 2 minutes. Cool slightly, then stir in 5 tablespoons of the sugar and the egg yolks and pour into the pastry shell. Whisk the egg whites in a separate bowl until stiff. Gradually whisk in the remaining sugar and spread over the pie. Bake in the oven for 40 minutes, or until the meringue is light brown. Remove from the oven and serve with light cream.

Rich Vanilla Ice Cream

Serves 4–6

ingredients
- 2½ cups whipping cream
- 1 vanilla bean
- 4 extra-large egg yolks
- ½ cup superfine sugar

1 Pour the cream into a large heavy-bottom saucepan. Split open the vanilla bean and scrape out the seeds into the cream, then add the whole vanilla bean. Bring almost to a boil, then remove the pan from the heat and let stand to infuse for 30 minutes.

2 Place the egg yolks and sugar in a large bowl and whisk together until pale and the mixture leaves a trail when the whisk is lifted. Remove the vanilla bean from the cream, then slowly add the cream to the egg mixture, stirring continuously with a wooden spoon. Strain the mixture into the rinsed-out saucepan or a double boiler and cook over low heat for 10–15 minutes, stirring continuously, until the mixture thickens enough to coat the back of the spoon. Do not let the mixture boil or it will curdle. Remove the custard from the heat and let cool for at least 1 hour, stirring occasionally to prevent a skin from forming.

3 If using an ice cream machine, churn the cold custard in the machine following the manufacturer's directions. Alternatively, freeze the custard in a freezer-proof container, uncovered, for 1–2 hours, or until it begins to set around the edges. Turn the custard into a bowl and stir with a fork or beat in a food processor until smooth. Return to the freezer and freeze for another 2–3 hours, or until firm or required. Cover the container with a lid for storing.

Chocolate Fudge Brownies

Makes 16

ingredients

- 6 tbsp butter, plus extra for greasing
- heaping ¾ cup low-fat cream cheese
- ½ tsp vanilla extract
- heaping 1 cup superfine sugar
- 2 eggs
- 3 tbsp unsweetened cocoa
- heaping ¾ cup self-rising flour, sifted
- ½ cup chopped pecans

for the fudge topping

- 4 tbsp butter
- 1 tbsp milk
- ⅔ cup confections' sugar
- 2 tbsp unsweetened cocoa
- pecans, to decorate (optional)

1 Preheat the oven to 350°F/180°C. Lightly grease and line a shallow 8-inch/20-cm square cake pan.

2 Beat together the cream cheese, vanilla extract, and 5 teaspoons of superfine sugar until smooth, then set aside.

3 Beat the eggs and remaining superfine sugar together until light and fluffy. Place the butter and cocoa in a small pan and heat gently, stirring until the butter melts and the mixture combines, then stir it into the egg mixture. Fold in the flour and nuts.

4 Pour half of the cake batter into the prepared pan and smooth the top. Carefully spread the cheese mixture over it, then cover it with the remaining cake batter. Bake in the preheated oven for 40–45 minutes. Let stand to cool in the pan.

5 To make the topping, melt the butter in the milk. Stir in the confectioners' sugar and cocoa. Spread the topping over the brownies and decorate with pecans, if using. Let the topping set, then cut into rectangles or squares to serve.

Chocolate Mousse Pots

Makes 6

ingredients

- 3½ oz/100 g semisweet dark chocolate (minimum 70% cocoa solids), chopped
- 1 tbsp butter
- 2 extra-large eggs, separated
- 1 tbsp maple syrup
- 2 tbsp Greek yogurt
- ⅔ cup blueberries
- 1 tbsp water
- 1 oz/25 g white chocolate, grated

1 Put the chocolate and butter in a heatproof bowl, set the bowl over a saucepan of barely simmering water, and heat until melted. Let stand to cool slightly, then stir in the egg yolks, maple syrup, and yogurt.

2 Whisk the egg whites in a large, grease-free bowl until stiff, then fold into the chocolate mixture. Divide among 6 small ramekins and chill for 4 hours.

3 Meanwhile, put the blueberries in a small saucepan with the water and cook until the berries begin to pop and turn glossy. Let stand to cool, then chill.

4 To serve, top each mousse with blueberries and the grated white chocolate.

Crème Brûlée

Serves 4–6

ingredients

- 2–2½ cups mixed berries, such as blueberries, and/or pitted fresh cherries
- 1½–2 tbsp orange liqueur or orange flower water
- 9 oz/250 g mascarpone cheese
- scant 1 cup crème fraîche
- 2–3 tbsp dark brown sugar

1 Prepare the fruit, if necessary, and lightly rinse, then place in the bottoms of 4–6 individual ⅔-cup ramekin dishes. Sprinkle the fruit with the liqueur.

2 Cream the mascarpone cheese in a bowl until soft, then gradually beat in the crème fraîche.

3 Spoon the cheese mixture over the fruit, smoothing the surface and ensuring that the tops are level. Chill in the refrigerator for at least 2 hours.

4 Sprinkle the tops with the sugar. Using a chef's blowtorch, heat the tops until caramelized (about 2–3 minutes). Alternatively, cook under a preheated broiler, turning the dishes, for 3–4 minutes, or until the tops are lightly caramelized all over.

5 Serve immediately or chill in the refrigerator for 15–20 minutes before serving.

Tiramisu

Serves 4

ingredients

- scant 1 cup strong black coffee, cooled to room temperature
- 4 tbsp orange liqueur, such as Cointreau
- 3 tbsp orange juice
- 16 Italian ladyfingers
- 9 oz/250 g mascarpone cheese
- 1¼ cups heavy cream, lightly whipped
- 3 tbsp confectioners' sugar
- grated rind of 1 orange
- 2¼ oz/60 g dark semisweet chocolate, grated

to decorate

- chopped toasted almonds
- candied orange peel
- chocolate shavings

1 Pour the cooled coffee into a heatproof pitcher and stir in the orange liqueur and orange juice. Place 8 of the ladyfingers in the bottom of a serving dish, then pour in half of the coffee mixture.

2 Place the mascarpone in a separate bowl together with the cream, sugar, and orange rind and mix well. Spread half of the mascarpone mixture over the coffee-soaked ladyfingers, then arrange the remaining ladyfingers on top.

3 Pour the remaining coffee mixture over the top, then spread over the remaining mascarpone mixture. Scatter with the grated chocolate and let chill in the refrigerator for at least 2 hours.

4 Serve decorated with chopped toasted almonds, candied orange peel, and chocolate shavings.

Chapter 2
Fish & Seafood

INTRODUCTION

Fish and other seafood are very good for you: they are full of protein, iodine, and magnesium, which are essential for building tissue, regulating the metabolism, and keeping the bowel healthy. Oily fish, in particular, are rich in essential fatty acids, which help to lower cholesterol and support the immune system.

Sole

Trout

Buying and storing fresh fish

Nowadays there is a wide variety of fish available. You can buy fresh flat fish, such as flounder, sole, or halibut, or round fish, such as cod, salmon, or trout. You can also buy preserved fish, which have been smoked, dried, or salted. When buying fresh whole fish, choose those that smell fresh or that smell of the sea. Avoid any that smell of ammonia. They should have moist, clear eyes and shiny, firm bodies. You can ask your fish dealer to skin, gut, and fillet whole larger fish for you. Refrigerate the fish as soon as you get home. Fresh fish is best eaten on the day of purchase, but it will keep for 1–2 days, if necessary. Frozen fish will keep for up to 6 months in the freezer, but will need thawing in the refrigerator for at least 8 hours before use. Oily fish, such as mackerel, should be wrapped well in clean, damp cloths and stored in the refrigerator. Lower-fat white fish, such as cod, can be covered with plastic wrap. Use it before the expiration date on the packaging.

Smoked fish

You can buy a wide variety of smoked fish. Smoked salmon is very popular and is usually served cold with slices of lemon. Smoked trout has a mild flavor and is best partnered with horseradish or slices of lemon. Smoked mackerel has a rich flavor and needs a sharp sauce, such as dill or mustard. Smoked haddock is delicious served with a creamy sauce or in a kedgeree—a rice-based fish dish—while smoked cod is popular in pies. Fresh smoked fish should be wrapped well in plastic wrap and stored in the refrigerator. Smoked fish is often bought vacuum-packed. Store it in the refrigerator and use before the expiration date.

Preparing and cooking fresh fish

There is a wide range of white fish available these days. Some, such as cod, are low in fat, while other types of fish, such as sardines, are rich in healthy essential fatty acids.

Herring

Mackerel

Cod
This round fish has firm, white, flaky flesh and a mild flavor. It can be baked, broiled, poached, pan-fried, or deep-fried in batter or breadcrumbs.

Haddock
Like cod, this round fish has firm, white flesh and a mild flavor. It can be baked, broiled, poached, pan-fried, or deep-fried, and in many recipes is interchangeable with cod.

Hake
With a milder flavor than cod, this round fish can be fried, baked, or steamed and is also useful in soups.

Pollock
This is a close, although smaller, relative of cod. It is cooked in the same way as cod or haddock and is often used in mixed fish soups.

Trout
Like salmon, this round fish is available farmed or wild, but the wild type is rare. It can be pan-fried, broiled, poached, steamed, grilled, or baked. This is an oily fish, which means that it is rich in essential fatty acids.

Halibut and turbot
These large flat fish both have firm flesh and an excellent flavor and are interchangeable in many recipes. You can fry, poach, steam, broil, or bake both these fish.

Mackerel
This is a round fish with a delicious flavor. It is at its best when simply broiled, but can also be fried or grilled. It is another oily fish that is good for your health.

Sole
This flat fish has an excellent flavor and needs little added flavoring to bring out its best qualities. You can pan-fry, deep-fry, bake, steam, or grill (whole fish only) sole. Lemon sole, also called English sole, is not a true sole but a species of flounder. It's suitable for poaching, frying, broiling, and baking.

Herrings, sardines, sprats, and smelt
These small fish have a lot of bones, so it is best to ask your fish dealer to remove the innards and as many bones as possible. They can be grilled, deep-fried, baked, or broiled. They are also oily fish, and, therefore, rich in essential fatty acids.

Flounder
This flat fish needs extra flavoring but is good when pan-fried or deep-fried, baked, broiled, poached, or steamed.

Salmon
This round fish is available farmed or wild. A popular fish, it can be pan-fried, broiled, poached, steamed, grilled, or baked. Salmon en croûte or en papillote (salmon baked in pastry or in parchment) are popular dishes. Salmon is an oily fish.

Tuna
This is a round, oily fish with firm, meaty flesh that makes wonderful steaks with only a very mild fish flavor. The steaks are excellent grilled or broiled for about 3 minutes each side (do not overcook). You can also bake, broil, grill, braise, or stew fresh tuna.

Fresh and frozen shellfish

You can buy fresh shellfish from fish dealers and supermarkets. In some cases, shrimp, for example, you can also buy them already prepared, cooked, and frozen.

Lobster

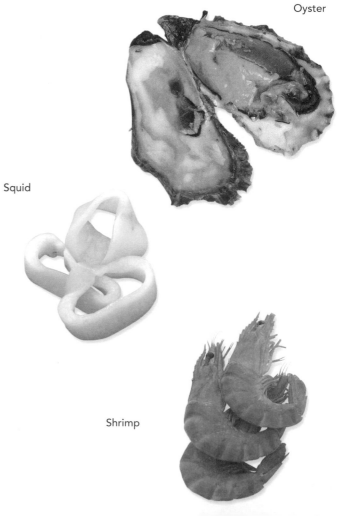

Oyster

Squid

Shrimp

Buying and storing shellfish

Shellfish can cause food poisoning, so always buy them as fresh as possible from a reputable supplier. Shellfish should smell fresh or sweet—avoid any that smell of chlorine or sulfur.

If you are buying mussels, clams, or oysters, the shells should be tightly closed and not cracked or damaged. Refrigerate shellfish in a covered container as soon as you get home and use on the day of purchase. If you buy live lobster or crabs, place something heavy on top of the container to stop them from escaping. Handle shellfish as little as possible and prepare with thoroughly clean equipment and hands.

Preparation and cooking techniques

Preparation techniques vary greatly, depending on the type of shellfish you are using. If you are in any doubt, your local fish dealer will be able to give you advice. Shellfish does not need to cook for long periods of time so stick to the recommended cooking times. Do not overcook it or you could impair the texture and/or taste. Squid, for example, becomes unpleasantly rubbery if cooked for too long.

Crab and lobster

You can buy crabs and lobsters alive or cooked. If you buy them live, make sure the claws are tied with string. Put them in the freezer for 1 hour before cooking to desensitize. To cook, take a large saucepan and pour in enough water or stock to cover the crab or lobster. Bring it to a boil, add the crab or lobster, cover the pan, and boil until it turns red. Plan 5 minutes of cooking for every 1 lb/450 g of crab. For a lobster, plan 5 minutes for the first 1 lb/450 g, plus an extra 3 minutes for each additional 1 lb/450 g. To remove the cooked meat from the crab, crack the claws and remove and reserve the white meat. Snap off the tail, then use your hands to break the shell. Lift out the body, cut it in half lengthwise, and scoop out the meat. Then lift out the brown meat from the shell. The edible parts of a lobster are the meat in the tail and claws, the liver, and the roe, if the lobster is female. Cooking a lobster and removing the meat can be fussy, however, so it is usually best to ask your fish dealer to do this for you.

Mussels

You should use fresh mussels on the day of purchase and keep them in lightly salted water until you are ready to use them. To clean and debeard them, use a small knife to scrape off any barnacles from the shells, then pull out and discard any clumps of hair (these are called "beards"). Use a stiff brush to scrub the shells under cold running water, then tap each mussel sharply with the handle of the knife and discard any that do not close tightly. To steam them, heat a little liquid (water, stock, or wine) in a large saucepan, add the cleaned mussels, cover the pan, and steam them, shaking the pan occasionally, for 5–6 minutes. Remove from the heat and discard any mussels that remain closed. You can also broil or bake them half shelled, or stew them shelled.

Oysters

These shellfish are usually eaten raw. Use a stiff brush to scrub the shells under cold running water, and discard any that are open. To open an oyster, insert a knife blade between the two shell halves and twist it to pry them open. Use a spoon to lift out the oyster inside (you will need to cut it from the muscle underneath). Serve it on a half shell. You can also bake or broil oysters in their half shells, or stew them shelled.

Shrimp

These come in different sizes and you can buy them peeled or unpeeled, cooked or raw. Cooked, peeled shrimp are also available frozen. To peel and devein a raw shrimp, carefully peel off the shell (you can remove the tail or leave it on for decorative effect). Using a small knife, make a shallow cut along the dark vein to reveal it, then remove it with the knife's tip. Discard the vein, then rinse the shrimp under cold running water and pat dry with paper towels. Shrimp require very little cooking—for example, you need to stir-fry them for only 2–3 minutes, until they turn pink. You can pan-fry, stir-fry, broil, bake, grill, or steam them.

Scallops

These have a delicate flavor and are becoming increasingly popular. They should be creamy white with pink corals. They need a minimal amount of cooking, usually 1–2 minutes on each side if you are pan-frying them shelled. You can also broil or bake them in their half shells.

Squid

You can buy squid whole or prepared. The edible parts are the tentacles, fins, pouch, and the ink. Sauté the squid for only 2–3 minutes—do not overcook it or it will go rubbery. You can also deep-fry, bake, poach, and stew it.

Clams

Use a stiff brush to scrub the shells under cold running water, and discard any that stay open when tapped. To open a clam, insert a knife blade between the two shell halves and twist it to pry them open. Use a spoon to lift out the soft flesh inside. You can eat clams raw, or you can steam them in their shells for 4 minutes or until they have opened. You can also bake or broil them in their half shells, or stew them shelled.

Mussels

Seafood Chowder

Serves 6

ingredients

- 2 lb 4 oz/1 kg mussels
- 12 oz/350 g skinless white fish fillets, such as cod, sole, or haddock
- 1 tbsp butter
- 1 large onion, finely chopped
- 6 cups fish stock
- ¼ cup all-purpose flour
- 7 oz/200 g cooked or raw, peeled shrimp
- 1¼ cups whipping cream or heavy cream
- salt and pepper
- snipped fresh dill, to garnish

1 Discard any mussels with broken shells or any that refuse to close when tapped. Rinse and pull off any beards. Put the mussels in a large, heavy-bottom saucepan. Cover tightly and cook over high heat for about 4 minutes, or until the mussels open, shaking the pan occasionally. Discard any that remain closed. When they are cool enough to handle, remove the mussels from their shells and set aside.

2 Meanwhile, lightly poach the fish fillets in a saucepan of gently simmering water for 4–5 minutes (if in one piece), or until just cooked but still moist. Using a fork, flake the flesh into a bowl.

3 Melt the butter in a heavy-bottom saucepan over medium–low heat. Add the onion, cover, and cook for 3 minutes, stirring frequently, until it softens.

4 Add the fish stock and bring to a boil. Slowly whisk in the flour until well combined and bring back to the boil, whisking continuously. Season with salt, if needed, and pepper. Reduce the heat and simmer, partially covered, for 15 minutes.

5 Add the poached fish and mussels and stir to combine. Stir in the shrimp and cream.

6 Taste and adjust the seasoning. Simmer for a few minutes longer to heat through. Ladle into warm bowls, sprinkle with dill, and serve.

Creamy Salmon Baked Potatoes

Serves 4

ingredients

- 4 large baking potatoes, scrubbed
- 9 oz/250 g skinless salmon fillet
- 1 cup reduced-fat cream cheese
- 2–3 tbsp skim milk
- 2 tbsp chopped or snipped fresh herbs, such as dill or chives
- ½ cup grated sharp cheddar cheese
- salt and pepper

1 Preheat the oven to 400°F/200°C. Prick the skins of the potatoes and put on the top shelf of the preheated oven. Bake for 50–60 minutes, until the skins are crisp and the centers are soft when pierced with a sharp knife or skewer.

2 Meanwhile, lightly poach the salmon fillet in a saucepan of gently simmering water for 4–5 minutes (if in one piece), or until just cooked but still moist. Alternatively, cut into 2–3 even pieces and cook in a microwave oven on medium for 2 minutes, then turn the pieces around so that the cooked parts are in the center, and cook for an additional 1 minute, or until just cooked but still moist. Using a fork, flake the flesh into a bowl.

3 In a separate bowl, blend the cream cheese with just enough of the milk to loosen, then stir in the herbs and a little salt and pepper.

4 When the potatoes are cooked, preheat the broiler to high. Cut the potatoes in half lengthwise. Carefully scoop the potato flesh out of the skins, reserving the skins, add to the cream cheese mixture, and mash together. Lightly stir in the salmon flakes.

5 Spoon the filling into the potato skins and top with the cheddar cheese. Cook under the preheated broiler for 1–2 minutes until the cheese is bubbling and turning golden. Serve immediately.

Smoked Fish Pie

Serves 6

ingredients
- 2 tbsp olive oil
- 1 onion, finely chopped
- 1 leek, thinly sliced
- 1 carrot, diced
- 1 celery stalk, diced
- 1⅔ cups halved button mushrooms
- grated rind of 1 lemon
- 12 oz/350 g skinless, boneless smoked cod or haddock fillet, cubed
- 12 oz/350 g skinless, boneless white fish, cubed
- 8 oz/225 g cooked, peeled shrimp
- 2 tbsp chopped fresh parsley
- 1 tbsp chopped fresh dill
- salt and pepper

for the sauce
- 4 tbsp butter
- ¼ cup all-purpose flour
- 1 tsp dry mustard
- 2½ cups milk
- ¾ cup grated Gruyère cheese

for the topping
- 3 large potatoes (about 1 lb 8 oz/ 675 g), unpeeled
- 4 tbsp butter, melted
- ¼ cup grated Gruyère cheese

1 For the sauce, heat the butter in a large saucepan and, when melted, add the flour and mustard. Stir until smooth and cook over very low heat for 2 minutes, without coloring. Slowly beat in the milk until smooth. Simmer gently for 2 minutes, then stir in the cheese until smooth. Remove from the heat and place some plastic wrap over the surface of the sauce to prevent a skin from forming. Reserve.

2 Meanwhile, for the topping, boil the whole potatoes in plenty of salted water for 15 minutes. Drain well and let stand until the potatoes are cool enough to handle.

3 Preheat the oven to 400°F/200°C. Heat the oil in a clean saucepan. Add the onion and cook for 5 minutes, until softened. Add the leek, carrot, celery, and mushrooms and cook for an additional 10 minutes, or until the vegetables have softened. Stir in the lemon rind and cook briefly.

4 Add the softened vegetables with the fish, shrimp, parsley, and dill to the sauce. Season to taste with salt and pepper and transfer to a greased 7-cup casserole dish.

5 Peel the cooled potatoes and grate them coarsely. Mix with the melted butter. Cover the filling with the grated potato and sprinkle with the grated Gruyère cheese.

6 Cover loosely with foil and bake in the preheated oven for 30 minutes. Remove the foil and bake for an additional 30 minutes, or until the topping is tender and golden and the filling is bubbling.

Sweet Potato & Tuna Fish Cakes

Serves 4

ingredients

- 1⅓ cups peeled and chopped sweet potatoes
- 6 oz/175 g canned tuna, drained
- 4 scallions, trimmed and chopped
- 1 tbsp grated lemon rind
- 1 tbsp chopped fresh cilantro
- pepper
- lemon wedges, to garnish
- freshly cooked green beans, to serve

1 Cook the sweet potatoes in a saucepan of boiling water for 10–12 minutes, or until tender when pierced with a fork. Drain and mash.

2 Flake the tuna, then add to the mashed potatoes together with the chopped scallions, lemon rind, chopped cilantro, and pepper to taste.

3 Mix the ingredients lightly together then, using slightly dampened hands, shape into 4 patties. Place on a plate, cover loosely, and let chill in the refrigerator for at least 30 minutes, longer if time permits.

4 Preheat the oven to 375°F/190°C. Place the fish cakes on a large nonstick baking sheet and cook for 20 minutes, or until piping hot. Transfer to serving plates, garnish with lemon wedges, and serve with freshly cooked green beans.

Baked Salmon with Wild Rice

Serves 4

ingredients

- 1½ cups wild rice, rinsed and drained
- 5½ tbsp butter
- 1 tbsp olive oil, plus extra for greasing
- 5¾ cups wiped and thinly sliced button mushrooms
- 1 tbsp chopped fresh tarragon, or ½ tbsp dried tarragon
- 3⅓ cups trimmed and thinly sliced leeks
- 12 thin lemon slices
- 4 salmon fillets, any small bones removed
- 4 tbsp dry white vermouth
- 4½ oz/125 g crème fraîche
- salt and pepper

1 Bring 5 cups of water to a boil in a large saucepan. Add the rice and 1½ teaspoons of salt and return the water to a boil. Cover the pan, reduce the heat to low, and simmer for 45–50 minutes, until all the liquid has been absorbed and the rice is tender. Add 2 tablespoons of the butter and fluff with a fork.

2 Meanwhile, preheat the oven to 425°F/220°C. Cut 4 circles of wax paper large enough to hold a salmon fillet with some mushrooms and leeks spooned on top. Fold the circles in half and brush the bottom halves with oil.

3 Melt 2 tablespoons of the remaining butter with the oil in a large skillet over high heat. Add the mushrooms and cook, stirring, for about 6 minutes, until they start to give off their liquid. Add the tarragon and salt and pepper to taste and stir. Transfer the mushrooms from the pan and set aside. Melt the remaining butter in the wiped-out pan. Add the leeks with salt and pepper to taste and cook, stirring, for 6 minutes, or until tender.

4 Arrange 3 lemon slices in a row along the fold on each of the paper circles. Place a salmon fillet on top, top with one-quarter of the mushrooms and the leeks, and add a tablespoon of vermouth, 2 tablespoons of crème fraîche, and some salt and pepper. Fold over the circles and crimp the edges so the bundles are sealed and none of the juices can escape. Transfer to a baking sheet, place in the oven, and bake for 12 minutes, or until the flesh flakes.

5 Place the salmon on a bed of wild rice and serve.

Cod & Fries

Serves 4

ingredients
- 4 large potatoes
- vegetable oil, for deep-frying
- 4 thick cod pieces, about 6 oz/ 175 g each, preferably from the head end
- salt and pepper
- lemon wedges, to serve (optional)

for the batter
- ½ oz/15 g fresh yeast cake
- 1¼ cups beer
- 1¾ cups all-purpose flour
- 2 tsp salt

for the mayonnaise
- 1 egg yolk
- 1 tsp whole-grain mustard
- 1 tbsp lemon juice
- scant 1 cup light olive oil
- salt and pepper

1 For the batter, cream the yeast with a little beer to a smooth paste. Gradually stir in the remaining beer. Sift the flour and salt into a bowl, make a well in the center, add the yeast, and whisk to a smooth batter. Cover and let stand at room temperature for 1 hour.

2 For the mayonnaise, process all the ingredients except the oil in a food processor for 30 seconds, until frothy. With the machine still running, gradually add the oil, drop by drop, until the mixture begins to thicken. Continue adding in a steady stream until it has been incorporated. Adjust the seasoning. Thin with a little hot water if too thick, then chill.

3 Cut the potatoes into strips about ⅝ inch/1.5 cm thick. Heat a large saucepan filled halfway with vegetable oil to 275°F/140°C, or until a cube of bread browns in 1 minute. Cook the fries in 2 batches for 5 minutes, or until cooked through but not browned. Drain on paper towels and reserve.

4 Increase the heat to 325°F/160°C, or until a cube of bread browns in 45 seconds. Season the fish, then dip into the batter. Deep-fry 2 pieces at a time for 7–8 minutes, until golden brown and cooked through. Drain on paper towels and keep warm while you cook the remaining fish and the fries.

5 Increase the heat to 375°F/190°C, or until a cube of bread browns in 30 seconds. Deep-fry the fries again, in 2 batches, for 2–3 minutes, until crisp and golden. Drain on paper towels and sprinkle with salt. Serve the fish with the fries, mayonnaise, and lemon wedges.

Baked Sea Bass with White Bean Puree

Serves 4

ingredients
- 2 tbsp olive oil
- 1 tbsp fresh thyme leaves
- 4 large sea bass fillets, about 6 oz/175 g each
- cherry tomatoes on the vine, to serve
- salt and pepper

for the white bean puree
- 3 tbsp olive oil
- 2 garlic cloves, chopped
- 1 lb 12 oz/800 g canned cannellini or lima beans, drained and rinsed
- juice of 1 lemon
- 2–3 tbsp water
- ¼ cup chopped fresh flat-leaf parsley

1 Preheat the oven to 400°F/200°C. Mix the oil, thyme, and a little salt and pepper to taste together in a small bowl or pitcher. Arrange the sea bass fillets on a baking sheet, pour the oil mixture over the top, and carefully turn to coat well. Put the sheet on the top shelf of the preheated oven and bake for 15 minutes.

2 Meanwhile, make the bean puree. Heat the oil in a saucepan over medium heat, add the garlic, and cook, stirring, for 1 minute. Add the beans and heat through for 3–4 minutes, then add the lemon juice and a little salt and pepper to taste. Transfer to a blender or food processor, add the water, and blend lightly until you have a puree. Alternatively, mash thoroughly with a fork. Stir the parsley into the puree.

3 Serve the sea bass fillets on top of the warm bean puree with a drizzle of any pan juices. Serve with vine tomatoes.

Mediterranean Fish Casserole

Serves 6

ingredients
- 2 tbsp olive oil
- 1 red onion, peeled and sliced
- 2 garlic cloves, peeled and chopped
- 2 red bell peppers
- 14 oz/400 g canned chopped tomatoes
- 1 tsp chopped fresh oregano or marjoram
- a few saffron strands soaked in 1 tbsp warm water for 2 minutes
- 1 lb/450 g white fish (cod, haddock, or hake), skinned and boned
- 1 lb/450 g prepared squid, cut into rings
- 1¼ cups fish or vegetable stock
- 4 oz/115 g cooked, shelled shrimp
- 6 cooked whole shrimp in their shells, to garnish
- 2 tbsp chopped fresh flat-leaf parsley, to garnish
- salt and pepper
- crusty bread, to serve

1 Heat the oil in a skillet and fry the onion and garlic over medium heat for 2–3 minutes, until beginning to soften.

2 Seed and thinly slice the bell peppers and add to the skillet. Continue to cook over alow heat for another 5 minutes. Add the tomatoes with the herbs and saffron and stir well.

3 Preheat the oven to 400°F/ 200°C. Cut the white fish into 1¼-inch/ 3-cm pieces and place with the squid in a casserole dish. Pour in the fried vegetable mixture and the stock, stir well, and season to taste.

4 Cover and cook in the center of the preheated oven for about 30 minutes, until the fish is tender and cooked. Add the shrimp at the last minute and just heat through.

5 Transfer to warm bowls, garnish with the whole shrimp and chopped parsley, and serve with crusty bread.

Paella

Serves 4

ingredients

- 3 tbsp olive oil
- 2 tbsp butter
- 2 garlic cloves, chopped
- 1 onion, chopped
- 2 large tomatoes, seeded and diced
- heaping ½ cup frozen peas
- 1 red bell pepper, seeded and chopped
- ¾ cup risotto rice
- 2 tsp dried mixed herbs
- 1 tsp saffron powder
- 1¾ cup chicken stock
- 4 skinless, boneless chicken breasts
- 5½ oz/150 g lean chorizo, skinned
- 7 oz/200 g cooked lobster meat
- 7 oz/200 g shrimp, peeled and deveined
- 1 tbsp chopped fresh flat-leaf parsley, plus extra to garnish
- salt and pepper

1 Heat the oil and butter in a large skillet pan over medium heat. Add the garlic and onion and cook, stirring, for 3 minutes, or until slightly softened.

2 Add the tomatoes, peas, red bell pepper, rice, mixed herbs, and saffron and cook, stirring, for 2 minutes. Pour in the stock and bring to a boil. Reduce the heat to low and cook, stirring, for 10 minutes.

3 Chop the chicken into bite-size pieces and add to the skillet. Cook, stirring occasionally, for 5 minutes. Chop up the chorizo, add to the skillet, and cook for 3 minutes. Chop up the lobster meat and add to the pan with the shrimp and parsley. Season with salt and pepper and cook, stirring, for an additional 2 minutes.

4 Remove the skillet from the heat, transfer the paella to a large serving dish or individual plates, garnish with the chopped parsley, and serve.

Seafood Gratin

Serves 4

ingredients

- 1 lb/450 g cod fillets
- 8 oz/225 g shirmp, peeled and deveined
- 8 oz/225 g scallops
- 3 tbsp extra virgin olive oil
- 1 garlic clove, chopped
- 4 scallions, chopped
- 1 zucchini, sliced
- 15 oz/425 g canned plum tomatoes
- 2 tbsp chopped fresh basil
- 1 cup fresh breadcrumbs
- ⅔ cup grated cheddar cheese
- salt and pepper

1 Preheat the oven to 375°F/190°C. Bring a large saucepan of water to a boil, then reduce the heat to medium. Rinse the cod, pat dry with paper towels, and add to the pan. Cook for 5 minutes. Add the shrimp and cook for 3 minutes, then add the scallops and cook for another 2 minutes. Drain, refresh under cold running water, and drain again.

2 Heat 2 tablespoons of the oil in a skillet over low heat. Add the garlic and scallions and cook, stirring, for 3 minutes. Add the zucchini and cook for 3 minutes, then add the tomatoes with their juices and the basil. Season to taste with salt and pepper and let simmer for 10 minutes.

3 Brush a shallow baking dish with the remaining oil and arrange the seafood in it. Remove the saucepan from the heat and pour the sauce over the fish. Scatter with the breadcrumbs and top with cheese. Bake in the oven for 30 minutes until golden. Transfer to warm plates and serve.

Warm Tuna & Kidney Bean Salad

Serves 4

ingredients
- 4 fresh tuna steaks, about 6 oz/175 g each
- 1 tbsp olive oil
- 7 oz/200 g canned kidney beans, rinsed and drained
- 3½ oz/100 g canned corn kernels
- 2 scallions, trimmed and thinly sliced
- salt and pepper
- lime wedges, to garnish

for the dressing
- 5 tbsp extra virgin olive oil
- 3 tbsp balsamic vinegar
- 1 tbsp lime juice
- 1 garlic clove, chopped
- 1 tbsp chopped fresh cilantro
- salt and pepper

1 Preheat a ridged grill pan. While the pan is heating, brush the tuna steaks with olive oil, then season with salt and pepper. Cook the steaks for 2 minutes, then turn them over and cook on the other side for another 2 minutes, or according to your taste, but do not overcook. Remove from the heat and let stand to cool slightly.

2 While the tuna is cooling, heat the kidney beans and corn kernels according to the directions on the cans, then drain.

3 To make the dressing, put all the ingredients into a small bowl and stir together well.

4 Put the kidney beans, corn kernels, and scallions into a large bowl, pour in half of the dressing, and mix together well. Divide the bean-and-corn salad among individual serving plates, then place a tuna steak on each one. Drizzle with the remaining dressing, garnish with the lime wedges, and serve.

Pan-Fried Shrimp

Serves 4

ingredients
- 4 garlic cloves
- 20–24 unshelled large raw shrimp
- heaping ½ cup butter
- 4 tbsp olive oil
- 6 tbsp brandy
- salt and pepper
- 2 tbsp chopped fresh flat-leaf parsley, to garnish
- lemon wedges, to serve

1 Using a sharp knife, peel and slice the garlic.

2 Wash the shrimp and pat dry using paper towels.

3 Melt the butter with the oil in a large skillet, add the garlic and shrimp, and fry over high heat, stirring, for 3–4 minutes, until the shrimp are pink.

4 Drizzle with brandy and season with salt and pepper to taste. Sprinkle with the chopped parsley and serve immediately with lemon wedges.

Flounder Fish Sticks

Serves 2

ingredients
- 2 flounder fillets, about 6 oz/175 g each, skinned
- 2 tbsp all-purpose flour
- 1 egg, beaten
- 2½ cups white or whole wheat breadcrumbs, made from one-day-old bread
- 1 tbsp finely chopped fresh flat-leaf parsley
- 1 garlic clove, peeled and crushed (optional)
- 1 cup vegetable oil, for frying
- salt and pepper
- lemon wedges, to serve
- aioli, to serve

1 Cut the fillets across diagonally into thin strips, about ½ inch/1 cm wide.

2 Season the flour well and put onto a plate. Roll the strips of fish in the flour until well covered.

3 Place the beaten egg in a shallow dish and then dip the fish into it.

4 Mix the breadcrumbs with the parsley and garlic, if using, and season well. Put the mixture into a plastic bag, add the fish, and toss to coat thoroughly. Chill in the refrigerator for at least 30 minutes.

5 Heat the oil in a skillet and fry half of the coated fish pieces over medium heat for 2–3 minutes, turning them with a slotted spoon. Remove from the pan and drain on paper towels. Keep warm. Repeat using the remaining fish.

6 Serve at once with lemon wedges and a bowl of aioli.

Linguine with Clams

Serves 4

ingredients
- 7 oz/200 g dried linguine pasta
- 3 tbsp extra virgin olive oil
- 4 garlic cloves, finely chopped
- 2 shallots, finely chopped
- ½ fresh red chile, finely chopped
- ½ cup white wine
- 2 lb 4 oz/1 kg fresh clams, cleaned
- 1 tbsp fresh chopped flat-leaf parsley
- zest of 1 lemon
- salt and pepper

1 Cook the linguine according to the package directions, drain, and toss with a splash of olive oil. Cover and keep warm.

2 Add half of the olive oil to a large saucepan with a lid and place over high heat. Add the garlic, shallots, and chile and cook gently for 8–10 minutes, until soft. Add the wine, bring to a boil, and cook for 2 minutes. Add the clams, cover, and cook for another 2–5 minutes, or until all the clams have opened. Discard any clams that remain closed. Add the drained linguine, parsley, lemon zest, the remaining olive oil, and some salt and pepper and mix through.

3 Serve in warm bowls, with another bowl for discarded shells.

Chapter 3
Meat

Introduction

Meat is rich in protein and easy to cook. It makes an
excellent centerpiece to any meal, and you can choose
from a wide range of roasts and cuts, from the economical
to the indulgent, to suit any occasion.

Beef

Lamb

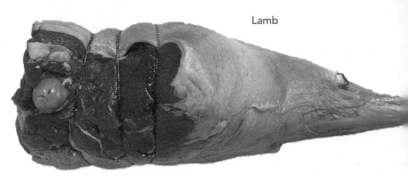

Buying and storing meat

Always buy your fresh meat from a reputable supplier. For
beef, look for meat that is deep burgundy red, not bright red;
the fat should be a cream color, not yellow. Choose beef
that has a marbling of fat through it—this will ensure that the
meat stays moist during cooking. For veal, the flesh should
be a very pale pink and the fat white. If it is turning red, it
means that the meat is older than it should be. For lamb,
choose firm, pinkish, marbled meat; avoid any that looks
dark and soggy. The fat should be a cream color, not yellow.
For pork, choose moist, pinkish meat with white fat. Avoid
any meat that looks oily or that has yellow fat.

If you are purchasing meat for roasting, plan 6–12 oz/
175–350 g per person, depending on whether the meat is
on or off the bone.

As soon as you get the meat home, unwrap it and transfer
it to a clean dish (the dish should have a lip deep enough to
catch any juices). Cover it with plastic wrap and store in the
refrigerator away from any cooked meats in order to prevent
cross-contamination. Leave any packaged meat in its
wrapping in the refrigerator and use by the expiration date.
Unpackaged ground lamb, beef, and pork is best used within
1–2 days of purchase. Fresh cuts of beef and pork will keep
in the refrigerator for 2–3 days, and cooked beef and pork
can be refrigerated for 4–5 days. Fresh lamb cuts will keep
for up to 4 days in the refrigerator. Before cooking, bring out
the meat (keep it covered) and let it reach room temperature
for about 30 minutes before cooking. You can freeze
small cuts of beef or pork for up to 6 months, and lamb
for up to 3 months. Make sure you thaw the meat
thoroughly in a refrigerator or cool room before cooking;
plan 6 hours per 1 lb/450 g.

Preparation techniques

There is a range of techniques you can use to prepare
and/or improve your chosen cuts of meat before cooking.
Some of them are done purely for presentation, while
other techniques help to tenderize the meat or facilitate
thorough cooking.

Lamb chops

Use a sharp knife to remove the excess fat around the
edge.

Pork chops and sirloin steaks

Use a sharp knife to make incisions in the fat at intervals
of 1 inch/2.5 cm around the edge. This helps prevent the
meat from curling up at the sides during cooking.

Chuck steak

Use a sharp knife to remove any excess fat. Slice the meat
across the grain, then cut across the slices to form smaller
pieces or cubes of meat.

Pork

Choosing cuts of meat

There are many different cuts of meat available. Choosing the right cut will help to ensure the perfect result for your chosen recipe. When in doubt, ask your local butcher for advice.

Tenderize thin cuts of meat
Put the meat between sheets of wax paper and pound with either a meat mallet or the bottom of a saucepan.

Stuff and tie a boneless roast
Put it skin-side down and arrange the stuffing evenly over the surface. Roll up the roast from the thick end, tie a piece of clean string lengthwise around the meat, then knot it and trim off the ends. Now tie additional pieces of string widthwise around the meat at intervals of about 1 inch/ 2.5 cm. Knot each one in turn and trim the ends.

Butterfly a leg of lamb
Push a chef's knife into the cavity of the bone, then cut sideways to part the meat. Open it out and make a light incision down the center of the meat so that it stays open and flat.

Prepare a rack of lamb
Remove the skin and excess fat, leaving a layer of fat about ⅝ inch/1.5 cm thick. Cut off the bone at the back, then remove the fat from the ends of the bones (to a length of about 2 inches/5 cm). Use a knife to scrape out the meat from between the bones.

Beef
For roasting, choose tenderloin, rib-eye roast, or standing rib roast. T-bone, porterhouse, top loin, and sirloin are excellent steaks for broiling, pan-frying, or grilling. For braising and stewing, use chuck, rump, or short rib.

Pork
For roasting, broiling, and frying, choose tender cuts from the loin and tenderloin that stand up to dry heat. Cuts from the shoulder and leg are tougher, so these are best cooked by slow, moist heat methods, such as braising and stewing. Chops, steaks, and cutlets are all terms referring to a slice of meat, but a steak may be thicker and a cutlet thinner. Medallions are boneless slices from the center loin.

Veal
Much of the veal found in supermarkets is limited to roasts, chops, and cutlets, but occasionally veal breast and ground veal are available, too. If availability is a problem, order ahead from a butcher.

Lamb
The leg is the most popular choice for roasting, but you can also roast cuts from the shoulder, rack, and loin. For broiling, try chops and steaks. Rib and loin chops are tender cuts; shoulder, arm, and blade chops from the arm and shoulder are noted by the lines of fat running through the meat. Finally, for stewing, braising, or casseroles, choose stew meat from the shoulder and neck for the best flavor.

Cooking and carving techniques

Techniques for cooking and carving meat are not difficult, but they do have to be performed properly in order to get the best out of the meat. Follow the instructions given here for perfect results every time.

Roasting and carving a boned roast

This technique is suitable for boned roasts of lamb, pork, and beef. Rub the surface with a little oil, followed by some salt and some crushed peppercorns (use a mortar and pestle for this). Place on a rack in a roasting pan, then roast in the oven, basting once or twice during cooking. Remove from the oven and cut off the strings. Wrap the meat in foil and let stand for 15–20 minutes. To carve, steady the meat with a fork, then carve slices downward from one end.

Roasting and carving a leg of lamb

Using a sharp knife, score a crisscross pattern in the fat, then rub all over the surface with a little oil, followed by some salt and freshly ground black pepper. Put the meat on a rack in a roasting pan and roast in the oven, basting once or twice during cooking.

To test if the meat is cooked all the way through, pierce a skewer or knife into the thickest part. The juices that run out will be clear if the meat is cooked. If not, return it to the oven and cook until it is done. Remove from the oven and wrap the meat in foil. Let stand for 15–20 minutes. To carve, turn the leg meat-side up, then steady the meat with a fork. Start carving from the knuckle end. When you have finished, turn over the leg and carve horizontal slices.

Using a meat thermometer

A meat thermometer is a useful device for testing whether a roast of meat is cooked thoroughly. Thorough cooking is particularly important in the case of pork, which can carry harmful bacteria and cause food poisoning if not cooked all the way through. Simply insert the thermometer into the thickest part of the meat at the start of cooking. Be careful to ensure that the thermometer does not come into contact with any bone, because this could produce a false reading. When the thermometer reaches the required temperature, the meat is cooked. The recommended temperatures for different meats are shown below.

COOKING TEMPERATURES

Lamb	Medium rare	165°F/75°C
	Well done	175°F/80°C
Pork	Well done	195°F/90°C
Beef	Rare	150°F/65°C
	Medium rare	160°F/70°C
	Well done	165°F/75°C

OVEN TEMPERATURES AND ROASTING TIMES

PLEASE NOTE THAT INDIVIDUAL OVEN TEMPERATURES AND COOKING TIMES VARY, SO THE FOLLOWING COOKING TIMES ARE ONLY APPROXIMATE. REMEMBER TO PREHEAT THE OVEN BEFORE COOKING FOR THE BEST RESULTS.

Meat	Cut	Weight	Temperature	Cooking time
Lamb	Whole leg	5 lb 8 oz/2.5 kg	350°F/180°C	2¼ hours (medium rare) or 2½ hours (well done)
Lamb	Whole shoulder	5 lb 8 oz/2.5 kg	350°F/180°C	2¼ hours (medium rare) or 2½ hours (well done)
Pork	Loin (boned)	5 lb 8 oz/2.5 kg	350°F/180°C 425°F/220°C	3 hours at lower temperature, then 20 minutes at higher temperature (well done)
Pork	Shoulder (boned)	5 lb 8 oz/2.5 kg	350°F/180°C 425°F/220°C	3 hours at lower temperature, then 20 minutes at higher temperature (well done)
Beef	Sirloin	5 lb 8 oz/2.5 kg	400°F/200°C	1¾ hours (rare), 2¼ hours (medium rare), or 2½ hours (well done)
Beef	3-rib prime roast	5 lb/2.25 kg	450°F/230°C 350°F/180°C	15 minutes at higher temperature, then 1 hour at lower temperature (rare)

OVEN TEMPERATURES AND HEAT DESCRIPTIONS

YOU MAY COME ACROSS RECIPES THAT DO NOT GIVE A SPECIFIC TEMPERATURE: INSTEAD THEY WILL SIMPLY RECOMMEND COOKING IN A "MODERATE" OR "HOT" OVEN. HERE IS A LIST OF THESE HEAT DESCRIPTIONS AND THEIR CORRECT TEMPERATURES.

Oven heat description	Fahrenheit	Celsius	Gas mark
Very cool	225–250°	110–120°	¼–½
Cool	275–300°	140–150°	1–2
Moderate	325–350°	160–180°	3–4
Moderately hot	375–400°	190–200°	5–6
Hot	425°	220°	7
Very hot	450–475°	230–240°	8–9

Roasted Beef

Serves 8

ingredients
- 6 lb/2.7 kg prime rib of beef
- 2 tsp dry English mustard
- 3 tbsp all-purpose flour
- 1¼ cups red wine
- 1¼ cups beef stock
- 2 tsp Worcestershire sauce (optional)
- salt and pepper

for the Yorkshire pudding
- ¾ cup all-purpose flour
- pinch of salt
- 1 egg, beaten
- ⅔ cup milk
- ⅔ cup water
- 2 tbsp roasted beef dripping or olive oil

1 Preheat the oven to 450°F/230°C (see step 3 to calculate when you will need to turn on the oven).

2 Season the meat with the salt and pepper and rub in the mustard and 1 tablespoon of the flour.

3 Place the meat in a roasting pan large enough to hold it comfortably and roast for 15 minutes. Reduce the heat to 375°F/190°C and cook for 15 minutes per 1 lb/450 g, plus 15 minutes (1 hour 45 minutes for this roast) for rare beef or 20 minutes per 1 lb/450 g, plus 20 minutes (2 hours 20 minutes) for medium beef. Baste the meat from time to time to keep it moist. If the pan becomes too dry, add a little stock or red wine.

4 Increase the oven temperature to 425°F/220°C. To make the Yorkshire pudding, beat together the flour, salt, egg, milk, and water until a batter forms. Let stand for 30 minutes. Heat 2 tablespoons of roasted beef dripping in an 8-inch/ 20-cm square roasting pan in the top of the oven. Remove the pan from the oven, pour in the batter, and bake for 25–30 minutes, until it is puffed up and golden brown.

5 Remove the meat from the oven and place on a hot serving plate, cover with foil, and let stand in a warm place for 10–15 minutes.

6 To make the gravy, pour off most of the fat from the pan, leaving behind the meat juices and sediments. Place the pan on the top of the stove over medium heat and scrape all the sediments from the bottom of the pan. Sprinkle in the remaining flour and quickly mix it into the juices with a small whisk. When you have a smooth paste, gradually add the wine and most of the stock, whisking all the time. Bring to a boil, then turn down the heat to a gentle simmer and cook for 2–3 minutes. Season with salt and pepper and add the remaining stock, if needed, and a little Worcestershire sauce, if liked.

7 When ready to serve, carve the meat into slices and serve on hot plates. Pour the gravy into a warm pitcher and take direct to the table. Serve with Yorkshire pudding.

Beef en Daube with Mustard Mashed Potatoes

Serves 2

ingredients
- 2 tsp vegetable oil
- 8 oz/225 g extra-lean chuck steak, cut into 8 pieces
- 10 small shallots, peeled but left whole
- 1 clove garlic, peeled and crushed
- 1 medium tomato, chopped
- 1½ cups finely sliced mushrooms
- ⅔ cup red wine
- ½ cup chicken stock
- 1 small bouquet garni
- 1 tsp cornstarch
- salt and pepper

for the mustard mashed potatoes
- 2 medium floury potatoes, peeled and sliced
- 1½–2 tbsp skim milk, heated
- 1 tsp Dijon-style mustard, to taste

1 Preheat the oven to 350°F/180°C.

2 Heat the oil in a heavy-bottom flameproof casserole. Add the meat and shallots and cook over high heat, stirring, for 4–5 minutes, browning the meat on all sides. Add the garlic, tomato, mushrooms, wine, and stock, and tuck the bouquet garni in well.

3 Bring to a simmer on the stove, cover, and transfer to the oven to cook for 45–60 minutes, or until everything is tender.

4 Make the mustard mashed potatoes about 30 minutes before the beef is ready. Place the potatoes in boiling water and simmer for 20 minutes, or until just tender. Remove from heat, drain well, and put in a bowl. Add the milk and mash well. Stir in the mustard to taste, and keep warm.

5 Use a slotted spoon to transfer the meat and vegetables to a warm serving dish. Cook the sauce on the stove over high heat until reduced by half. Reduce the heat, remove and discard the bouquet garni, and check the seasoning.

6 Mix the cornstarch with a little cold water to form a paste, then add the mixture to the sauce, stirring well, and bring back to a simmer. Pour the sauce over the meat and serve with the mustard mashed potatoes.

Classic Beef Fajitas

Serves 4–6

ingredients
- 1 lb 9 oz/700 g beef skirt steak, cut into strips
- 6 garlic cloves, chopped
- juice of 1 lime
- large pinch mild chili powder
- large pinch paprika
- large pinch ground cumin
- 1–2 tbsp extra virgin olive oil
- 12 flour tortillas
- butter, for greasing
- vegetable oil, for frying
- 1–2 avocados, pitted, sliced, and tossed with lime juice
- ½ cup sour cream
- salt and pepper

for the salsa
- 8 ripe tomatoes, diced
- 3 scallions, sliced
- 1–2 fresh green chiles, such as jalapeño or serrano, seeded and chopped
- 3–4 tbsp chopped fresh cilantro
- 5–8 radishes, diced
- ground cumin

1 Combine the beef with the garlic, lime juice, chili powder, paprika, cumin, and olive oil. Add salt and pepper, mix well, and let marinate for at least 30 minutes at room temperature, or overnight in the refrigerator.

2 To make the salsa, place the tomatoes in a bowl with the scallions, green chiles, cilantro, and radishes. Season to taste with cumin, salt, and pepper. Set aside.

3 Heat the tortillas one by one in a lightly greased nonstick skillet, wrapping each in foil as you work, to keep it warm.

4 Heat a little oil in a large, heavy-bottom skillet over high heat. Add the meat and stir-fry until browned and just cooked through.

5 Serve the sizzling hot meat with the warm tortillas and the salsa, avocado, and sour cream for each person to make their own fajitas.

Chili con Carne

Serves 6

ingredients

- 4 tbsp sunflower oil
- 2 onions, chopped
- 1 garlic clove, chopped
- 1 tbsp all-purpose flour
- 2 lb/900 g chuck steak, diced
- 1¼ cups beef stock
- 1¼ cups red wine
- 2–3 fresh red chiles, seeded and chopped
- 1 lb 12 oz/800 g canned red kidney beans, drained and rinsed
- 14 oz/400 g canned chopped tomatoes
- salt and pepper
- tortilla chips, to serve

1 Heat half of the oil in a heavy-bottom saucepan. Add half of the chopped onion and the garlic and cook, stirring occasionally, for 5 minutes, until softened. Remove with a slotted spoon.

2 Place the flour on a plate and season well with salt and pepper, then toss the meat in the flour to coat. Cook the meat, in batches, until browned all over, then return the meat and the onion mixture to the saucepan. Pour in the stock and wine and bring to a boil, stirring. Reduce the heat and simmer for 1 hour.

3 Meanwhile, heat the remaining oil in a skillet. Add the remaining onion and the chiles and cook, stirring occasionally, for 5 minutes. Add the beans and tomatoes with their juices and break up with a wooden spoon. Simmer for 25 minutes, until thickened.

4 Divide the meat among individual plates, top with the bean mixture, and serve with tortilla chips.

Broiled Steak with Tomatoes & Garlic

Serves 4

ingredients

- 3 tbsp olive oil, plus extra for brushing
- 4 cups peeled and chopped tomatoes
- 1 red bell pepper, seeded and chopped
- 1 onion, chopped
- 2 garlic cloves, finely chopped
- 1 tbsp chopped fresh flat-leaf parsley
- 1 tsp dried oregano
- 1 tsp sugar
- 4 entrecôte (flesh from ribs) steaks or sirloin steaks, about 6 oz/175 g each
- salt and pepper
- green beans and new potatoes, to serve

1 Place the oil, tomatoes, red bell pepper, onion, garlic, parsley, oregano, and sugar in a heavy-bottom saucepan and season to taste with salt and pepper. Bring to a boil, reduce the heat, and simmer for 15 minutes.

2 Meanwhile, preheat the broiler to high. Snip any fat around the outsides of the steaks. Season each generously with pepper (no salt) and brush with oil. Broil for 1 minute on each side, then reduce the heat to medium and cook according to taste: 1½–2 minutes each side for rare; 2½–3 minutes each side for medium; 3–4 minutes on each side for well done.

3 Transfer the steaks to warm individual plates. Serve immediately with green beans, new potatoes, and the sauce for pouring on top.

Shepherd's Pie

Serves 4

ingredients

- 1 lb 9 oz/700 g fresh lean ground lamb
- 2 onions, chopped
- 1½ cups diced carrots
- 1–2 garlic cloves, crushed
- 1 tbsp all-purpose flour
- scant 1 cup lamb stock
- 7 oz/200 g canned chopped tomatoes
- 1 tsp Worcestershire sauce
- 1 tsp chopped fresh sage
- 9 potatoes (about 2 lb 4 oz/1 kg)
- 2 tbsp margarine
- 3–4 tbsp skim milk
- 4½ oz/125 g button mushrooms (optional)
- salt and pepper

1 Preheat the oven to 400°F/200°C. Place the ground lamb in a heavy-bottom saucepan with no extra fat and cook gently until the meat begins to brown.

2 Add the onions, carrots, and garlic and continue to cook gently for 10 minutes. Stir in the flour and cook for 1–2 minutes, then gradually stir in the stock and chopped tomatoes and bring to a boil.

3 Add the Worcestershire sauce, seasoning, and sage, cover, and simmer gently for 25 minutes, giving an occasional stir.

4 Meanwhile, cook the potatoes in boiling salted water until tender, then drain thoroughly and mash, beating in the margarine, seasoning, and enough milk to produce a piping consistency. Place in a pastry bag fitted with a large star tip.

5 Slice the mushrooms (if using), stir into the meat, then taste and adjust the seasoning, if necessary. Turn into a shallow ovenproof dish.

6 Pipe the potatoes evenly over the meat. Cook in the preheated oven for 30 minutes, or until piping hot and the potato is golden brown.

Moussaka

Serves 4

ingredients

- 2 eggplants, thinly sliced
- 1 lb/450 g fresh lean ground lamb
- 2 onions, thinly sliced
- 1 tsp finely chopped garlic
- 14 oz/400 g canned tomatoes
- 2 tbsp chopped fresh parsley
- 2 eggs
- 1¼ cups low-fat plain yogurt
- 1 tbsp freshly grated Parmesan cheese
- salt and pepper

1 Preheat the oven to 350°F/180°C. Dry-fry the eggplant slices, in batches, in a nonstick skillet on both sides until browned. Remove from the skillet.

2 Add the ground lamb to the skillet and cook for 5 minutes, stirring, until browned. Stir in the onions and garlic and cook for 5 minutes, or until browned. Add the tomatoes, parsley, and salt and pepper, then bring to a boil and simmer for 20 minutes, or until the meat is tender.

3 Arrange half of the eggplant slices in a layer in an ovenproof dish. Add the meat mixture, then a final layer of the remaining eggplant slices.

4 Beat the eggs in a bowl, then beat in the yogurt and add salt and pepper to taste. Pour the mixture over the eggplants and sprinkle the grated cheese on top. Bake the moussaka in the preheated oven for 45 minutes, or until golden brown. Serve straight from the dish.

Rack of Lamb

Serves 2

ingredients
- 9–10½ oz/250–300 g rack of lamb, trimmed
- 1 garlic clove, crushed
- ⅔ cup red wine
- 1 fresh rosemary sprig, crushed to release the flavor
- 1 tbsp olive oil
- ⅔ cup lamb stock
- 2 tbsp red currant jelly
- salt and pepper

for the mint sauce
- small bunch of fresh mint leaves, chopped
- 2 tsp superfine sugar
- 2 tbsp boiling water
- 2 tbsp white wine vinegar

1 Place the rack of lamb in a nonmetallic bowl and rub all over with the garlic. Pour in the wine and place the rosemary sprig on top. Cover and let marinate in the refrigerator for 3 hours, or overnight, if possible.

2 To make the mint sauce, combine the mint leaves with the sugar in a small bowl. Add the boiling water and stir to dissolve the sugar. Add the white wine vinegar and let stand for 30 minutes before serving with the lamb.

3 Preheat the oven to 425°F/220°C.

4 Remove the lamb from the marinade, reserving the marinade, dry the meat with paper towels, and season well with salt and pepper. Place in a small roasting pan, drizzle with the oil, and roast in the oven for 15–20 minutes, depending on whether you like your meat rare or medium. Remove the lamb from the oven and let rest, covered with foil, in a warm place for 5 minutes.

5 Meanwhile, place the marinade in a small pan, bring to a boil over medium heat, and let simmer for 2–3 minutes. Add the lamb stock and red currant jelly and simmer until a syrupy consistency is achieved.

6 Carve the lamb into cutlets and serve on warm plates with the stock and red currant jelly sauce spooned over the top. Serve the mint sauce separately.

Irish Stew

Serves 4

ingredients
- 4 tbsp all-purpose flour
- 3 lb/1.3 kg neck of lamb, trimmed of visible fat
- 3 large onions, chopped
- 3 carrots, sliced
- 4 potatoes, quartered
- ½ tsp dried thyme
- 3¼ cups hot beef stock
- salt and pepper
- 2 tbsp chopped fresh parsley, to garnish

1 Preheat the oven to 325°F/160°C. Spread the flour on a plate and season with salt and pepper. Roll the pieces of lamb in the flour to coat, shaking off any excess, and arrange in the bottom of a casserole.

2 Layer the onions, carrots, and potatoes on top of the lamb.

3 Sprinkle in the thyme and pour in the stock, then cover and cook in the preheated oven for 2½ hours. Garnish with the chopped fresh parsley and serve straight from the casserole.

Lamb Shanks with Roasted Onions

Serves 4

ingredients

- 4 lamb shanks, about 12 oz/ 350 g each
- 6 garlic cloves
- 2 tbsp extra virgin olive oil
- 1 tbsp fresh rosemary, very finely chopped
- 4 red onions
- 4 carrots, cut into thin sticks
- 4 tbsp water
- salt and pepper

1 Preheat the oven to 350°F/180°C. Trim off any excess fat from the lamb. Using a small, sharp knife, make 6 incisions in each shank. Cut the garlic cloves lengthwise into 4 slices. Insert 6 garlic slices in the incisions in each lamb shank.

2 Place the lamb in a single layer in a roasting pan, drizzle with the olive oil, sprinkle with the rosemary, and season with pepper. Roast in the preheated oven for 45 minutes.

3 Wrap each of the onions in a piece of foil. Remove the roasting pan from the oven and season the lamb with salt. Return to the oven and place the wrapped onions on the shelf next to it. Roast for an additional 1–1¼ hours, until the lamb is very tender.

4 Meanwhile, bring a large saucepan of water to a boil. Add the carrot sticks and blanch for 1 minute. Drain and refresh in cold water.

5 Remove the roasting pan from the oven when the lamb is meltingly tender and transfer it to a warm serving dish. Skim off any fat from the roasting pan and place it over medium heat. Add the carrots and cook for 2 minutes, then add the water, bring to a boil, and simmer, stirring continuously and scraping up the glazed sediment from the bottom of the pan.

6 Transfer the carrots and sauce to the serving dish. Remove the onions from the oven and unwrap. Cut off and discard about ½ inch/1 cm off the tops and add the onions to the dish. Serve immediately.

Pork Pot Roast

Serves 4

ingredients
- 1 tbsp sunflower oil
- 4 tbsp butter
- 2 lb 4 oz/1 kg boned and rolled pork loin roast
- 4 shallots, chopped
- 6 juniper berries
- 2 fresh thyme sprigs, plus extra to garnish
- ⅔ cup dry cider
- ⅔ cup chicken stock or water
- 8 celery stalks, chopped
- 2 tbsp all-purpose flour
- ⅔ cup heavy cream
- salt and pepper

1 Heat the oil with half of the butter in a large, heavy-bottom saucepan or flameproof casserole. Add the pork and cook over medium heat, turning frequently, for 5–10 minutes, or until browned. Transfer to a plate.

2 Add the shallots to the saucepan and cook, stirring frequently, for 5 minutes, or until softened. Add the juniper berries and thyme sprigs and return the pork to the saucepan with any juices that have collected on the plate. Pour in the cider and stock, season to taste with salt and pepper, then cover and simmer for 30 minutes. Turn the pork over and add the celery. Re-cover the pan and cook for an additional 40 minutes.

3 Meanwhile, make a beurre manié by mashing the remaining butter with the flour in a small bowl. Transfer the pork and celery to a platter with a slotted spoon and keep warm. Remove and discard the juniper berries and thyme. Whisk the beurre manié, a little at a time, into the simmering cooking liquid. Cook, stirring continuously, for 2 minutes, then stir in the cream and bring to a boil.

4 Slice the pork and spoon a little of the sauce over it. Garnish with the thyme sprigs and serve immediately. Hand around the remaining sauce separately.

Meatloaf

Serves 4

ingredients

- 1 thick slice white bread, crusts removed
- 1 lb 9 oz/700 g fresh ground beef, pork, or lamb
- 1 medium egg
- 1 tbsp finely chopped onion
- 1 beef bouillon cube, crumbled
- 1 tsp dried herbs
- salt and pepper
- sauce or gravy, mashed potatoes, and freshly cooked green beans, to serve

1 Preheat the oven to 350°F/180°C.

2 Put the bread into a small bowl and add enough water to soak. Let stand for 5 minutes, then drain and squeeze well to get rid of all the water.

3 Combine the bread and all the other ingredients in a bowl. Shape into a loaf, then place on a baking sheet or in a loaf pan or ovenproof dish. Put the meatloaf in the preheated oven and cook for 30–45 minutes, until the juices run clear when it is pierced with a skewer.

4 Serve in slices with your favorite sauce or gravy, mashed potatoes, and green beans.

Sausage & Bean Casserole

Serves 4

ingredients

- 8 Italian link sausages
- 3 tbsp olive oil
- 1 large onion, chopped
- 2 garlic cloves, chopped
- 1 green bell pepper, seeded and sliced
- 8 oz/225g canned whole tomatoes, skinned and chopped or 14 oz/400 g canned chopped tomatoes
- 2 tbsp sun-dried tomato paste
- 14 oz/400 g canned cannellini beans

1 Prick the sausages all over with a fork. Heat 2 tablespoons of the oil in a large, heavy-bottom skillet. Add the sausages and cook over low heat, turning frequently, for 10–15 minutes, until evenly browned and cooked through. Remove them from the skillet and keep warm. Drain off the oil and wipe out the skillet with paper towels.

2 Heat the remaining oil in the skillet. Add the onion, garlic, and bell pepper to the skillet and cook for 5 minutes, stirring occasionally, or until softened.

3 Add the tomatoes to the skillet and let the mixture simmer for about 5 minutes, stirring occasionally, or until slightly reduced and thickened.

4 Stir the sun-dried tomato paste, cannellini beans, and Italian sausages into the mixture in the skillet. Cook for 4–5 minutes, or until the mixture is piping hot. Add 4–5 tablespoons of water if the mixture becomes too dry during cooking.

5 Transfer to serving plates and serve.

Macaroni with Sausage,
Pepperoncini & Olives

Serves 6

ingredients

- 1 tbsp olive oil
- 1 large onion, finely chopped
- 2 garlic cloves, very finely chopped
- 1 lb/450 g pork link sausage, peeled and roughly chopped
- 3 canned pepperoncini, or other hot red peppers, drained and sliced
- 14 oz/400 g canned chopped tomatoes
- 2 tsp dried oregano
- ½ cup chicken stock or red wine
- 1 lb/450 g dried macaroni
- 12–15 pitted black olives, quartered
- ⅔ cup freshly grated cheddar or Gruyère cheese
- salt and pepper

1 Heat the oil in a large skillet over medium heat. Add the onion and cook for 5 minutes, until softened. Add the garlic and cook for a few seconds, until just beginning to color. Add the sausage and cook until evenly browned.

2 Stir in the pepperoncini, tomatoes, oregano, and stock. Season to taste with salt and pepper. Bring to a boil, then simmer over medium heat for 10 minutes, stirring occasionally.

3 Meanwhile, bring a large saucepan of lightly salted water to a boil. Add the pasta, bring back to a boil, and cook for 8–10 minutes, or according to the package directions, until tender but still firm to the bite. Drain and transfer to a warm serving dish.

4 Add the olives and half of the cheese to the sauce, then stir until the cheese has melted.

5 Pour the sauce over the pasta. Toss well to mix. Sprinkle with the remaining cheese and serve immediately.

Chapter 4
Poultry & Game

Introduction

Poultry is rich in protein, and quick and easy to prepare and cook. Some birds, such as chicken and turkey, can be a low-fat choice as long as the fatty skin is removed, and they are very versatile. Duck is fattier, but makes a good dinner-party choice. Game birds and animals are becoming more widely available and make impressive dishes for entertaining.

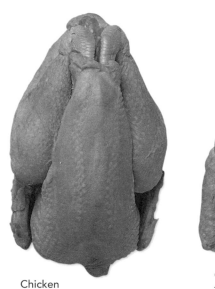

Chicken

Guinea fowl

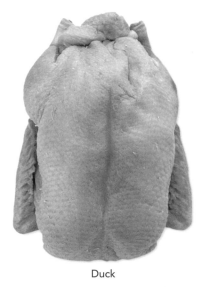

Duck

Quail

Buying and storing poultry and game

Always buy your poultry and game as fresh as possible and from a reputable supplier. Choose plump birds that have unblemished skin, and make sure that any wrapping or packaging is intact.

As soon as you get it home, remove the packaging (if it is a fresh bird) and transfer the giblets (if any) to a separate bowl. Place the bird on a rack in a dish, then cover it and any giblets loosely with plastic wrap and store in the refrigerator. Keep it well away from cooked meats to prevent any cross-contamination. Whole birds will keep for 1–2 days in the refrigerator, but giblets no longer than 1 day.

Frozen birds can be stored in the freezer in their original packaging. Thaw in the refrigerator thoroughly before cooking: you will need to plan 5 hours per 1 lb/450 g for a chicken and 6 hours per 1 lb/450 g for a turkey.

Game birds are available fresh when in season and frozen all year round. If they are truly wild birds and not farmed, they will have a lower fat content and should, therefore, be wrapped in bacon during roasting. Older birds are not recommended for roasting—they are more suited to soups, casseroles, and stews. Game animals, such as venison and rabbit, tend to be less tender than farmed animals because they get more exercise in the wild. They should be cooked slowly until tender, but not overcooked. Braising is a good method for keeping the meat moist, or it can be roasted if wrapped first in bacon.

Types of bird

In addition to the flavor, the choice of bird may depend on the occasion, how many people you are catering for, and how much preparation you are willing to do.

Chicken

There are many different varieties of chicken available, including free range, organic, and corn-fed. You can buy whole birds already prepared for the oven or frozen. You can also buy a variety of cuts—wing, breast, leg, thigh, or drumstick—or you can cut up a whole bird yourself. Chicken is delicious roasted, steamed, poached, broiled, casseroled, grilled, stir-fried, pan-fried, or deep-fried. A Rock Cornish game hen is a small chicken, at 2½ lb/ 1.1 kg, suitable for a single serving. Broiler-fryers are young birds typically weighing 3½ lb/1.6 kg that are best for frying and broiling; they have the best flavor. Roasters weigh 2½–5 lb/ 1.1–2.25 kg and are best for roasting.

Poussin

A French term for a young, small chicken weighing up to I lb/450 g. If a recipe calls for poussin, use a game hen

Guinea fowl

This bird is related to the chicken and the partridge, and has light and dark meat and a strong flavor. It is available fresh and frozen. Because guinea fowl has a low fat content, it is most suited to moist cooking methods, such as casseroling. Alternatively, you can wrap it in bacon slices and roast it.

Turkey

These birds are much larger than chickens—some can grow to a massive 70 lb/31.5 kg/70 lb—but the trend nowadays is for much smaller birds. This is because turkey suppliers would like to encourage their use all year round, instead of just during Thanksgiving and Christmas. Turkeys have similar uses to chickens, and you can often interchange them with chickens in recipes. You can buy whole birds already prepared for the oven or frozen. You can also buy separate cuts, such as cutlets or drumsticks. Turkey is particularly suitable for roasting, casseroling, braising, stir-frying, or pan-frying.

Duck

Ducks are available whole, fresh, and frozen. Breast and leg cuts are also available. Duck is fattier than chicken or turkey, and is, therefore, particularly suitable for roasting, broiling, or pan-frying. Duck is often served with a tart fruit sauce, such as orange, to cut through any fatty aftertaste.

Partridge

This game bird has dark flesh and an earthy flavor. Its flesh can be tough so is best braised, stewed, or casseroled. It can also be roasted.

Goose

Geese are larger than ducks, and can be bought fresh, although they are more often bought frozen. Although they are popular during holidays and at Christmas time, especially in Europe, they have become less popular year-round because of their very high-fat content. Geese are best roasted, pot roasted, braised, or stewed. It is also a good idea to serve them with a tart fruit sauce to cut through any fatty aftertaste.

Grouse

These are small game birds, so plan one bird per person. If you are going to roast them, wrap them in bacon before cooking. You can pot roast, braise, casserole, or stew them.

Pheasant

These are medium-size game birds. The male has more brilliant plumage than the female, but the female is juicier and more tender. Young pheasants can be roasted, but older birds should be wrapped in bacon for roasting; they can also be braised, casseroled, or stewed.

Quail

These small game birds are related to the partridge. The American type has lean but lighter flesh, whereas the European type has lean, medium-dark flesh. Both types have a sweet flavor. Quails are suitable for roasting, pot roasting, braising, broiling, casseroling, or grilling. Their small eggs have a speckled brown shell and a rich flavor.

Venison

Deer is a popular game animal and the meat is available wild or farmed. It is low in cholesterol, and usually available as leg or saddle joints, or as steaks. The best meat comes from a male deer under the age of two years. Venison meat is dry and is, therefore, more suited to casseroles.

Rabbit

This game animal has fine white meat and is available fresh or frozen; you can also buy it whole or boned and cut into pieces. Tender young rabbits are suitable for broiling, frying, or roasting; older or wild rabbits should be braised, casseroled, or stewed.

Preparation and cooking techniques

It is essential to cook poultry all the way through in order to kill off any potentially harmful bacteria. If a bird is not cooked through when tested, return it to the oven to finish cooking, even if you have to exceed the recommended cooking time.

Making chicken stock

Chicken stock is easy to prepare and is ideal for adding to soups and sauces. It can be stored, covered with plastic wrap, in the refrigerator for 2–3 days. You can also freeze it for up to 6 months. Put the chicken carcass into a large saucepan with 1 chopped onion, 1 sliced carrot, 1 chopped celery stalk, and 1 chopped leek. Add 1 bay leaf and 1 sprig of thyme, 3 stalks of parsley, and some cracked black peppercorns. Cover with water and bring to a boil, then use a slotted spoon to skim off any scum from the surface. Reduce the heat, cover, and let simmer for 2–3 hours. Strain into a large bowl and discard the solids. Use the stock as required.

Butterflying a small bird

Butterflying helps to flatten the bird before broiling or grilling, ensuring quicker and more even cooking. Place the bird breast-side down (the legs are under the bird, the wings on top) on a clean cutting board. Cut along either side of the backbone and remove it (you can save it for making chicken stock or discard it). Open the bird out and turn it over. Using your palms, press down on the bird to flatten it against the cutting board. You can insert skewers crisscrossed to hold the bird flat.

Roasting a large chicken or a turkey

First wipe the bird inside and out with paper towels. If you will be stuffing it, pull back the skin around the neck cavity and insert the stuffing into only the neck end (do not overfill the bird or it will not cook through properly). If you are not stuffing the bird, simply season the cavity. Pull the skin over the top, then pull up the wings and tie with string. Pull the legs together and tie with string. Rub butter or oil over the skin of the bird, and season to taste with salt and pepper. Transfer to a wire rack in a roasting pan, and roast in a preheated oven, basting occasionally, until cooked through and tender. To test, insert a sharp knife or skewer into the thickest part of the bird. If the juices run clear, the bird is cooked; if not, return it to the oven and cook until done. Remove the bird from the oven and let rest, covered in foil, for 15–20 minutes before carving.

OVEN TEMPERATURES AND ROASTING TIMES

INDIVIDUAL OVEN TEMPERATURES AND COOKING TIMES VARY, SO COOKING TIMES ARE APPROXIMATE. PREHEAT THE OVEN BEFORE COOKING.

Bird	Weight	Temperature	Cooking Time
Chicken	6 lb 8 oz/3 kg	400°F/200°C	2¼ hours
Turkey	11 lb/5 kg	350°F/180°C	3½ hours
	18 lb/8 kg	350°F/180°C	4¾–5 hours
Quail	1 lb/450 g	400°F/200°C	30 minutes
Goose	11 lb/5 kg	425°F/220°C	30 minutes at higher temperature, then
		350°F/180°C	for 2–3 hours at lower temperature
Duck	5 lb 8 oz/2.5 kg	425°F/220°C	20 minutes at higher temperature, then for
		350°F/180°C	2 hours at lower temperature

Roasting a goose

Wipe the goose inside and out with paper towels and pull out any excess fat from inside it. Season well with salt and pepper. If you will be stuffing the goose, insert the stuffing as far as possible in the neck flap end, securing the flap with a skewer. Prick the goose all over with a fork, lay on a rack in a roasting pan, and place in a preheated oven. To test that it is cooked all the way through, insert a skewer into the thickest part of the bird; if the juices run clear, the bird is cooked. Remove from the oven and let rest for 20 minutes before carving.

Carving a large bird

Place the cooked bird breast-side up on a clean cutting board. Use a carving knife to cut between one wing and the side of the breast. Remove the wing and cut thin, downward slices through the breast meat. Repeat with the other side, reserving the wings and the breast slices. Pull out one leg and cut through the joint. Repeat with the other side. Slice the meat from the thighs and drumsticks. Serve the wings and the meat slices.

Roasting and carving a duck

Wipe the duck inside and out with paper towels. Duck has a high-fat content, so remove any surplus fat. Season inside the tail cavity and insert a bay leaf. Transfer the bird to a wire rack in a roasting pan. Use a fork to prick holes all over it, then season with salt and pepper. Roast in a preheated oven until cooked through and tender (turn and baste it halfway through the cooking time).

To test that the bird is cooked all the way through, insert a sharp knife or skewer into the thickest part of the bird; if the juices run clear, the bird is cooked. To serve the duck, cut it up by cutting it in half lengthwise. Alternatively, use a sharp knife to separate the legs from the body, then cut off the wings. Remove the breast meat and slice it. Serve the legs, wings, and slices of breast meat.

CUTTING UP A WHOLE BIRD

1 TO CUT A LARGE RAW BIRD INTO PIECES, REMOVE ANY STRING AND PLACE IT ON A CLEAN CUTTING BOARD, BREAST-SIDE UP, WITH THE LEGS POINTING TOWARD YOU.

2 USING A SHARP KNIFE, CUT THE SKIN BETWEEN ONE LEG AND THE SIDE OF THE BREAST, THEN USE YOUR HAND TO PRESS THE LEG DOWN FLAT TO THE BOARD. DO THE SAME WITH THE OTHER LEG. CUT THROUGH THE JOINT ATTACHING ONE OF THE LEGS AND REMOVE THE LEG FROM THE BODY. DO THE SAME FOR THE OTHER SIDE.

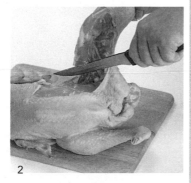

3 TURN THE BIRD TO FACE THE OTHER WAY AND LOCATE THE RIDGE ALONG THE MIDDLE OF THE BACK. USING A KNIFE, CUT AWAY ONE BREAST, TAKING A WING OFF WITH IT. DO THE SAME WITH THE OTHER BREAST.

4 TO DIVIDE THE LEGS INTO THIGHS AND DRUMSTICKS, PUT THEM SKIN-SIDE DOWN ON THE CUTTING BOARD. CUT THROUGH THE LINE TO SEPARATE THE JOINT. RESERVE THE CARCASS FOR MAKING STOCK.

Traditional Roasted Chicken

Serves 4

ingredients

- 2 tbsp butter, softened
- 1 garlic clove, finely chopped
- 3 tbsp finely chopped toasted walnuts
- 1 tbsp chopped fresh parsley
- 4 lb/1.8 kg oven-ready chicken
- 1 lime, cut into quarters
- 2 tbsp vegetable oil
- 1 tbsp cornstarch
- 2 tbsp water
- salt and pepper
- roasted potatoes, to serve

1 Preheat the oven to 375ºF/190ºC. Mix 1 tablespoon of the butter with the garlic, walnuts, and parsley together in a small bowl. Season well with salt and pepper. Loosen the skin from the breast of the chicken without breaking it. Spread the butter mixture evenly between the skin and breast meat. Place the lime quarters inside the body cavity.

2 Pour the oil into a roasting pan. Transfer the chicken to the pan and dot the skin with the remaining butter. Roast for 1¾ hours, basting occasionally, until the chicken is tender and the juices run clear when a skewer is inserted into the thickest part of the meat. Lift out the chicken and place on a serving platter to rest for 10 minutes.

3 Blend the cornstarch with the water, then stir into the juices in the pan. Transfer to the stove. Stir over low heat until thickened. Add more water, if necessary. Spoon the thickened juices over the chicken and serve with roasted potatoes.

Thai Green Chicken Curry

Serves 4

ingredients

- 2 tbsp peanut or sunflower oil
- 2 tbsp prepared Thai green curry paste
- 1 lb 2 oz/500 g skinless, boneless chicken breasts, cut into cubes
- 2 kaffir lime leaves, roughly torn
- 1 lemongrass stalk, finely chopped
- 1 cup canned coconut milk
- 16 baby eggplants, halved
- 2 tbsp Thai fish sauce
- fresh Thai basil sprigs and kaffir lime leaves, thinly sliced, to garnish

1 Heat 2 tablespoons of oil in a preheated wok or large, heavy-bottom skillet. Add 2 tablespoons of the curry paste and stir-fry briefly until all the aromas are released.

2 Add the chicken, lime leaves, and lemongrass and stir-fry for 3–4 minutes, until the meat is beginning to color. Add the coconut milk and eggplants and simmer gently for 8–10 minutes, or until tender.

3 Stir in the fish sauce and serve immediately, garnished with Thai basil sprigs and lime leaves.

Chicken & Spinach Lasagne

Serves 4

ingredients

- 12 oz/350 g frozen chopped spinach, thawed and drained
- ½ tsp freshly grated nutmeg
- 3¼ cups skinned and diced lean, cooked chicken
- 4 oven-ready lasagna verde noodles
- 1½ tbsp cornstarch
- scant 2 cups milk
- ⅔ cup freshly grated Parmesan cheese
- salt and pepper

for the tomato sauce

- 14 oz/400 g canned chopped tomatoes
- 1 onion, finely chopped
- 1 garlic clove, crushed
- ⅔ cup white wine
- 3 tbsp tomato paste
- 1 tsp dried oregano
- salt and pepper

1 To make the tomato sauce, put the tomatoes into a pan and stir in the onion, garlic, wine, tomato paste, and oregano. Bring to a boil and simmer for 20 minutes, until thick. Season well with salt and pepper.

2 Preheat the oven to 375°F/190°C. Drain the spinach again and spread it out on paper towels to make sure that as much water as possible is removed. Layer the spinach in the bottom of a large ovenproof baking dish. Sprinkle with ground nutmeg and season to taste with salt and pepper.

3 Arrange the diced chicken over the spinach and spoon the tomato sauce over the top. Arrange the lasagna noodles over the tomato sauce.

4 Blend the cornstarch with a little of the milk to make a paste. Pour the remaining milk into a pan and stir in the paste. Heat, stirring, until the sauce thickens. Season well.

5 Spoon the sauce over the lasagna noodles and transfer the dish to a baking sheet. Sprinkle the grated Parmesan cheese over the sauce and bake in the preheated oven for 25 minutes until golden, then serve.

Chicken Kiev

Serves 4

ingredients
- ½ cup butter, softened
- 3–4 garlic cloves, finely chopped
- 1 tbsp chopped fresh parsley
- 1 tbsp snipped fresh chives
- finely grated rind and juice of ½ lemon
- 8 skinless, boneless chicken breasts, about 4 oz/115 g each
- scant ½ cup all-purpose flour
- 2 eggs, lightly beaten
- 1¾ cups dry breadcrumbs
- peanut oil or sunflower oil, for deep-frying
- salt and pepper

1 Beat the butter in a bowl with the garlic, herbs, and lemon rind and juice. Season to taste with salt and pepper. Divide into 8 pieces, then shape into cylinders. Wrap in foil and chill for about 2 hours, until firm.

2 Place the chicken between 2 sheets of plastic wrap. Pound gently with a rolling pin to flatten the chicken to an even thickness. Place a butter cylinder on each chicken piece and roll up. Secure with toothpicks.

3 Place the flour, eggs, and breadcrumbs in separate shallow dishes. Dip the rolls into the flour, then the egg, and, finally, the breadcrumbs. Place on a plate, cover, and chill for 1 hour.

4 Heat the oil in a saucepan or deep-fat fryer to 350–375°F/180–190°C, or until a cube of bread browns in 30 seconds. Deep-fry the chicken in batches for 8–10 minutes, or until cooked through and golden brown. Drain on paper towels. Serve immediately.

Coq au Vin

Serves 4

ingredients
- 4 tbsp butter
- 2 tbsp olive oil
- 4 lb/1.8 kg chicken pieces
- 4 oz/115 g rindless smoked bacon, cut into strips
- 4 oz/115 g pearl onions
- 4 oz/115 g cremini mushrooms, halved
- 2 garlic cloves, finely chopped
- 2 tbsp brandy
- 1 cup red wine
- 1¼ cups chicken stock
- 1 bouquet garni
- 2 tbsp all-purpose flour
- salt and pepper
- bay leaves, to garnish (optional)

1 Melt half of the butter with the olive oil in a large, flameproof casserole. Add the chicken and cook over medium heat, stirring, for 8–10 minutes, or until golden brown all over. Add the bacon, onions, mushrooms, and garlic.

2 Pour in the brandy and set it alight with a match or taper. When the flames have died down, add the wine, stock, and bouquet garni and season to taste with salt and pepper. Bring to a boil, reduce the heat, and simmer gently for 1 hour, or until the chicken pieces are cooked through and tender. Meanwhile, make a beurre manié by mashing the remaining butter with the flour in a small bowl.

3 Remove and discard the bouquet garni. Transfer the chicken to a large plate and keep warm. Stir the beurre manié into the casserole, a little at a time. Bring to a boil, return the chicken to the casserole, and serve immediately, garnished with bay leaves (but make sure the bay leaves are not consumed—they are only for decoration).

Peking Duck

Serves 4

ingredients
- 4 lb/1.8 kg duck
- 7½ cups boiling water
- 4 tbsp honey
- 2 tsp dark soy sauce
- carrot strips, to garnish

for the sauce
- 2 tbsp sesame oil
- ½ cup hoisin sauce
- ⅔ cup superfine sugar
- ½ cup water

to serve
- Chinese pancakes
- cucumber matchsticks
- shredded scallions

1 Place the duck on a rack set over a roasting pan and pour 5 cups of the boiling water over it. Remove the duck and rack and discard the water. Pat dry with clean paper towels, replace the duck and rack, cover, and reserve for several hours.

2 Mix the honey, remaining boiling water, and soy sauce together. Brush the mixture as a glaze over the skin and inside the duck. Reserve the remaining glaze. Set aside for 1 hour, until the glaze has dried.

3 Coat the duck with another layer of glaze. Let dry and repeat until all of the glaze is used.

4 Preheat the oven to 375°F/190°C. For the sauce, heat the oil in a saucepan. Add the hoisin sauce, sugar, and water. Simmer for 2–3 minutes, until thickened. Cool and chill until required.

5 Cook the duck in the preheated oven for 30 minutes. Turn the duck over and cook for 20 minutes. Turn the duck again and cook for 20–30 minutes, or until the meat is cooked through and the skin is crisp.

6 Remove the duck from the oven and let stand for 10 minutes. Meanwhile, heat the Chinese pancakes in a bamboo steamer for 5–7 minutes. Cut the duck skin and meat into strips and divide between individual serving plates. Garnish with carrot strips and serve with the pancakes, cucumber matchsticks, shredded scallions, and sauce.

Duck Breasts with Chili & Lime

Serves 4

ingredients
- 4 boneless duck breasts
- 1 tsp vegetable oil
- ½ cup chicken stock
- 2 tbsp plum preserve or jam
- salt and pepper

for the marinade
- 2 garlic cloves, crushed
- 4 tsp light brown sugar
- 3 tbsp lime juice
- 1 tbsp soy sauce
- 1 tsp chili sauce

to serve
- lime wedges
- freshly cooked rice

1 To make the marinade, mix the garlic, sugar, lime juice, soy sauce, and chili sauce together.

2 Using a small, sharp knife, cut deep slashes in the skin of the duck breasts to make a diamond pattern. Place the duck breasts in a wide, nonmetallic dish.

3 Spoon the marinade over the duck breasts, turning to coat them evenly in the mixture. Cover the dish with plastic wrap and let marinate in the refrigerator for at least 3 hours, or overnight, if possible.

4 Drain the duck, reserving the marinade. Heat a large, heavy-bottom pan until very hot and brush with the oil. Add the duck breasts, skin-side down, and cook for 4–5 minutes until the skin is browned and crisp. Pour off the excess fat.

5 Turn the duck breasts and cook on the other side for 2–3 minutes to brown. Add the reserved marinade and the stock and preserve, then simmer for 2 minutes. Adjust the seasoning to taste and spoon the juices over the meat. Serve with lime wedges and freshly cooked rice.

Roasted Duck with Apple

Serves 4

ingredients
- 4 duck pieces, about 12 oz/350 g each
- 4 tbsp dark soy sauce
- 2 tbsp light brown sugar
- 2 red apples
- 2 green apples
- juice of 1 lemon
- 2 tbsp honey
- a few bay leaves
- salt and pepper
- assorted freshly cooked vegetables, to serve

for the apricot sauce
- 14 oz/400 g canned apricots in fruit juice
- 4 tbsp sweet sherry

1 Preheat the oven to 375°F/190°C. Wash the duck and trim away any excess fat. Place on a wire rack over a roasting pan and prick all over with a fork or a clean, sharp needle.

2 Brush the duck with the soy sauce. Sprinkle with the sugar and season with pepper. Cook in the preheated oven, basting occasionally, for 50–60 minutes, or until the meat is cooked through and the juices run clear when a skewer is inserted into the thickest part of the meat.

3 Meanwhile, core the apples and cut each into 6 wedges, then place in a small bowl and mix with the lemon juice and honey. Transfer to a small roasting pan, add a few bay leaves, and season to taste with salt and pepper. Cook alongside the duck, basting occasionally, for 20–25 minutes, until tender. Remove and discard the bay leaves.

4 To make the sauce, place the apricots in a blender or food processor with the can juices and the sherry. Process until smooth. Alternatively, mash the apricots with a fork until smooth and mix with the juice and sherry.

5 Just before serving, heat the apricot sauce in a small saucepan. Remove the skin from the duck and pat the flesh with paper towels to absorb any fat. Serve the duck with the apple wedges, apricot sauce, and freshly cooked vegetables.

Roasted Turkey with Bread Sauce

Serves 8

ingredients
- 4 tbsp stuffing
- 11 lb/5 kg turkey
- 3 tbsp butter
- holly leaves (optional), to decorate

for the bread sauce
- 1 onion, peeled
- 4 cloves
- 2½ cups milk
- 2½ cups fresh white breadcrumbs
- 4 tbsp butter
- salt and pepper for the bread sauce

to serve
- cranberry sauce
- cooked vegetables
- roasted potatoes

1 Preheat the oven to 425°F/220°C. If you are stuffing the turkey, spoon the stuffing into the neck cavity and close the flap of skin with a skewer. If you prefer to cook the stuffing separately, cook according to the recipe's directions.

2 Place the bird in a large roasting pan and rub it all over with the butter. Roast in the preheated oven for 1 hour, then lower the oven temperature to 350°F/180°C and roast for an additional 2½ hours. You may need to pour off the fat from the roasting pan occasionally.

3 Meanwhile, make the bread sauce. Stud the onion with the cloves, then place in a saucepan with the milk, breadcrumbs, and butter. Bring just to boiling point over low heat, then remove from the heat and let stand in a warm place to infuse. Just before serving, remove the onion and cloves and reheat the sauce gently, beating well with a wooden spoon. Season to taste with salt and pepper.

4 Check that the turkey is cooked by inserting a skewer or the point of a sharp knife into the thigh—if the juices run clear, it is ready. Transfer the bird to a carving board, cover loosely with foil. and let stand to rest.

5 Carve the turkey and serve with the warm bread sauce, stuffing, cranberry sauce, vegetables, and potatoes, and decorate with holly leaves, if liked.

Lemon & Mint Turkey Burgers

Serves 6

ingredients

- 1 lb 2 oz/500 g fresh ground turkey
- ½ small onion, grated
- finely grated rind and juice of 1 small lemon
- 1 garlic clove, finely chopped
- 2 tbsp finely chopped fresh mint
- ½ tsp pepper
- 1 tsp sea salt
- 1 egg, beaten
- 1 tbsp olive oil, plus extra for frying
- lemon wedges, to serve

1 Place all the ingredients in a bowl and mix well with a fork. Shape the mixture into 12 balls, rolling them with the palm of your hand. Flatten into patties about ¾ inch/2 cm thick. Cover and let stand in the refrigerator for at least 1 hour, or overnight.

2 Heat about 5 tablespoons of oil in a large, heavy-bottom skillet. When the oil starts to look hazy, add the burgers, cooking in batches, if necessary. Cook over medium–high heat for 4–5 minutes on each side, until golden brown and cooked through.

3 Drain the burgers on paper towels and transfer to a warm serving dish. Serve with lemon wedges.

Roasted Goose with Cinnamon-Spiced Red Cabbage

Serves 6

ingredients

- 10 lb/4.5 kg oven-ready goose
- 2 onions, quartered
- 2 bay leaves
- 1 bunch fresh thyme
- salt and pepper

for the red cabbage

- 3 tbsp olive oil
- 1 large onion, sliced
- 1 red cabbage, shredded
- 1 large cooking apple, peeled, cored, and chopped
- 3 tbsp raisins
- 2½ cups red wine
- 4 tbsp red wine vinegar
- 2 tsp superfine sugar, or to taste
- 1 cinnamon stick

1 Preheat the oven to 400°F/200°C. Cut away any excess fat from the tail area of the goose. Season the goose cavity to taste with salt and pepper and push in the onion quarters, bay leaves, and thyme, reserving a few sprigs for the garnish. Put the goose on a rack set over a roasting pan and prick the skin all over with a skewer. Season the outside of the goose to taste with salt and pepper. Roast in the preheated oven for 15 minutes per 1 lb/450 g, plus an extra 15 minutes. Remove from the oven, cover loosely with foil, and let rest for 15 minutes before carving.

2 While the goose is roasting, prepare the red cabbage. Heat the oil in a large skillet over medium heat, add the onion, and cook, stirring frequently, for 3–4 minutes, until softened but not colored. Add all the remaining ingredients, cover, and cook for 30–40 minutes, until the cabbage is tender and the liquid has reduced. Remove the cinnamon stick before serving.

3 Carve the goose and serve in slices, alongside the red cabbage and garnished with the reserved thyme.

Roasted Pheasant with Red Wine & Herbs

Serves 4

ingredients

- scant ½ cup butter, slightly softened
- 1 tbsp chopped fresh thyme
- 1 tbsp chopped fresh parsley
- 2 oven-ready young pheasants
- 4 tbsp vegetable oil
- ½ cup red wine
- salt and pepper

to serve

- roasted parsnips
- sautéed potatoes

1 Preheat the oven to 375°F/190°C. Place the butter in a small bowl and mix in the chopped herbs. Lift the skins off the pheasants, being careful not to tear them, and push the herb butter under the skins. Season to taste with salt and pepper.

2 Pour the oil into a roasting pan, add the pheasants, and cook in the preheated oven for 45 minutes, basting occasionally. Remove from the oven, pour the red wine over the birds, then return to the oven and cook for an additional 15 minutes, or until cooked through. Check that each bird is cooked by inserting a knife between the legs and body. If the juices run clear, they are cooked.

3 Remove the pheasants from the oven, cover with foil, and let stand for 15 minutes. Divide between individual serving plates, and serve with roasted parsnips and sautéed potatoes.

Quails with Grapes

Serves 4

ingredients
- 4 tbsp olive oil
- 8 quails, gutted
- 1¾ cups green seedless grapes
- 1 cup grape juice
- 2 cloves
- about ⅔ cup water
- 2 tbsp Spanish brandy
- salt and pepper

for the potato pancake
- 5 unpeeled potatoes
- 2½ tbsp unsalted butter
- 1½ tbsp olive oil

1 Preheat the oven to 450°F/230°C. For the pancake, parboil the potatoes for 10 minutes. Drain and let cool completely, then peel, coarsely grate, and season with salt and pepper to taste. Reserve until required.

2 Take a heavy-bottom skillet or flameproof casserole large enough to hold the quails in a single layer and heat the oil over medium heat. Add the quails and fry on all sides until they are golden brown.

3 Add the grapes, grape juice, cloves, enough water to come halfway up the side of the quails, and salt and pepper to taste. Cover and simmer for 20 minutes. Transfer the quails and all the juices to a roasting pan or casserole, and sprinkle with brandy. Roast, uncovered, in the preheated oven for 10 minutes.

4 Meanwhile, to make the potato pancake, melt the butter with the oil in a 12-inch/30-cm nonstick skillet over high heat. When the fat is hot, add the grated potato and spread into an even layer. Reduce the heat and simmer for 10 minutes. Place a plate over the skillet and, wearing oven mitts, invert them so the potato pancake drops onto the plate. Slide the potato back into the skillet and continue cooking on the other side for 10 minutes, or until cooked through and crisp. Slide out of the skillet and cut into 4 wedges. Keep the pancake warm until the quail is ready.

5 Place a pancake wedge and 2 quails on each individual serving plate. Taste the grape sauce and adjust the seasoning, if necessary. Spoon the sauce over the quails and serve immediately.

Game Pie

Serves 4–6

ingredients

- oil, for greasing
- 1 lb 9 oz/700 g mixed game, cut into 1¼-inch/3-cm pieces
- 2 tbsp all-purpose flour, plus extra for dusting
- 3 tbsp vegetable oil
- 1 onion, coarsely chopped
- 1 garlic clove, finely chopped
- 12 oz/350 g large portobello mushrooms, sliced
- 1 tsp crushed juniper berries
- ½ cup port or Marsala
- 2 cups chicken or game stock
- 1 bay leaf
- 14 oz/400 g prepared puff pastry
- 1 egg, beaten
- salt and pepper

1 Preheat the oven to 325°F/160°C. Grease a 5-cup pie dish. Put the meat into a large plastic bag with the flour and salt and pepper and shake to coat the meat.

2 Heat the oil in a large flameproof casserole dish over high heat and brown the meat in batches. Remove with a slotted spoon and keep warm. Fry the onion and garlic for 2–3 minutes, until softened, then add the mushrooms and cook for about 2 minutes, stirring continuously, until they start to wilt. Add the juniper berries, then the port, and then scrape the sediment from the bottom of the casserole. Add the stock, stirring continuously, and bring to a boil. Let simmer for 2–3 minutes. Add the bay leaf and return the meat to the casserole. Cover and cook in the oven for 1½–2 hours, until the meat is tender. Check for seasoning and add more salt and pepper, if necessary. Remove from the oven and cool. Chill overnight in the refrigerator to develop the flavors. Remove and discard the bay leaf.

3 Preheat the oven to 400°F/200°C. Roll out the pastry on a lightly floured work surface to about 2¾ inches/7 cm larger than the pie dish. Cut off a 1¼-inch 3-cm strip around the edge. Moisten the rim of the dish and press the pastry strip onto it. Place a pie funnel in the center of the dish and spoon in the meat filling. Don't overfill; keep any extra gravy to serve separately.

4 Moisten the pastry collar with a little water and put on the pastry lid. Crimp the edges of the pastry firmly and glaze with the egg.

5 Bake the pie on a baking sheet near the top of the oven for about 30 minutes. If necessary, cover it with foil and reduce the oven temperature a little. The pie should be golden brown and the filling bubbling hot.

Chapter 5
Vegetables & Salads

Introduction

Vegetables are very nutritious: they are rich in vitamins and minerals and low in fat. They are also very quick and easy to prepare and cook. You can also use surplus or leftover vegetables in other dishes, such as stock or stews.

Buying and storing vegetables

Choose vegetables when they are in season because this is when they are at their best. Try to buy them in small quantities on a frequent basis to ensure a constant fresh supply—the fresher the vegetables, the better they will taste and the more nutrients they will have. Here are some of the main varieties.

Root vegetables

Root vegetables are delicious and vary greatly in terms of flavor. They provide a colorful contrast to leafy green vegetables and are particularly good roasted or in casseroles or stews.

Carrots

These are available all year round. Carrots should be peeled first, then you can grate them raw into salads, or slice and boil them. After boiling, you can mash them, if desired. You can also steam, stir-fry, or roast them.

Beets

These are available all year round and are excellent washed and grated raw into salads. Alternatively, you can boil or roast them whole. You can also buy beets already cooked.

Radishes

These are available in many sizes, shapes, and colors all year round, the most common variety being the small red radish, which is either round or oval. Washed, trimmed, and served raw, radishes give a distinctive, peppery taste to salads and make excellent garnishes, whole or sliced.

Celeriac

This knobbly vegetable, also called celery root, is usually available in fall, winter, and spring. It is very good peeled and boiled, then mashed. You can also parboil and roast celeriac.

Parsnips

Fresh parsnips are best during fall and winter, although they are available all year round. They should always be cooked. You can boil and mash, or parboil and roast them. You can also steam or sauté parsnips, and they are very good in soups.

Potatoes

Available all year round and usually classified as either floury or waxy, this versatile and popular vegetable comes in many shapes, sizes, and colors, including long and round, white, red, and blue. Potatoes range in size from small new potatoes, which are ideal for boiling and for salads, to large baking potatoes, which are excellent for baking in their skins or for making fries. When cooking potatoes, you can either peel them first, or simply scrub them and leave them unpeeled. Potato skins are very nutritious, and delicious when cooked, so it is often a good idea to leave the skins on, unless you are making mashed potatoes, when it is better to remove them.

Potatoes are excellent boiled, mashed, fried, baked, and roasted. You can serve them hot or cold. After buying your potatoes, store them in a cool, dark place.

Sweet potatoes

They are not botanically related to the potato, but sweet potatoes, which have a delicious sweet flavor, can be substituted for potatoes in many recipes.

Rutabaga

This root vegetable is best in fall and winter. It should always be peeled and cooked. You can boil and mash it or parboil and roast it. It is delicious mashed with carrots.

Turnips

Although available all year round, the peak season for turnips is in winter. Like rutabagas, these root vegetables are best peeled and boiled, then mashed. You can also parboil and roast them.

Carrots

Radishes

Parsnips

Baby new potatoes

Floury baking potato

Spinach

Waxy potatoes

Red potatoes

Leafy vegetables and salad greens

Leafy vegetables and salad greens are very good for us, which is why nutritionists recommend eating plenty of them. They also make attractive accompaniments to many dishes.

Salad greens

Our appetite for salad greens has grown in recent years. Different varieties of lettuce include iceberg, romain, frisée, and Boston, as well as red leaf and radicchio. Lettuce is rich in iron, calcium, and vitamins A and C, yet is very low in calories and fat. It is a popular favorite in salads, makes a good garnish, and is delicious lightly sautéed. Other popular salad greens include arugula, a member of the brassica family, and watercress, a rich source of vitamin C.

Spinach

Although a good source of iron and vitamins A and C, the oxalic acid content of spinach actually prevents the body's absorption of iron and calcium, so it is probably best eaten in moderation. Baby spinach leaves can be washed and used raw in salads, or you can boil, stir-fry, steam, or sauté the leaves. When spinach is cooked, it reduces in volume considerably, so you'll need to plan substantially more raw spinach to ensure that you have enough when it is cooked. It is best lightly steamed. You can also buy spinach frozen or canned.

Lettuce

Brassicas

These members of the cabbage family are excellent boiled, steamed, or stir-fried. Be careful to avoid overcooking them—brassicas are best when tender but still slightly crisp to the bite.

Chinese cabbage

Broccoli

Savoy cabbage

Brussels sprouts

Cauliflower

Brussels sprouts

These look like tiny cabbages and are, in fact, related to the cabbage family. They are available fresh during fall and winter, or frozen all year round. They are very good boiled or steamed, or shredded and added to stir-fries. However, due to their sulfur content, they have a strong flavor that some people dislike.

Cauliflower

Like cabbage, cauliflower comes in different colors: white, green, and red, although the white type is the most popular. You can eat it raw, or cook it by boiling, steaming, stir-frying, sautéeing, or baking.

Bok choy

This is available all year round. It looks a little like celery and has crunchy white stalks and dark green leaves. It is related to Chinese cabbage botanically, and is often confused with them but is not the same. However, it does have similar uses and can be used raw in salads, or stir-fried, sautéed, steamed, braised, or baked.

Cabbage

These come in many shapes and colors, ranging from white and green to red and the purplish-black cavolo nero (black kale, sometimes called Tuscan kale). Look for cabbage that is crisp and fresh. You can wash and eat it raw in salads and coleslaw, or cook it in a variety of ways such as boiling, steaming, or stir-frying.

Broccoli

This popular vegetable is available all year round and is nutritious. It can be boiled, steamed, stir-fried, sautéed, or baked.

Chinese cabbage

The crinkly, cream-color leaves with green tips of Chinese cabbage are at their best in the fall. They can be used raw in salads, or sautéed, steamed, braised, or baked. They are also popular in stir-fries.

The onion family

These members of the onion family contain sulfuric compounds that give them their unmistakable aroma and flavour. Their taste varies from mild to pungent.

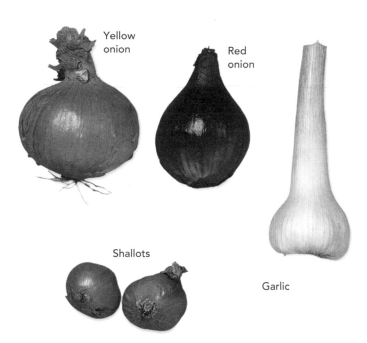

Yellow onion

Red onion

Shallots

Garlic

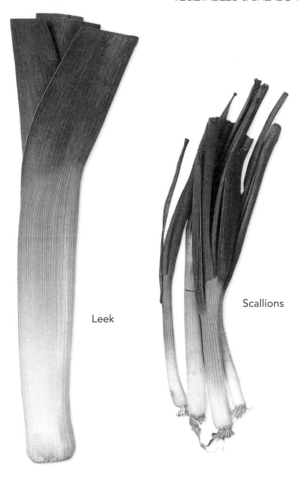

Leek

Scallions

Shallots
These are small onions that resemble large garlic cloves when they are peeled. Use shallots when you need a milder onion flavor. They are particularly good in stir-fries and casseroles, and in kebabs.

Scallions
These very small onions are available all year round but their peak season is during the spring and summer. They can be used raw in salads or sliced to make an attractive garnish, or they can be boiled, steamed, sautéed, or baked. Scallions are also excellent in stir-fries and soups.

Garlic
This versatile bulb was popular with the ancient Egyptians for its medicinal qualities and has many uses in modern cooking. It has an unmistakable taste, due to its sulfur content, and adds a delicious flavor to many different recipes. It can be boiled, steamed, sautéed, stir-fried, baked, and roasted. When garlic is cooked with wine, it produces a wonderful flavor and the combination is excellent in soups and sauces. It can also be used to liven up dressings and marinades.

Leeks
These have a very mild onion flavor and range in size from small baby leeks to large. They can be boiled, steamed, sautéed, stir-fried, or baked, and can be substituted for onions in most recipes.

Onions
These are available all year round in a variety of colors, from yellow and white to red. They also range in size from tiny pearl onions to the large Bermuda onions, and they vary in flavor from mildly pungent to very strong. Once peeled and trimmed, they can be eaten raw in salads or as a garnish, or they can be cooked in a wide variety of dishes, from stir-fries to casseroles. You can also pickle onions.

Heat-loving vegetables

The tastes of the vegetables in this category vary from the mild, creamy flavor of avocados, to the sweet freshness of tomatoes and the fiery heat of chiles. They are popular in a wide range of international dishes.

Eggplants

These come in different sizes and colors, from the large, deep-purple type, to the tiny green pea eggplant. Eggplants must always be cooked, and unless you are using them in a moist recipe with a lot of liquid, you should degorge them to remove bitter juices first. Simply cut the eggplant into slices about ½ inch/1 cm thick, spread them out in a large, shallow dish, and sprinkle with plenty of salt. Let the slices stand for 30 minutes, then transfer to a colander and rinse off the salt with plenty of cold running water. Pat dry with paper towels, then use.

Avocados

These green or purplish-black vegetables are shaped like pears but have a soft, buttery interior. Look for avocados that are just beginning to yield to the touch when pressed and have no bruises. You can use them halved as an appetizer, sliced in salads, or mashed in dips. Avocados discolor quickly when cut, so use them right away after cutting, or brush them with lemon juice to prevent discoloration.

Chiles

These fiery vegetable fruits usually come in red or green, and in many different sizes and shapes, from ¼ inch/5 mm to 30 cm/12 inches in length. Generally, the smaller the chilli, the hotter the flavor; the small ones can be so fiery that they can burn the skin. Always wear protective gloves when handling chiles, and keep them away from your eyes. Chiles add a spicy kick to many recipes and are particularly good in sauces and stir-fries, and in dishes such as chili con carne. Seed chiles before use in order to reduce their fiery heat.

Bell peppers

When sweet peppers are young, they are green and quite bitter, then as they ripen and get sweeter, they turn red. You can also get yellow, orange, purple, and brown peppers, or peppers in different shapes, such as the long, pointed red Mediterranean peppers. Once sliced and seeded, they can be used raw in salads or as crudités, or cooked in a variety of dishes. Roasting or broiling brings out their sweet flavor. They can also be sautéed, stir-fried, steamed, braised and baked.

Tomatoes

These are available all year round and come in many different sizes and shapes, from tiny cherry tomatoes to large beef tomatoes. Make sure your tomatoes are firm when you buy them. Tomatoes left on the vine are particularly flavorful: in order to preserve their flavor, store them on the vine until you intend to use them. You can eat tomatoes raw in salads and snacks, or cook them. You can also stuff them. They make excellent sauces, soups, and pizza toppings, and are delicious sautéed, stir-fried, broiled, and baked.

Beans and peas

These legumes have a delicious flavor, and some varieties, such as sugar snap peas, are tender enough to have an edible pod, so you can eat them whole. They are very good stir-fried.

Pods

These are young vegetables that have edible pods, such as sugar snap peas, snow peas, green beans, and runner beans. They have a delicious sweet flavor and can be steamed, boiled, sautéed, or stir-fried.

Shelled peas and beans

These are seeds that are grown in the pod, then are served shelled. They include garden peas, as well as young baby peas, and fava beans, which are green and slightly kidney shaped. All of them can be boiled or steamed.

Peas

Green beans

Snow peas

Squash

Vine-growing members of the large squash family are suitable for use in a variety of dishes. Smaller varieties tend to be more flavorful.

Other vegetables

Mushrooms and corn are delicious in salads, risottos, and stir-fries, but try experimenting with more exotic varieties of vegetables, too, such as Asian vegetables and seaweeds.

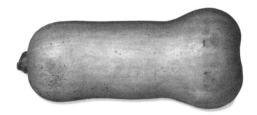

Butternut squash

Corn

Button mushrooms

Zucchini

This is one of the summer squash varieties and comes in various shades of green, sometimes with yellow stripes. It also comes in a variety of sizes, starting with the babies at 4 inches/10 cm long. The smaller varieties tend to have the most flavor. You can also get small, round zucchini, ideal for stuffing. Zucchini are available all year round, and are very versatile. They can be steamed, broiled, charbroiled, stir-fried, sautéed, deep-fried, baked, and roasted, or you can eat them raw in salads. Zucchini flowers, if you can get them, are wonderful stuffed and cooked, or battered and fried.

Cucumbers

Although best known as a salad vegetable, the cucumber is, in fact, a member of the squash family. It can be cut into crudités, with or without its skin, served raw with dips, or lightly sautéed or stir-fried.

Pumpkins

This large squash is available in fall and winter. The large varieties are popular at Halloween, when they are carved out and made into masks or lanterns. The smaller, orange varieties have a sweeter flavor and are more suitable for cooking. Pumpkin pie is a particular favorite. You can also use pumpkin in soups and casseroles.

Other squashes

Butternut, acorn, and spaghetti squashes are classed as winter squashes. They are large and have thick skins and firm flesh. Once seeded, they can be roasted, baked, or steamed. Summer squashes, such as patty pans, are smaller and can be sautéed, steamed, or baked.

Corn

The most popular type of corn these days is the yellow corn. The husks and silks need to be removed before cooking, then you can simply cook the corn whole on the cob, or remove the kernels and cook them on their own. Corn comes into season in the summer months, but you can also buy it frozen or canned all year round. It is delicious boiled on the cob, or the kernels can be cooked and used in soups, salads, and casseroles. You can also buy baby corn, which can be boiled, steamed, or stir-fried.

Mushrooms

Mushrooms vary greatly in size, shape, and color. Both cultivated or wild mushrooms are available all year round. The more common fresh mushrooms are the white button, the brown cremini, and the large, flat portobello mushrooms; Exotic mushrooms include shiitake and porcini, which are available fresh or dried. Do not pick wild mushrooms yourself unless you are positive you can identify them correctly—many wild mushrooms are poisonous. Mushrooms can absorb a lot of water, so it is better to wipe them with a clean, damp cloth instead of washing them. They can be sautéed, stir-fried, deep-fried in batter, broiled, or baked.

Exotic vegetables

There is a great variety of exotic vegetables available nowadays, and they come from all over the world. Some of the most popular include kombu, which is a dried form of kelp that is used in Japanese cooking; daikon, a long white radish (also called mooli) that is used in Asian cooking; and wakame, an edible seaweed popular in Asia.

Chunky Vegetable Soup

Serves 6

ingredients

- 2 carrots, sliced
- 1 onion, diced
- 1 garlic clove, crushed
- 2⅓ cups diced new potatoes
- 2 celery stalks, sliced
- 1⅔ cups quartered closed-cup mushrooms
- 14 oz/400 g canned chopped tomatoes
- 1¼ cups vegetable stock
- 1 bay leaf
- 1 tsp dried mixed herbs or 1 tbsp chopped fresh mixed herbs
- ½ cup frozen corn kernels or ⅓ cup drained, canned corn kernels
- ½ cup shredded green cabbage
- freshly ground black pepper
- sprigs of fresh basil, to garnish (optional)

1 Put the carrots, onion, garlic, potatoes, celery, mushrooms, tomatoes, and stock into a large saucepan. Stir in the bay leaf and herbs. Bring to a boil, then reduce the heat, cover, and simmer for 25 minutes.

2 Add the corn kernels and cabbage and return to a boil. Reduce the heat, cover, and simmer for 5 minutes, or until the vegetables are tender. Remove and discard the bay leaf. Season to taste with pepper.

3 Ladle into warm soup bowls, garnish with basil, if using, and serve immediately.

Leek & Potato Soup

Serves 4

ingredients

- 2 tbsp butter
- 2 garlic cloves, chopped
- 3 large leeks
- 4 potatoes
- 2 tbsp chopped fresh parsley
- 1 tbsp chopped fresh oregano
- 1 bay leaf
- 3½ cups vegetable stock
- scant 1 cup light cream
- 1 cup grated smoked firm cheese
- salt and pepper
- snipped chives, to garnish

1 Melt the butter in a large saucepan over medium heat. Add the garlic and cook, stirring, for 1 minute. Trim and slice the leeks. Peel the potatoes and cut into bite-size chunks. Add the leeks and cook, stirring, for 2 minutes. Add the potatoes, half of the parsley, all the oregano, and the bay leaf and stock, then season to taste with salt and pepper. Bring to a boil, then reduce the heat, cover the saucepan, and let simmer for 25 minutes. Remove from the heat, let cool for 10 minutes, then remove and discard the bay leaf.

2 Transfer half of the soup to a food processor and process until smooth (you may need to do this in batches). Return to the saucepan with the rest of the soup, stir in the cream, and reheat gently. Adjust the seasoning, if necessary.

3 Remove from the heat and stir in the cheese. Ladle into warm soup bowls, garnish with the snipped chives and remaining parsley, and serve.

Niçoise Pasta Salad

Serves 4

ingredients

- 12 oz/350 g dried conchiglie
- 1 cup green beans
- 1¾ oz/50 g canned anchovy fillets, drained
- 2 tbsp milk
- 2 small crisp lettuce
- 3 large beefsteak tomatoes
- 4 hard-cooked eggs
- 8 oz/225 g canned tuna, drained
- 1 cup pitted black olives
- salt

for the vinaigrette dressing

- 3 tbsp extra virgin olive oil
- 2 tbsp white wine vinegar
- 1 tsp whole-grain mustard
- salt and pepper

1 Bring a large pan of lightly salted water to a boil over medium heat. Add the pasta and cook for 8–10 minutes, until tender but still firm to the bite. Drain and refresh in cold water.

2 Bring a small pan of lightly salted water to a boil over medium heat. Add the green beans and cook for 10–12 minutes, or until tender but still firm to the bite. Drain, refresh in cold water, drain again, and reserve.

3 Put the anchovies in a shallow bowl, pour in the milk, and let stand for 10 minutes. Meanwhile, tear the lettuce into large pieces. Blanch the tomatoes in boiling water for 1–2 minutes, then drain, skin, and coarsely chop the flesh. Shell the eggs and cut into quarters. Flake the tuna into large chunks.

4 Drain the anchovies and the pasta. Put all the salad ingredients into a large bowl and gently mix together.

5 To make the vinaigrette dressing, beat together the oil, vinegar, and mustard and season to taste with salt and pepper. Chill in the refrigerator until required. Just before serving, pour the vinaigrette dressing over the salad.

Caesar Salad

Serves 4

ingredients
- 1 extra-large egg
- 2 romaine lettuce or 3 Boston lettuce
- 6 tbsp olive oil
- 2 tbsp lemon juice
- 8 canned anchovy fillets, drained and coarsely chopped
- 85 g/3 oz fresh Parmesan cheese, shaved
- salt and pepper

for the garlic croutons
- 4 tbsp olive oil
- 2 garlic cloves
- 5 slices white bread, crusts removed, cut into ½-inch/1-cm cubes

1 Bring a small, heavy-bottom saucepan of water to a boil.

2 Meanwhile, make the garlic croutons. Heat the olive oil in a heavy-bottom skillet. Add the garlic and diced bread and cook, stirring and tossing frequently, for 4–5 minutes, or until the bread is crispy and golden all over. Remove from the skillet with a slotted spoon and drain on paper towels.

3 While the bread is frying, add the egg to the boiling water and cook for 1 minute, then remove from the saucepan and reserve.

4 Arrange the lettuce leaves in a salad bowl. Mix the olive oil and lemon juice together, then season to taste with salt and pepper. Crack the egg into the dressing and whisk to blend. Pour the dressing over the lettuce, toss well, then add the croutons and chopped anchovies and toss the salad again. Sprinkle with Parmesan cheese shavings and serve.

Greek Feta Salad

Serves 4

ingredients
- a few grape leaves
- 4 tomatoes, sliced
- ½ cucumber, peeled and sliced
- 1 small red onion, sliced thinly
- 4 oz/115 g feta cheese, cubed
- 8 black olives

for the dressing
- 3 tbsp extra virgin olive oil
- 1 tbsp lemon juice
- ½ tsp dried oregano
- salt and pepper

1 To make the dressing, put the oil, lemon juice, oregano, and salt and pepper in a screw-top jar and shake together until blended.

2 Arrange the grape leaves on a serving dish and then the tomatoes, cucumber, and onion. Scatter the cheese and olives on top. Pour the dressing over the salad and serve.

Roasted Summer Vegetables

Serves 4

ingredients
- 2 tbsp olive oil
- 1 fennel bulb
- 2 red onions
- 2 beefsteak tomatoes
- 1 eggplant
- 2 zucchini
- 1 yellow bell pepper
- 1 red bell pepper
- 1 orange bell pepper
- 4 garlic cloves
- 4 fresh rosemary sprigs
- pepper
- crusty bread, to serve (optional)

1 Preheat the oven to 400°F/200°C. Brush a large ovenproof dish with a little of the oil. Prepare the vegetables. Cut the fennel, red onions, and tomatoes into wedges. Slice the eggplant and zucchini thickly, then seed all the bell peppers and cut into chunks. Arrange the vegetables in the dish and tuck the garlic cloves and rosemary sprigs among them. Drizzle with the remaining oil and season to taste with pepper.

2 Roast the vegetables in the preheated oven for 10 minutes. Remove the dish from the oven and turn the vegetables over with a slotted spoon. Return to the oven and roast for another 10–15 minutes, until tender and beginning to turn golden brown.

3 Serve the vegetables straight from the dish, or transfer to a warm serving plate. Serve with crusty bread, if desired.

Crisp Noodle & Vegetable Stir-Fry

Serves 4

ingredients

- peanut oil, for deep-frying
- 4 oz/115 g rice vermicelli, broken into 3-inch/7.5-cm lengths
- 1 cup green bean pieces
- 2 carrots, cut into thin sticks
- 2 zucchini, cut into thin sticks
- 4 oz/115 g shiitake mushrooms, sliced
- 1-inch/2.5-cm piece fresh ginger, shredded
- ½ small head Chinese cabbage, shredded
- 4 scallions, shredded
- 1 cup bean sprouts
- 2 tbsp dark soy sauce
- 2 tbsp Chinese rice wine
- large pinch of sugar
- 2 tbsp coarsely chopped fresh cilantro

1 Fill a wok or deep, heavy-bottom skillet halfway with oil. Heat to 350–375°F/180–190°C, or until a cube of bread browns in 30 seconds.

2 Add the noodles, in batches, and cook for 1½–2 minutes, or until crisp and puffed up. Remove and drain on paper towels. Pour off all but 2 tablespoons of oil from the wok.

3 Heat the remaining oil over high heat. Add the green beans and stir-fry for 2 minutes.

4 Add the carrot and zucchini sticks, sliced mushrooms and ginger, and stir-fry for another 2 minutes.

5 Add the shredded Chinese cabbage and scallions with the bean sprouts and stir-fry for another 1 minute.

6 Add the soy sauce, rice wine, and sugar and cook, stirring continuously, for 1 minute.

7 Add the noodles and chopped cilantro and toss well. Serve immediately.

Ratatouille

Serves 4

ingredients

- 1 eggplant (about 9 oz/250 g)
- 4 tbsp olive oil
- 2 garlic cloves, chopped
- 1 large onion, chopped
- 2 red bell peppers, seeded and cut into bite-size chunks
- 1 lb 12 oz/800 g canned chopped tomatoes
- 2 zucchini, sliced
- 1 celery stalk, sliced
- 1 tsp sugar
- 2 tbsp chopped fresh thyme
- salt and pepper

1 Trim the eggplant and cut it into bite-size chunks, then place it in a colander. Sprinkle with salt and let stand for 30 minutes.

2 Heat the oil in a large saucepan over medium heat. Add the garlic and onion and cook, stirring, for 3 minutes, until softened slightly. Rinse the eggplant and drain well, then add it to the saucepan with the red bell peppers. Reduce the heat and cook gently, stirring frequently, for an additional 10 minutes.

3 Stir in the tomatoes, zucchini, celery, sugar, and thyme, and season to taste with salt and pepper. Bring to a boil, then reduce the heat, cover the saucepan, and let simmer gently for 30 minutes.

4 Remove the saucepan from the heat, transfer to bowls, and serve.

Vegetable Cannelloni

Serves 4

ingredients
- 12 dried cannelloni tubes
- 1 eggplant
- ½ cup olive oil, plus extra
  for brushing
- 8 oz/225 g spinach
- 2 garlic cloves, crushed
- 1 tsp ground cumin
- 1¼ cups chopped mushrooms
- 2 oz/55 g mozzarella cheese,
  sliced
- salt and pepper
- mâche, to garnish

for the tomato sauce
- 1 tbsp olive oil
- 1 onion, chopped
- 2 garlic cloves, crushed
- 1 lb 12 oz/800 g canned
  chopped tomatoes
- 1 tsp superfine sugar
- 2 tbsp chopped fresh basil

1 Preheat the oven to 375°F/190°C. Bring a large, heavy-bottom saucepan of lightly salted water to a boil. Add the cannelloni tubes, return to a boil, and cook for 8–10 minutes, or until tender but still firm to the bite. Transfer the pasta to a plate and pat dry with paper towels. Brush a large ovenproof dish with oil.

2 Cut the eggplant into small dice. Heat the oil in a skillet over medium heat. Add the eggplant and cook, stirring frequently, for about 2–3 minutes.

3 Add the spinach, garlic, cumin, and mushrooms and reduce the heat. Season to taste with salt and pepper and cook, stirring, for about 2–3 minutes. Spoon the mixture into the cannelloni tubes and put into the dish in a single layer.

4 To make the sauce, heat the oil in a pan over medium heat. Add the onion and garlic and cook for 1 minute. Add the tomatoes, sugar, and basil and bring to a boil. Reduce the heat and simmer for about 5 minutes. Spoon the sauce over the cannelloni tubes.

5 Arrange the mozzarella cheese on top of the sauce and bake in the preheated oven for about 30 minutes, or until the cheese is golden brown and bubbling. Serve garnished with mâche.

Grilled Zucchini Bruschetta

Serves 4

ingredients

- 1 tbsp olive oil, plus extra for drizzling
- ½ tsp ground cumin
- 2 zucchini (about 10½ oz/300 g), cut in half widthwise, then thinly sliced lengthwise
- 1 red onion, thinly sliced
- 2 large plum or vine-ripened tomatoes, thickly sliced (each cut into 4 slices)
- 8 slices (each about ¾ inch/2 cm thick) plain ciabatta bread (or 8 slices cut from a large French baguette)
- 1 garlic clove, halved
- salt and pepper

1 In a large bowl, whisk together the olive oil, cumin, and seasoning. Add the zucchini and onion slices and toss gently to coat all over. Heat a nonstick, ridged grill pan over medium heat. Place a layer of zucchini and onion slices on the pan and cook for about 6–8 minutes, or until lightly browned and tender, turning occasionally. When the first batch is cooked, remove and keep warm, then add the remaining zucchini and onion slices to the grill pan and cook as before. Remove and keep warm.

2 Add the tomato slices to the grill pan and cook briefly on both sides (about 1 minute on each side), then remove and keep warm. Carefully wipe out any stray tomato seeds from the pan using paper towels, if necessary. Add the bread slices to the grill pan and toast each side, turning once. Remove from the pan to warm serving plates.

3 Rub the toasts on one side with the cut garlic halves, then drizzle with a little olive oil. Arrange the grilled vegetables on top of the garlicky toasts and serve immediately.

Stuffed Red Bell Peppers with Basil

Serves 4

ingredients

- ¾ cup long-grain white or brown rice
- 4 large red bell peppers
- 2 tbsp olive oil
- 1 garlic clove, chopped
- 4 shallots, chopped
- 1 celery stalk, chopped
- 3 tbsp chopped toasted walnuts
- 2 tomatoes, peeled and chopped
- 1 tbsp lemon juice
- ⅓ cup raisins
- ¼ cup freshly grated cheddar cheese
- 2 tbsp chopped fresh basil
- salt and pepper

1 Preheat the oven to 350°F/180°C. Cook the rice in a saucepan of lightly salted boiling water for 20 minutes if using white rice, or 35 minutes if using brown. Drain, rinse under cold running water, then drain again.

2 Meanwhile, using a sharp knife, cut the tops off the bell peppers and reserve. Remove the seeds and white cores, then blanch the bell peppers and reserved tops in boiling water for 2 minutes. Remove from the heat and drain well. Heat half of the oil in a large skillet. Add the garlic and shallots and cook, stirring, for 3 minutes. Add the celery, walnuts, tomatoes, lemon juice, and raisins and cook for an additional 5 minutes. Remove from the heat and stir in the rice, cheese, chopped basil, and seasoning.

3 Stuff the bell peppers with the rice mixture and arrange them in a baking dish. Place the tops on the bell peppers, drizzle with the remaining oil, loosely cover with foil, and bake in the preheated oven for 45 minutes. Remove from the oven and serve.

Classic Roasted Potatoes

Serves 4

ingredients
- 8 medium or 4 large floury potatoes, peeled
- ½ tsp salt
- paprika
- scant ½ cup vegetable oil
- pepper

1 Preheat the oven to 400ºF/200ºC. Using a sharp knife, cut the potatoes in half, or into quarters if very large, then arrange in a roasting pan. Sprinkle with the salt, then season to taste with pepper and paprika.

2 Pour the oil over the potatoes, then turn them in the oil until well coated. Transfer to the preheated oven and roast, basting occasionally, for 1½ hours, or until golden brown and tender. Remove from the oven and serve immediately.

Braised Red Cabbage

Serves 6

ingredients

- 2 tbsp sunflower oil
- 2 onions, thinly sliced
- 2 apples, peeled, cored, and thinly sliced
- 1 large red cabbage, cored and shredded
- 4 tbsp red wine vinegar
- 2 tbsp sugar
- ¼ tsp ground cloves
- ⅓ cup raisins
- ½ cup red wine
- 2 tbsp red currant jelly
- salt and pepper

1 Heat the oil in a large saucepan. Add the onions and cook, stirring occasionally, for 10 minutes, or until softened and golden. Stir in the apple slices and cook for 3 minutes.

2 Add the cabbage, vinegar, sugar, cloves, raisins, and red wine and season to taste with salt and pepper. Bring to a boil, stirring occasionally. Reduce the heat, cover, and cook, stirring occasionally, for 40 minutes, or until the cabbage is tender and most of the liquid has been absorbed.

3 Stir in the red currant jelly, transfer to a warm dish, and serve.

Risotto with Artichoke Hearts

Serves 4

ingredients
- 8 oz/225 g canned artichoke hearts
- 1 tbsp olive oil
- 3 tbsp butter
- 1 small onion, finely chopped
- 1½ cups risotto rice
- 5 cups hot vegetable stock
- scant 1 cup freshly grated Parmesan cheese or Grana Padano cheese
- salt and pepper
- fresh flat-leaf parsley, to garnish

1 Drain the artichoke hearts, reserving the liquid, and cut them into quarters.

2 Heat the oil with 2 tablespoons of the butter in a deep saucepan over medium heat until the butter has melted. Stir in the onion and cook gently, stirring occasionally, for 5 minutes, or until soft and starting to turn golden. Do not brown.

3 Add the rice and mix to coat in oil and butter. Cook, stirring continuously, for 2–3 minutes, or until the grains are translucent.

4 Gradually add the artichoke liquid and the hot stock, a ladle at a time. Stir continuously and add more liquid as the rice absorbs each addition. Increase the heat to medium so that the liquid simmers. Cook for 15 minutes, then add the artichoke hearts. Cook for an additional 5 minutes, or until all the liquid is absorbed and the rice is creamy. Season to taste with salt and pepper.

5 Remove the risotto from the heat and add the remaining butter. Mix well, then stir in the cheese until it melts. Season, if necessary. Spoon the risotto into warm bowls, garnish with parsley, and serve immediately.

Chapter 6
Herbs & Spices

Introduction

There is a wide range of fresh herbs available all year round in your local supermarket, as well as a tempting array of fragrant and exotic spices. You can also buy frozen herbs, which are a good substitute when fresh herbs are unavailable. It is a good idea to keep some flowerpots of fresh herbs on a windowsill and a selection of dried herbs and spices in your pantry. Note that if you are substituting a dried herb for fresh, you will need only one-third of the quantity, because the flavor is more concentrated.

Buying and storing herbs and spices

If you buy fresh herbs in flowerpots, place them on a windowsill where they can get plenty of light, and water them regularly. Basil, in particular, needs a lot of water, so make sure you do not let it dry out. Packaged fresh herbs should be stored in their wrapping in the refrigerator. If you grow herbs in your garden, after picking, keep them in a glass of clean water until you are ready to use them. Store dried herbs and ground spices in a cool, dark place—an airy pantry is ideal. Use all fresh herbs by their expiration date, and go through your pantry regularly and throw out any dried herbs and spices that are past their best.

Basil
There are many varieties of this herb. It thrives in a warm, Mediterranean climate, and, therefore, in cold climates it will do better indoors on a windowsill with plenty of sunshine and water. It has a sweet, aromatic flavor, and is particularly good with tomatoes and mozzarella cheese. It is also delicious with poultry, fish and seafood, salads, and sauces. This herb is fragile, so it should be added to recipes toward the end of the cooking time.

Tarragon
The dark green pointed leaves of tarragon have an aromatic, anise seedlike flavor. It adds a distinctive taste to poultry, fish, eggs, sauces, salads, and dressings. It is best to use this herb on its own, because its strong flavor can overpower other herbs if mixed with them.

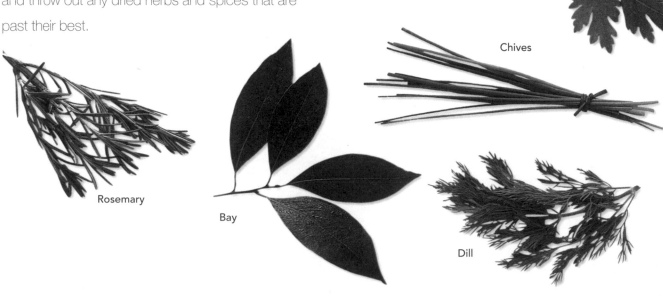

Cilantro

Chives

Rosemary

Bay

Dill

Thyme

This herb comes in different varieties, and several of them are commonly used in cooking. The leaves add a pungent, aromatic flavor to meat, poultry, egg, and potato dishes, and are good in soups, sauces, roasts, casseroles, and stews.

Oregano

This green herb is related to marjoram. It has a pungent flavor and should be used sparingly. It is popular in Italian cookery, particularly on pizzas, and adds an aromatic flavor to meat and poultry, eggs, and cheese.

Cilantro

This pungent herb has bright green leaves and is very popular in Mediterranean and Asian cooking. It adds a distinctive flavor to salads, cooked vegetables, and stir-fries.

Fennel

There are two types of fennel. One has a bulbous base, which can be cooked and used like a vegetable; the other variety has no bulb. Fennel has a strong anise seed flavor. The leaves of both types can be snipped into soups and sauces, and are excellent with fish and egg dishes.

Marjoram

This ancient herb has pale green leaves and a delicate, sweet flavor. It is ideal with meat, poultry, cheese, tomatoes, eggs, and dressings.

Rosemary

The silvery, needle-shape leaves of rosemary have a strong aromatic flavor. It is used in soups, salads, roasts, stuffings, dressings, and marinades, as well as on pizzas. The herb also makes delicious skewers for kebabs. It pairs particularly well with potatoes and bread, as well as meat, poultry, fish, and eggs.

Bay

The leaves of this aromatic herb come from the Mediterranean laurel tree. The fresh leaves, if you can get them, have more flavor than the dried, but either type will add a good, pungent flavor to soups, sauces, stocks, and casseroles. They are usually removed from the dish and discarded once the food has absorbed their flavor.

Sage

This herb has grayish oval leaves and a pungent, slightly bitter taste. It is common in stuffings, especially those containing onion, and is excellent with pork, poultry, beans, cheese, rice, and pasta. It is also used to flavor drinks.

Chervil

The dark green, curly leaves of chervil have an aromatic flavor with a hint of anise seed. It is especially good in chicken, fish, and egg dishes.

Mint

There are many species of mint, the two best-known being peppermint and spearmint. Peppermint has a more peppery flavor, while spearmint has a fresher mint taste. Mint is a hardy plant and can take over a herb garden if not carefully controlled. Use it to flavor cooked potatoes, peas, sauces, soups, meat dishes, desserts, and drinks.

Dill

This herb has feathery green leaves, called dill weed, and a mild flavor. Dill is excellent with fish, as well as in salads, cheese dishes, and sauces.

Chives

These relatives of the onion family have long, hollow stems and edible purple flowers. The fresh stems are snipped into small pieces and added to salads, soups, cream cheese, and egg dishes. You can also buy them frozen and dried.

Parsley

This versatile herb is rich in vitamins A and C and comes in many varieties. The two most popular types have green leaves that are either curly or flat. Curly parsley is common all year round, while Italian flat-leaf parsley may be found only in some supermarkets and specialty delicatessens. Parsley is used in a wide range of dishes, including soups, salads, sauces, stir-fries, and casseroles, as well as stuffings, dressings, and marinades. It adds a spicy, lingering flavor to meat, poultry, fish, eggs, and vegetables, and helps to offset the sulfur aftertaste of garlic. It also makes an attractive garnish, particularly the flat-leaf variety.

Oregano

Thyme

Basil

Types and uses of spices

Spices used to be costly when international travel was comparatively slow and difficult—now they are less expensive and more widely available.

Cardamom pods

Chili powder

Ground cinnamon

Cinnamon sticks

Paprika

This spice is made from ground red pepper pods and its flavor can vary from mild, sweet, and pungent to fiery hot. It is excellent in salads and as a garnish. It also goes well with meat, poultry, eggs, vegetables, cream cheese, pasta, rice, and beans.

Cardamom

This aromatic spice is related to ginger and has a pungent lemon flavor. You can grind and use the whole pod, or use just the seeds inside. Cardamom is widely used in Asian and Middle Eastern dishes, and adds a distinctive flavor to soups, stews, curries, pastry, bread, and cakes.

Allspice

This small berry comes from the West Indies and South America and has a sweet flavor of nutmeg, cinnamon, and cloves. You can buy it whole or ground. It is used with meat, onions, and fruit desserts, as well as in cakes and bread.

Mustard

This hot, acrid spice is available as whole seeds, ground, or processed into a paste that ranges in intensity from mild to strong. It goes well with meat, poultry, seafood, eggs, beans, potatoes, cheese, cream and butter sauces, bread, marinades, chutneys, and relishes.

Chili powder

This powdered mixture of spices includes dried chiles, cumin, coriander, and cloves. It has a fiery heat but you can also buy mild chili powder. Use it to flavor soups and stews. It goes well with seafood, meat, poultry, vegetables, beans, and eggs.

Fennel seeds

You can buy fennel seeds whole or ground. They have a sweet, mildly anise seed flavor and can be used in savory and sweet dishes, including marinades, pizzas, stuffings, bread, cakes, cookies, and a variety of desserts and drinks. Fennel goes particularly well with meat, poultry, fish, beet, onions, potatoes, tomatoes, cucumber, beans, pasta, rice, cheese, eggs, and fruit.

Star anise

This star-shape brown pod comes from an Asian tree. It has a warm, aromatic, slightly bitter anise seed flavor and is available whole or ground. It is popular in Chinese cooking, and is used in marinades, stir-fries, casseroles, cakes, fruit, and some drinks. It goes particularly well with pork, poultry, and fish.

Caraway

These seeds have a nutty, anise seed flavor and can be bought whole or ground. They are popular in German and Austrian cookery, and are used to flavor soups, stews, meat, cheese, vegetables, sauerkraut, bread, cakes, and the liqueur kümmel.

Juniper

These berries are available dried and are usually crushed to release their pungent pine flavor. Use them to flavor various meats as well as pâtés, stuffings, and sauces.

Mace

This sweet, fragrant spice is most often sold ground and is used to flavor a wide range of savory and sweet dishes, including beef, chicken, fish, vegetables, pasta, beans, cheese, chocolate, fruit, cakes, marinades, cookies, chutneys, and mulled wine.

Cayenne pepper

This type of pepper is made from tropical chiles and it has a hot, spicy flavor. Use it to add a kick to South American and Caribbean dishes. It is especially good with seafood and chutneys.

Peppercorns

The dried berries from the pepper plant come in black, white, and green. Black peppercorns are the most widely used, and are available whole, cracked, or ground. They deteriorate quickly when ground, so it is best to buy them whole and grind them yourself. They have an aromatic flavor and can be used in almost every savory recipe and some sweet fruit dishes, such as balsamic strawberries.

Cinnamon

This spice comes from the bark of a tropical tree. The bark is dried and curled into quills or sticks; it can also be bought ground. Cinnamon has a sweet, aromatic smell and flavor, and is popular in Middle Eastern dishes. It is used to flavor a wide range of savory and sweet dishes, such as stews, curries, pies, bread, and cakes, and a host of desserts and drinks.

Garam masala

Ground ginger

Coriander seeds

Whole
nutmeg

Nutmeg
Nutmeg has a sweet, fragrant flavor and is available whole or ground. It is used in a wide variety of savory and sweet dishes, from meat, poultry, vegetables, beans, rice, cheese, and eggs to chocolate, fruit, cream sauces, and drinks.

Coriander
The dried seeds of the coriander plant are fragrant and lemony and can be used whole or ground. They are popular in marinades, chutneys, curries and casseroles, and go well with meat, poultry, fish, cheese, vegetables, beans, chocolate, and preserves.

Saffron
This spice has a pungent, slightly bitter flavor. It comes from the purple crocus and is available in threads or powdered. It is used to tint and flavor marinades, soups, stews, rice dishes, breads, and casseroles. This is the spice that gives the rice in Spanish paella its characteristic yellow color. Saffron is expensive, so the less expensive turmeric is often used in its place.

Cloves
These come from the buds of the tropical clove tree. The dried brown buds are sold whole or powdered, and have a sweet, pungent flavor. Push whole cloves into ham, pork, onions, and oranges to flavor them, or use them ground in soups, stews, bread, cakes, desserts, and chutneys. You can also use them whole in drinks, such as mulled wine (but you should always remove whole cloves before serving).

Apple pie spice
This blend of spices usually consists of cinnamon, nutmeg, and cardamom. You can make your own by using 4 parts cinnamon, 2 parts nutmeg, and 1 part cardamom. It has a warm, sweet flavor and is delicious in fruit desserts, bread, cakes, cookies, and drinks.

Cumin
These dried seeds have a pungent, nutty flavor and are also available ground. Cumin is popular in Asian and Mexican cooking, and goes well with beef, pork, salmon, shellfish, beans, pasta, eggs, cheese, and rice.

Five-spice powder
Chinese five-spice powder is, as its name implies, a blend of five spices, usually cloves, cinnamon, fennel seeds, Sichuan peppercorns, and star anise. It has a sweet, pungent flavor and is popular in Chinese and Vietnamese cooking. It is especially good in stir-fries. It can be found in many supermarkets as well as in Asian grocery stores.

Curry powder
This powder contains a mixture of spices that include cardamom, chiles, cloves, coriander, fenugreek, and turmeric. It is available mild or hot, and is used in curries, cream sauces, and chutneys. It also goes well with beef, chicken, turkey, seafood, root vegetables, rice, eggs, and cheese.

Turmeric
This spice comes from the root of a tropical plant and has a pungent, somewhat bitter flavor. The powdered variety has a bright orange-yellow color, so is used to tint foods as well as to flavor them. Turmeric is often used as a cheaper alternative to saffron to color food. Use this spice to color or flavor seafood, poultry, pasta, cheese, eggs, curries, risottos, chutneys, marinades, bread, and beans.

Garam masala
The blend of spices in garam masala varies, but it often includes cumin, cinnamon, cloves, cardamom, chiles, fennel, fenugreek, garlic, ginger, and black pepper. It is popular in Indian cooking, especially in curries, and also goes well with vegetables, eggs, cheese, and rice.

Ginger
Ginger is available fresh or dried. The fresh root has a warm, lemon flavor and can be used chopped or grated. It is especially useful in marinades, salads, soups, stews, and stir-fries; it can also be preserved in syrup. Ginger powder has a more pungent, spicy flavor, and is particularly good with chocolate, cream, fruit, gingerbread, cakes, cookies, preserves, chutneys, and drinks.

Minted Pea & Bean Soup

Serves 4–6

ingredients

- 1½ tbsp olive oil
- 1 bunch scallions, trimmed and chopped
- 1 large celery stalk, chopped
- 1 garlic clove, crushed
- 1 potato, peeled and diced
- 5 cups vegetable stock
- 1 bay leaf
- 1 cup peas
- 14 oz/400 g canned flageolet beans, drained and rinsed
- salt and pepper
- finely shredded fresh mint, to garnish
- multigrain bread rolls, to serve

1 Heat the oil in a large saucepan over medium–high heat. Add the scallions, celery, and garlic and cook, stirring, for about 3 minutes, until soft. Add the potato and stir for an additional minute.

2 Add the stock, bay leaf, and salt and pepper to taste and bring to a boil, stirring. Reduce the heat to low, cover the pan, and simmer for 20 minutes, or until the potatoes are tender.

3 Add the peas and beans and return the soup to a boil. Reduce the heat, re-cover the pan, and continue to simmer until the peas are tender.

4 Remove and discard the bay leaf, then put the soup into a food processor or blender and blend until smooth. Place a metal strainer over the rinsed-out pan and use a wooden spoon to push the soup through the strainer.

5 Add salt and pepper to taste and reheat. Ladle the soup into warm bowls, sprinkle with mint, and serve with the bread rolls.

Basil & Pine Nut Pesto

Serves 4

ingredients
- about 40 fresh basil leaves
- 3 garlic cloves, crushed
- 3 tbsp pine nuts
- ½ cup finely grated Parmesan cheese, plus extra to garnish
- 2–3 tbsp extra virgin olive oil
- 1 lb 8 oz/675 g fresh pasta or 12 oz/350 g dried pasta
- salt and pepper

1 Rinse the basil leaves and pat them dry with paper towels.

2 Place the basil leaves, garlic, pine nuts, and grated Parmesan cheese in a food processor and process for 30 seconds, or until smooth. Alternatively, pound all of the ingredients by hand, using a mortar and pestle.

3 If you are using a food processor, keep the motor running and slowly add the olive oil. Alternatively, add the oil drop by drop while stirring briskly. Season to taste with salt and pepper.

4 Bring a large, heavy-bottom saucepan of water to a boil. Add the pasta, return to a boil, and cook for 3–4 minutes for fresh pasta or 8–10 minutes for dried, or according to the package directions, until tender but still firm to the bite. Drain the pasta thoroughly and stir in the pesto.

5 Transfer to warm serving bowls, garnish with the Parmesan cheese, and serve hot.

Tarragon Chicken

Serves 4

ingredients

- 4 skinless, boneless chicken breasts, about 6 oz/175 g each
- ½ cup white wine
- 1–1¼ cups chicken stock
- 1 garlic clove, finely chopped
- 1 tbsp dried tarragon
- ¾ cup heavy cream
- 1 tbsp chopped fresh tarragon
- salt and pepper
- green vegetables, to serve

1 Season the chicken with salt and pepper and place in a single layer in a large, heavy-bottom skillet. Pour in the wine and enough chicken stock just to cover and add the garlic and dried tarragon. Bring to a boil, reduce the heat, and cook gently for 10 minutes, or until the chicken is tender and cooked all the way through.

2 Remove the chicken with a slotted spoon or tongs, cover, and keep warm. Strain the poaching liquid through a strainer into a clean skillet and skim off any fat from the surface. Bring to a boil and cook for 12–15 minutes, or until reduced by about two-thirds.

3 Stir in the cream, return to a boil, and cook until reduced by about half. Stir in the fresh tarragon.

4 Transfer the chicken breasts to warm plates. Spoon the sauce over the top and serve with green vegetables.

Herbed Mixed Bean Salad
with Fried Halloumi Cheese

Serves 4–6

ingredients

- 5 tbsp extra virgin olive oil
- 2 tbsp tarragon vinegar
- ½ tsp multigrain mustard
- pinch of sugar
- 1 cup green bean pieces
- ¾ cup shelled fava beans, gray outer skins removed if not young
- ¾ cup fresh or frozen shelled peas
- 14 oz/400 g canned cannellini beans, drained and rinsed
- 1 small red onion, thinly sliced
- 2 tbsp chopped fresh parsley
- 1 tbsp snipped fresh chives
- 3 oz/85 g arugula or watercress
- salt and pepper

for the fried halloumi cheese

- ½ tbsp olive oil, plus extra for drizzling
- 12 oz/350 g halloumi cheese or feta cheese, drained, cut into 12 slices
- all-purpose flour, for dusting

1 Put the olive oil, vinegar, mustard, sugar, and salt and pepper to taste in a small screw-top jar and shake until blended and emulsified. Set aside.

2 Prepare a bowl of iced water. Bring a saucepan of lightly salted water to a boil. Add the green beans and fava beans and blanch for 3 minutes, or until just tender. Use a slotted spoon to remove the beans from the water and immediately transfer them to the iced water.

3 Return the water to a boil and blanch the peas for 3 minutes, or until tender. Remove from the water and add to the iced water to cool. Drain the beans and peas and pat dry with paper towels. Transfer to a large bowl, add the dressing, cannellini beans, onion, and herbs and toss. Cover and chill.

4 To make the fried halloumi cheese, heat the oil in a pan over medium–high heat. Dust the cheese with flour, shaking off the excess and add to the pan. Fry for 3–6 minutes, or until golden. Flip the cheese over and cook the other side, then remove and keep warm while you fry the remaining pieces.

5 Divide the salad ingredients and the arugula between individual plates and arrange the hot cheese alongside. Drizzle the cheese with olive oil and serve.

Fusilli with Smoked Salmon & Dill

Serves 4

ingredients
- 1 lb/450 g dried fusilli
- 4 tbsp unsalted butter
- 1 small onion, finely chopped
- 6 tbsp dry white wine
- 2 cups heavy cream
- 8 oz/225 g smoked salmon
- 2 tbsp snipped fresh dill, plus extra sprigs to garnish
- 1–2 tbsp lemon juice
- salt and pepper

1 Bring a large, heavy-bottom saucepan of lightly salted water to a boil. Add the pasta, return to a boil, and cook for 8–10 minutes, or according to package directions, until tender but still firm to the bite.

2 Meanwhile, melt the butter in a heavy-bottom saucepan. Add the onion and cook over low heat, stirring occasionally, for 5 minutes, or until softened. Add the wine, bring to a boil, and continue boiling until reduced by two-thirds. Pour in the cream and season to taste with salt and pepper. Bring to a boil, reduce the heat, and simmer for 2 minutes, or until slightly thickened. Cut the smoked salmon into squares and stir into the saucepan with the snipped dill and lemon juice to taste.

3 Drain the pasta and transfer to a warm serving dish. Add the smoked salmon mixture, toss well, garnish with dill sprigs, and serve immediately.

Marinated Sardine Fillets
with Oregano & Fennel

Serves 6

ingredients

- 8 large sardines, gutted and scaled
- 6 tbsp extra virgin olive oil
- 1 tbsp white wine vinegar
- 1 tbsp dried oregano
- 2 garlic cloves, crushed
- 1 tsp black peppercorns, crushed
- ½ tsp sea salt
- ¼ tsp dried chili flakes
- ½ red onion, sliced thinly
- 1 fennel bulb, trimmed, quartered lengthwise, and sliced thinly
- 4 tomatoes, seeded and sliced into thin segments
- 2 tbsp shredded fresh basil

1 Preheat the oven to 350°F/180°C. Place the sardines in an ovenproof baking dish. Combine the oil, vinegar, oregano, and garlic, and season with the crushed pepper, sea salt, and chili flakes. Pour the mixture over the sardines. Bake for 20–25 minutes, until the flesh is no longer translucent around the backbone.

2 Remove the sardines from the oven and let cool in the baking dish. Sprinkle with the red onion slices, cover with plastic wrap, and let marinate in the refrigerator for up to 3 days. Remove from the refrigerator an hour or two before serving.

3 Arrange the fennel and tomato segments on top of the sardines, spooning over some of the oily juices from the dish. Sprinkle with the basil just before serving.

Tuna & Herbed Fusilli Salad

Serves 4

ingredients
- 7 oz/200 g dried fusilli
- 1 red bell pepper, seeded and quartered
- 1 red onion, sliced
- 4 tomatoes, sliced
- 7 oz/200 g canned tuna, drained and flaked

for the dressing
- 6 tbsp basil-flavored oil or extra virgin olive oil
- 3 tbsp white wine vinegar
- 1 tbsp lime juice
- 1 tsp mustard
- 1 tsp honey
- ¼ cup chopped fresh basil, plus extra sprigs to garnish

1 Preheat the broiler. Bring a large saucepan of lightly salted water to a boil. Add the pasta, return to a boil, and cook for 8–10 minutes, until tender but still firm to the bite.

2 Meanwhile, put the bell pepper quarters under the preheated hot broiler and cook for 10–12 minutes, until the skins begin to blacken. Transfer to a plastic bag, seal, and set aside.

3 Remove the pasta from the heat, drain, and set aside to cool. Remove the bell pepper quarters from the bag and peel off the skins. Slice the quarters into strips.

4 To make the dressing, put all the dressing ingredients in a large bowl and stir together well. Add the pasta, bell pepper strips, onion, tomatoes, and tuna. Toss together gently, then divide among serving bowls. Garnish with basil sprigs and serve.

Spicy Potato Fries

Serves 4

ingredients
- 4 large waxy potatoes
- 2 sweet potatoes
- 4 tbsp butter, melted
- ½ tsp chili powder
- 1 tsp garam masala
- salt

1 Cut both the potatoes and sweet potatoes into slices about ½ inch/ 1 cm thick, then cut them into finger-shape strips. Place the potatoes in a large bowl of cold salted water. Let soak for 20 minutes.

2 Preheat the oven to 400°F/200°C. Remove the potato strips with a slotted spoon and drain thoroughly. Pat with paper towels until they are completely dry.

3 Pour the melted butter onto a baking sheet. Transfer the potato strips to the baking sheet. Sprinkle with the chili powder and garam masala, turning the potato strips over to coat them with the spice mixture.

4 Cook the potatoes in the preheated oven, turning frequently, for about 40 minutes, until browned and cooked all the way through.

5 Drain the fries well on paper towels to remove the excess oil and serve immediately.

Vegetarian Samosas

Makes 8

ingredients

- 1 carrot, diced
- 1 large sweet potato, diced
- heaping ½ cup frozen peas
- 2 tbsp ghee or vegetable oil
- 1 onion, chopped
- 1 garlic clove, chopped
- 1-inch/2.5-cm piece fresh ginger, grated
- 1 tsp ground turmeric
- 1 tsp ground cumin
- ½ tsp chili powder
- ½ tsp garam masala
- 1 tsp lime juice
- salt and pepper
- lime wedges, to serve
- sweet chili dipping sauce, to serve

for the dough

- 1¼ cups all-purpose flour, plus extra for dusting
- 3 tbsp butter, diced
- 4 tbsp warm milk
- vegetable oil, for frying

1 Bring a saucepan of water to a boil, add the carrot, and cook for 4 minutes. Add the sweet potato and continue to cook for 4 minutes, then add the peas and cook for an additional 3 minutes. Drain.

2 Heat the ghee in a saucepan over medium heat, add the onion, garlic, ginger, spices, and lime juice and cook, stirring, for 3 minutes. Add the drained vegetables and season to taste with salt and pepper. Cook, stirring, for 2 minutes. Remove from the heat and let cool for 15 minutes.

3 To make the pastry, put the flour into a bowl and rub in the butter. Add the milk and mix to form a dough. Knead briefly and divide into 4 pieces. On a lightly floured work surface, form each piece into a ball and roll out into a circle measuring 6½ inches/17 cm in diameter. Halve each circle, divide the filling between them, and brush the edges with water, then fold over into triangles and seal the edges.

4 Heat 1 inch/2.5 cm of oil in a skillet to 350–375°F/180–190°C, or until a cube of bread browns in 30 seconds. Cook the samosas in batches for 3–4 minutes, or until golden. Remove the samosas with a slotted spoon and drain on paper towels.

5 Transfer to serving bowls and serve hot with the lime wedges and sweet chili dipping sauce.

Spicy Fragrant Black Bean Chili

Serves 4

ingredients
- 2¼ cups dried black beans
- 2 tbsp olive oil
- 1 onion, chopped
- 5 garlic cloves, roughly chopped
- ½–1 tsp ground cumin
- ½–1 tsp mild chili powder
- 1 red bell pepper, seeded and diced
- 1 carrot, diced
- 2¼ cups diced fresh tomatoes
- 1 bunch fresh cilantro leaves, coarsely chopped
- salt and pepper

1 Soak the beans overnight, then drain. Place in a saucepan, cover with water, and bring to a boil. Boil for 10 minutes, then reduce the heat and simmer for 1½ hours, or until tender. Drain well, reserving 1 cup of the cooking liquid.

2 Heat the oil in a skillet. Add the onion and garlic and cook for 2 minutes, stirring, until softened.

3 Stir in the cumin and chili powder and continue to cook for 20–30 seconds. Add the red bell pepper, carrot, and tomatoes. Cook over medium heat for 5 minutes.

4 Add half of the cilantro and the beans and their reserved liquid. Season to taste with salt and pepper. Simmer for 30–45 minutes, or until flavorful and thickened.

5 Season to taste with salt and pepper. Transfer to warm serving bowls, garnish with the remaining cilantro, and serve.

Spiced Mackerel with Tomato Salad

Serves 4

ingredients
- 4 garlic cloves, well crushed
- finely grated zest and juice of 1 lemon
- heaping 1 tsp ground cumin
- heaping 1 tsp smoked paprika
- 2–3 tbsp olive oil
- 4 large mackerel fillets, about 7 oz/200 g each, or 8 small mackerel fillets, about 3½ oz/ 100 g each

for the tomato salad
- 2 juicy ripe tomatoes
- 1 small red onion, thinly sliced
- heaping 1 tbsp chopped fresh herbs, such as thyme, mint, or parsley
- 2 tbsp olive oil
- 1 tbsp white wine vinegar
- pinch of superfine sugar
- salt and pepper

1 Mix the garlic, lemon zest and juice, cumin, paprika, and oil together in a small bowl. Put the mackerel fillets in a shallow, nonmetallic dish and thoroughly rub both sides with the spice mixture. Cover and let marinate in a cool place for 30 minutes, if possible.

2 Preheat the broiler to high. Lay the mackerel fillets in the broiler pan and cook under the preheated broiler for 3 minutes on one side, then turn over, drizzle with any remaining marinade, and cook for an additional 2–3 minutes, or until the mackerel is cooked through.

3 Meanwhile, prepare the salad. Slice the tomatoes and arrange with the onion on a serving platter. Put the herbs, oil, vinegar, sugar, and a little salt and pepper to taste in a screw-top jar and shake well to combine.

4 Drizzle the dressing over the salad and serve with the hot mackerel fillets.

Chicken Casserole with a Herb Crust

Serves 4

ingredients
- 4 whole chicken legs, dusted in flour
- 1 tbsp olive oil
- 1 tbsp butter
- 1 onion, chopped
- 3 cloves garlic, sliced
- 4 parsnips, peeled and cut into large chunks
- ⅔ cup dry white wine
- 3½ cups chicken stock
- 3 leeks, white parts only, sliced
- ⅔ cup halved, pitted dried plums or prunes (optional)
- 1 tbsp English mustard
- 1 bag store-bought bouquet garni
- 2¼ cups fresh breadcrumbs
- ⅔ cup grated cheddar cheese
- salt and pepper
- 1 cup mixed, chopped tarragon and flat-leaf parsley

1 Preheat the oven to 350°F/180°C.

2 Fry the chicken in a casserole with the olive oil and butter, until golden brown. Remove with a slotted spoon and keep warm. Add the onion, garlic, and parsnips to the casserole and cook for 20 minutes, or until the mixture is golden brown. Add the wine, stock, leeks, dried plums (if using), English mustard, and bouquet garni and season with salt and pepper.

3 Add the chicken to the casserole, place the lid on, and cook in the oven for 1 hour. Meanwhile, mix together the breadcrumbs, cheese, and herbs.

4 Remove the casserole from the oven and increase the heat to 400°F/200°C.

5 Remove the lid of the casserole and sprinkle the crust mixture over the top. Return to the oven for 10 minutes, uncovered, until the crust starts to brown slightly.

6 Remove from the oven and serve.

Spicy Red Lentil Soup

Serves 4–6

ingredients

- scant 1⅔ cups red lentils, picked over and rinsed
- 8 cups vegetable stock or water
- 2 fresh green chiles, halved lengthwise
- 1 tsp ground turmeric
- 2 tbsp sunflower oil
- 1½ onions, thinly sliced
- 2 large garlic cloves, crushed
- 2 tsp curry paste, mild, medium, or hot, to taste
- salt and pepper
- Greek yogurt and chopped fresh cilantro leaves, to garnish
- warmed naan, to serve

1 Put the lentils and stock into a large saucepan with a tight-fitting lid. Place over high heat and slowly bring to a boil, skimming the surface as necessary. Add the chiles and turmeric, reduce the heat to low, cover the pan, and let the lentils simmer for 25–30 minutes, until they are soft and mushy.

2 Meanwhile, heat the oil in a separate large saucepan over medium heat. Add the onions and garlic and fry for 5–7 minutes, until the onions are tender but not brown. Add the curry paste and cook, stirring, for about 1 minute.

3 Put the lentils and any remaining water into the pan with the onion mixture and stir together.

4 Put the mixture into a blender or food processor and process until blended. Return the mixture to the rinsed-out pan and add enough water to make a thin soup. Slowly bring to a boil. Reduce the heat, season to taste with salt and pepper, and simmer for 2 minutes.

5 Ladle into warm soup bowls, swirl in a spoonful of yogurt, and sprinkle with cilantro. Serve with the warmed naan.

Meatballs with Tomato Sauce

Serves 4

ingredients
- 3 tbsp olive oil
- 3 onions, finely chopped
- 3 garlic cloves, crushed
- heaping 2 tsp dried mixed herbs or oregano
- 1 lb/450 g fresh ground beef
- 1 extra-large egg, beaten
- salt and pepper
- 2–3 tbsp freshly grated Parmesan or mozzarella cheese, to serve

for the tomato sauce
- 14 oz/400 g canned chopped tomatoes
- 1 tbsp tomato paste
- pinch of light brown sugar

1 Heat 2 tablespoons of the oil in a saucepan over medium heat, add the onions, and cook, stirring occasionally, for 5 minutes, or until transparent. Add the garlic and cook, stirring, for an additional 1 minute, then stir in the herbs. Transfer half of the contents of the saucepan to a bowl and let cool slightly.

2 To make the tomato sauce, add all of the sauce ingredients, with salt and pepper to taste, to the saucepan, stir well, and bring to a simmer. Simmer for 20–30 minutes, stirring once or twice, until you have a rich sauce. Meanwhile, stir the beef, egg, and salt and pepper to taste into the onion mixture in the bowl. Combine thoroughly and then form into 16 small balls.

3 When the tomato sauce is nearly ready, heat the remaining oil in a nonstick skillet over medium–high heat, add the meatballs, and cook, turning a few times, for 5–6 minutes, or until golden on all sides and cooked through. Serve with the tomato sauce, with the cheese sprinkled over.

Chapter 7
Rice, Pasta, Beans & Grains

Introduction

Carbohydrates such as rice, pasta, noodles, and grains provide a good, inexpensive source of energy, especially the whole wheat/whole grain varieties, and are a valuable source of dietary fiber. Combine them with protein-rich pulses, and you have a delicious meal that is nutritious, satisfying, and healthy.

Buying and storing pasta

You can buy fresh and dried pasta in a wide variety of colors, shapes, and sizes. It is usually made with durum wheat or whole wheat flour. Fresh pasta usually keeps for up to 2 days in the refrigerator, and dried pasta for up to 2 years in the storecupboard. Always use them by their 'expiration' date.

Buying and storing noodles

In addition to Italian pasta, there are also different types of Asian noodles. Asian noodles should be stored in a cool, dry place, and used by their "expiration" date.

How to cook pasta

Cooking pasta is quick and easy. Simply bring a large saucepan of lightly salted water to a boil, add the pasta, and bring back to the boil, stirring at intervals to prevent it sticking together. Reduce the heat slightly and cook until it is tender but still firm to the bite; this is known as "al dente". Remove from the heat, drain, and serve tossed with olive oil or accompanied by your chosen sauce or recipe.

Cellophane noodles

These threadlike noodles are also known as Chinese vermicelli and are made from the starch of mung beans. Dried cellophane noodles should be soaked briefly before use, although this is not necessary in dishes that contain a lot of liquid, such as soups.

Egg noodles

These are very popular in Asian cooking, especially in Chinese stir-fries. Check the cooking instructions on the package: some need to be soaked in hot water for about 4–5 minutes, while others can be put straight into the wok.

Ramen noodles

These noodles are deep-fried and sold packaged, often accompanied by ready-to-use broth mix.

Rice noodles

These delicate, fine, white noodles are simply soaked in hot water for 4–5 minutes. They are very good added to soups and stir-fries, and when deep-fried they become deliciously crunchy. They make a good gluten-free alternative to wheat-based pasta shapes.

Soba noodles

These thin noodles are made from wheat flour and buckwheat. They are popular in Japanese cooking.

Udon noodles

These thick Japanese noodles are like spaghetti, except that they can be square as well as round. They are made from cornflour or wheat flour, and are available both fresh and dried.

Thick egg noodle

Fine egg noodle

Medium egg noodle

Conchigliette

Cannelloni

Lumaconi

Penne

Fusilli

Rigatoni

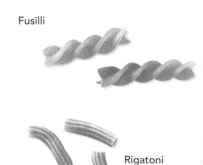

Making your own fresh pasta

You can buy good-quality fresh pasta nowadays, but if you prefer to make your own, the process is simple. You might also like to invest in a pasta machine in order to create perfect pasta shapes of your choice.

Homemade pasta

Serves 6

10 oz/280 g all-purpose flour,
  plus extra for dusting
1 tsp salt
2 eggs, lightly beaten
3 tbsp tomato paste (optional—use if you
  want a red, tomato-flavored pasta)

Lightly dust a clean work surface with flour. Sift the flour and salt into a mound on the work surface.

Make a well in the center of the flour, add the beaten eggs, and tomato paste if using, and mix to a stiff dough. If necessary, stir in a few tablespoons of water.

Knead the dough vigorously for about 8 minutes, then wrap it in plastic wrap and leave it to rest for 30 minutes, or for up to 2 days in the refrigerator if not required right away. Roll out the dough to the desired thickness, then use a sharp knife to cut it into pieces of the required shape and size.

Alternatively, use a pasta machine to cut the dough. The pasta is now ready to be cooked.

PASTA NAMES

Anelli Very small rings

Cannelloni Large, hollow tubes

Conchiglie Ridged shells

Farfalle Bows

Fettucine Long, narrow ribbons

Fusilli Spirals

Lasagne Large, flat rectangular sheets

Linguine Long, narrow ribbons with flattened edges

Lumaconi Snail shapes

Macaroni Long or short narrow tubes, often curved

Penne Hollow quills

Ravioli Square cushions

Spaghetti Long, narrow strings

Tagliatelle Long ribbons, a little wider than fettucine

Vermicelli Long, very fine, hairlike strings

Buying and storing dried beans

Beans, lentils, and peas all fall into the category of legumes. You can buy these protein-rich foods dried, or ready to use in cans if you are short of time. When buying dried beans, store them in airtight containers in a cool, dry place and use by the expiration date, or, if there is no date on the package, within 1 year for best results. Do not mix old and new beans because they will take different lengths of time to cook. Once cooked, refrigerate leftover beans and use within 3 days, or freeze them in an airtight container and use within 6 months.

Preparing and cooking dried beans

Most dried beans need soaking for at least 8 hours, then boiling rapidly for 10 minutes, followed by additional cooking for at least 45 minutes, or until they are tender. The main exceptions are soybeans, which need 12 hours to soak and 4 hours to cook, and chickpeas, which need 8 hours to soak and 2 hours to cook. Haricot beans need to soak overnight and need up to 1½ hours to cook. Lentils and split peas usually need no soaking and can be cooked in around 25–30 minutes.

Chickpeas
These round, cream-colored peas have a nutty flavor, and are excellent in soups, salads, dips, and stews, as well as pasta or grain dishes. Chickpeas can also be roasted for snacks, and are used in falafel, a Middle Eastern dish in which the mashed beans are formed into balls and deep-fried. Soak chickpeas for at least 8 hours before use. After soaking, drain and rinse them, then cover with fresh water and bring to a boil. Lower the heat and simmer for 2 hours, until they are thoroughly cooked.

Soybeans
The most common color of soybeans is pale yellow. These beans are good in soups and other savory dishes, such as curries. Remember that they need to be soaked for at least 12 hours. After soaking, drain and rinse them, then cover with fresh water and bring to a boil. Boil them for the first hour of cooking, then simmer for another 3 hours, until they are thoroughly cooked.

Aduki beans
These small red beans are good in soups and salads.

Cannellini beans
Add these long, creamy white beans to soups and salads.

Split peas
These disk-shaped yellow or green peas are split along a natural seam. They can be cooked and pureed, and used in soups, casseroles, and other savory dishes.

Lentils
These are small, disk-shaped legumes. Use red or orange lentils pureed and in soups and sauces; green or brown lentils are best in salads, sauces, stews, and other savory dishes.

Red kidney beans
These red, kidney-shape beans can be added to soups, salads, and stews. They must be boiled rapidly for 10 minutes, otherwise they can cause food poisoning. They should be precooked before being added to slow cookers, which do not reach a sufficiently high cooking temperature to eliminate the toxins.

Cannellini beans
These white beans can be used in a wide variety of savory dishes, including soups, salads, stews, and casseroles. They are also the beans commonly used as baked beans with tomato sauce.

Lima beans
These white, kidney-shape beans are excellent in soups and salads.

Flageolet beans
These small green beans are excellent in salads and as an accompaniment to meat dishes.

Borlotti beans
These oval beans vary in color from pale pink to maroon-streaked skin. Use them in soups, dips, and other savory dishes.

Black-eyed peas
These small beige beans have a circular black "eye." Use them in sauces, stir-fries, and soups.

Soybeans

Black-eyed peas

Chickpeas

Long-grain rice

Glutinous rice

Split peas

Buying and storing rice

There are many different varieties of rice available. Store rice in airtight containers for up to 3 years in a cool, dry place, or use by the expiration date if sooner.

Short-grain rice

This rice has short, fat grains that are more starchy and moist than medium- and long-grain rice. Varieties of short-grain rice include arborio and carnaroli rice, which are used in risottos.

Medium-grain rice

These grains are a little shorter than long-grain rice. They are more moist and, therefore, tend to clump together when cooked. Medium-grain rice is used in savory dishes.

Long-grain rice

Both white and brown long-grain rice are excellent for savory dishes because the grains stay separate when cooked.

Basmati rice

This Himalayan long-grain rice has a nutty flavor and is excellent in savory dishes. It is available in white or brown and the grains stay dry and separate when cooked.

Jasmine rice

This tender rice has a delicate, fragrant, aromatic flavor. It is popular in both Vietnamese and Thai cooking.

Arborio rice

This starchy, short-grain creamy rice is ideal in risottos.

Carnaroli rice

This short-grain Italian rice has often been called "the king of Italian rice." It has a high-starch content and makes a wonderful creamy risotto.

Glutinous rice

This rice has a high-starch content and becomes very sticky and creamy when cooked. It is popular in desserts, especially rice pudding.

Instant rice

These rice grains are polished and partially boiled so that they are quick to cook. They stay fluffy and separate when cooked, but have less flavor than white or brown rice.

Red rice

This rice is grown in the Camargue region of France and in China. It has a pale red color and a nutty flavor that is similar to brown rice.

Wild rice

This grain is in fact a marsh grass, not a rice. The grains are long and black, with a nutty flavor. It is often mixed with brown long-grain rice for reasons of economy.

How to cook long-grain and basmati rice

To cook rice for four people, put 1¼ cups rice into a strainer and rinse under cold running water. Transfer to a large saucepan and pour in 2½ cups cold water. Add a large pinch of salt, then bring to a boil. Reduce the heat, stir briefly, then cover the pan and simmer gently until the rice is tender and all the liquid has been absorbed (but do not let the rice burn). As a rough guide, white rice will need 15 minutes, and brown rice will need 25–30 minutes, but check the package directions. Remove from the heat and let stand for 5 minutes with the lid on. Fluff the grains with a fork and serve.

Other grains

It is always worthwhile experimenting with other types of grains. Try using them in salads, soups, and stews, or piling them onto a platter and topping them with tasty cooked vegetables and sauces.

Barley

The polished variety of barley, known as pearl barley, is the kind most widely available. You can also buy hulled barley, which is unpolished, from specialty stores and health-food stores. Barley is delicious and excellent in soups, casseroles, and stews.

Millet

This protein-rich grain is a staple in Africa and Asia, and is boiled in a similar way to rice.

Couscous

This is not a true grain, but pieces of semolina. Steam it in accordance with the directions on the package. It makes an excellent bed of grains on which to pile meats and vegetables.

Cornmeal

This yellow grain is made from corn and features widely in Southern cooking. Follow the cooking package directions because methods and cooking times vary. Polenta is a coarse grain Italian version. To serve polenta cold, once the mixture pulls away from the pan, pour it into a baking sheet, let cool, then cut it into squares and serve. To serve hot, at the same stage stir in a generous pat of butter, then remove it from the heat and stir vigorously until the polenta stays firm.

Bulgur wheat

This comprises wheat kernels that have been precooked. It is a golden-brown grain with a nutty flavor. Because it has already been cooked, you simply need to soak it in plenty of cold water for 20–30 minutes, then strain it in a strainer, pressing out as much water as possible. This grain is excellent in salads, especially in the Middle Eastern dish known as "tabbouleh." It is also good in pilafs.

Quinoa Salad with Sun-Dried Tomatoes, Olives & Feta

Serves 4

ingredients

for the salad
- 1½ cups quinoa
- 2¼ cups water
- 10 sun-dried tomatoes (in oil, drained)
- ⅓ cup crumbled feta cheese
- 2 scallions, white parts only, chopped
- ½ cup chopped mixed fresh herbs (basil, parsley, cilantro)
- ½ cup chopped pitted black olives

for the dressing
- 5 tbsp roasted tomato oil
- 3 tbsp fresh lemon juice
- 1 garlic clove, crushed
- salt and freshly ground black pepper

1 Spread the quinoa on a dish and pick out any pieces of grit. Rinse the grains thoroughly in a fine-mesh strainer and drain.

2 In a medium saucepan, bring the water to a boil over low heat, stir in the quinoa, and return to a boil. Lower the heat, cover, and simmer for about 15 minutes, or until all the liquid has been absorbed. Remove from the heat, fluff up the quinoa with a fork, and transfer to a bowl. Let stand to cool a little.

3 Add the remaining ingredients to the bowl and mix with the quinoa.

4 Whisk the dressing ingredients together, pour over the quinoa, toss, and serve.

Chicken & Butternut Casserole

Serves 4–6

ingredients

- 2 tbsp olive oil
- 4 skinless, boneless chicken thighs, about 3½ oz/100 g each, cut into bite-size pieces
- 1 large onion, sliced
- 2 leeks, chopped
- 2 garlic cloves, chopped
- 1 butternut squash, peeled, seeded, and cut into cubes
- 2 carrots, diced
- 14 oz/400 g canned chopped tomatoes and herbs
- 14 oz/400 g canned mixed beans, drained and rinsed
- ½ cup vegetable or chicken stock, plus extra if needed
- salt and pepper

1 Preheat the oven to 325°F/160°C.

2 Heat half of the oil in a large, flameproof casserole over high heat, add the chicken, and cook, turning frequently, for 2–3 minutes, until browned all over. Reduce the heat to medium, remove the chicken with a slotted spoon, and set aside.

3 Add the remaining oil to the casserole, add the onion and leeks, and cook, stirring occasionally, for 10 minutes, or until soft. Add the garlic, squash, and carrots and cook, stirring, for 2 minutes. Add the tomatoes and their juices, the beans, chicken pieces, and stock, stir well, and bring to a simmer.

4 Cover, transfer to the preheated oven, and cook for 1–1¼ hours, stirring once or twice—if the casserole looks too dry, add a little extra stock. Season with a tiny amount of salt and pepper to taste before serving.

Spiced Lentils with Spinach

Serves 4–6

ingredients

- 2 tbsp olive oil
- 1 large onion, finely chopped
- 1 large garlic clove, crushed
- ½ tbsp ground cumin
- ½ tsp ground ginger
- 1⅓ cups French green lentils
- about 2½ cups vegetable stock
- 3½ cups baby spinach leaves
- 2 tbsp fresh mint leaves
- 1 tbsp fresh cilantro leaves
- 1 tbsp fresh flat-leaf parsley
- lemon juice
- salt and pepper
- strips of lemon rind, to garnish

1 Heat the oil in a large skillet over medium heat. Add the onion and cook, stirring occasionally, for about 6 minutes. Stir in the garlic, cumin, and ginger and cook, stirring occasionally, until the onion starts to brown.

2 Stir in the lentils. Pour in enough stock to cover the lentils by 1 inch/2.5 cm and bring to a boil. Lower the heat and simmer for 20–30 minutes, until the lentils are tender.

3 Meanwhile, rinse the spinach leaves in several changes of cold water and shake dry. Finely chop the mint, cilantro, and parsley.

4 If there isn't any stock left in the pan, add a little extra. Add the spinach and stir through until it just wilts. Stir in the mint, cilantro, and parsley. Adjust the seasoning, adding lemon juice and salt and pepper. Transfer to a serving bowl and serve, garnished with lemon rind.

Vegetable Stew with Green Lentils

Serves 6

ingredients

- 1 tbsp olive oil
- 1 onion, finely chopped
- 1 garlic clove, finely chopped
- 1 carrot, halved and thinly sliced
- 1 small green cabbage, cored, quartered, and thinly sliced
- 14 oz/400 g canned chopped tomatoes
- ½ tsp dried thyme
- 2 bay leaves
- 6 cups chicken or vegetable stock
- 1 cup French green lentils
- 2 cups water
- salt and pepper
- chopped fresh flat-leaf parsley, to garnish

1 Heat the oil in a large saucepan over medium heat, add the onion, garlic, and carrot and cook for 3–4 minutes, stirring frequently, until the onion starts to soften. Add the cabbage and cook for an additional 2 minutes.

2 Add the tomatoes, thyme, and 1 bay leaf, then pour in the stock. Bring to a boil, reduce the heat to low, and cook gently, partially covered, for 45 minutes, until the vegetables are tender.

3 Meanwhile, put the lentils in another saucepan with the remaining bay leaf and the water. Bring just to a boil, reduce the heat, and simmer for about 25 minutes, until tender. Drain off any remaining water and set aside.

4 Let the stew cool, then transfer to a food processor or blender and process until smooth, working in batches, if necessary. (If using a food processor, strain off the cooking liquid and reserve. Puree the solids with enough cooking liquid to moisten them, then combine with the remaining liquid.)

5 Return the stew to the saucepan and add the cooked lentils. Taste and adjust the seasoning, and cook for about 10 minutes to heat through. Ladle into warm bowls and garnish with parsley.

Chinese Fried Rice

Serves 4

ingredients

- 3 cups water
- ½ tsp salt
- 1⅔ cups long-grain rice
- 2 eggs
- 4 tsp cold water
- 3 tbsp sunflower oil
- 4 scallions, sliced diagonally
- 1 red, green, or yellow bell pepper, cored, seeded, and thinly sliced
- 3–4 lean bacon slices, rind removed and cut into strips
- 2¼ cups fresh bean sprouts
- 1 cup frozen peas, thawed
- 2 tbsp soy sauce (optional)
- salt and pepper

1 Pour the water into the wok with the salt and bring to a boil. Rinse the rice in a strainer under cold running water until the water runs clear, drain thoroughly, and add to the boiling water. Stir well, then cover the wok tightly with the lid and simmer gently for 12–13 minutes. (Do not remove the lid during cooking or the steam will escape and the rice will not be cooked.)

2 Remove the lid, give the rice a good stir, and spread out on a large plate or baking sheet to cool and dry.

3 Meanwhile, beat each egg separately with salt and pepper and 2 teaspoons of cold water. Heat 1 tablespoon of oil in a preheated wok, pour in the first egg, swirl it around, and let cook undisturbed until set. Transfer to a cutting board and cook the second egg. Cut the omelets into thin slices.

4 Add the remaining oil to the wok and, when really hot, add the scallions and sliced bell pepper and stir-fry for 1–2 minutes. Add the bacon and continue to stir-fry for another 2 minutes. Add the bean sprouts and peas and toss together thoroughly. Stir in the soy sauce, if using.

5 Add the rice, along with salt and pepper to taste, and stir-fry for 1 minute, then add the omelet strips and continue to stir-fry for 2 minutes, or until the rice is piping hot. Serve immediately.

Parmesan Risotto with Mushrooms

Serves 6

ingredients

- 2 tbsp olive oil or vegetable oil
- scant 1¼ cups risotto rice
- 2 garlic cloves, crushed
- 1 onion, chopped
- 2 celery stalks, chopped
- 1 red or green bell pepper, seeded and chopped
- 3¾ cups thinly sliced mushrooms
- 1 tbsp chopped fresh oregano or 1 tsp dried oregano
- 4 cups vegetable stock
- ⅓ cup drained and chopped sun-dried tomatoes in olive oil (optional)
- ½ cup finely grated Parmesan cheese
- salt and pepper
- fresh flat-leaf parsley sprigs, to garnish

1 Heat the oil in a deep saucepan. Add the rice and cook over low heat, stirring continuously, for 2–3 minutes, until the grains are thoroughly coated in oil and translucent.

2 Add the garlic, onion, celery, and bell pepper and cook, stirring frequently, for 5 minutes. Add the mushrooms and cook for 3–4 minutes. Stir in the oregano.

3 Gradually add the hot stock, a ladle at a time. Stir continuously and add more liquid as the rice absorbs each addition. Increase the heat to medium so that the liquid simmers. Cook for 20 minutes, or until all the liquid is absorbed and the rice is creamy. Add the sun-dried tomatoes, if using, 5 minutes before the end of the cooking time and season to taste with salt and pepper.

4 Remove the risotto from the heat and stir in half of the Parmesan until it melts. Transfer the risotto to warm bowls. Top with the remaining cheese, garnish with flat-leaf parsley, and serve immediately.

Wok-Fried Soba Noodles

Serves 4

ingredients

- 10½ oz/300 g dry thin soba (buckwheat) noodles
- 3 tbsp sunflower or peanut oil
- 1 tsp ground ginger
- 1 tbsp Chinese rice wine vinegar
- 1½ tsp sesame oil
- 1 tsp light soy sauce
- 1 cup beans prouts
- 1 cup thinly sliced snow peas
- 4 scallions, chopped
- 2 garlic cloves, crushed
- 1 red bell pepper, halved, seeded, and thinly sliced
- ½ head cabbage, cored and thinly shredded
- small handful fresh cilantro leaves
- pepper
- toasted sesame seeds, to garnish

1 Bring a saucepan of water to a boil, add the noodles, and boil for 3 minutes, or according to the package directions. Drain well, then add to a bowl of cold water and use your hand to swish around to remove all the starch. Drain again, then put into another bowl of cold water and set aside.

2 Put 2 tablespoons of the sunflower oil into a large bowl and stir in the ginger. Beat in the vinegar, sesame oil, and soy sauce. Add pepper to taste.

3 Drain the noodles very well, shaking off any excess water, then add to the bowl with the oil. Add the bean sprouts, snow peas, scallions, garlic, red bell pepper, and cabbage and use your hands to mix together. Season to taste. If you're not cooking immediately, cover the bowl with plastic wrap and chill until 10 minutes before you want to cook.

4 When you are ready to cook, heat a wok over high heat until a splash of water "dances" on the surface. Add the remaining oil to the wok and heat until it shimmers.

5 Tip in the noodles and vegetables and stir-fry for 3–5 minutes, until all the vegetables are hot and just tender. Add the cilantro and stir them through. Taste and adjust the seasoning.

6 Transfer the noodles and vegetables to serving bowls and sprinkle with the sesame seeds.

Vegetable Couscous

Serves 4

ingredients

- 2 tbsp vegetable oil
- 1 large onion
- 1 carrot, chopped
- 1 turnip, chopped
- 2½ cups vegetable stock
- 1 cup couscous
- 2 tomatoes
- 1 red bell pepper
- 2 zucchini
- 1 cup green beans
- grated rind of 1 lemon
- pinch of turmeric (optional)
- 1 tbsp finely chopped
  fresh cilantro
- salt and pepper

1 Heat the oil in a large saucepan. Chop the onion, then add to the pan with the carrot and turnip and fry for 3–4 minutes. Add the stock, bring to a boil, cover, and let simmer for 20 minutes.

2 Meanwhile, place the couscous in a bowl and moisten with a little boiling water, stirring, until the grains have swollen and separated.

3 Peel and quarter the tomatoes, seed and chop the red bell pepper, then chop the zucchini and green beans.

4 Add the tomatoes, red bell pepper, zucchini, and green beans to the pan and stir. Stir the lemon rind into the couscous, add the turmeric, if using, and mix thoroughly. Place the couscous in a steamer and position it over the saucepan of vegetables. Simmer the vegetables so that the couscous steams for 8–10 minutes.

5 Pile the couscous onto warm serving plates. Ladle the vegetables and some of the liquid over the top. Season to taste, then scatter with the finely chopped cilantro and serve immediately.

Tabbouleh

Serves 4

ingredients
- 1¼ cups bulgur wheat
- 3 tbsp extra virgin olive oil
- 4 tbsp lemon juice
- 4 scallions
- 1 green bell pepper, seeded and sliced
- 4 tomatoes, chopped
- 2 tbsp chopped fresh parsley
- 2 tbsp chopped fresh mint
- 8 black olives, pitted
- salt and pepper

1 Place the bulgur wheat in a large bowl and add enough cold water to cover. Let stand for 30 minutes, or until the wheat has doubled in size. Drain well and press out as much liquid as possible. Spread out the wheat on paper towels to dry.

2 Place the wheat in a serving bowl. Mix the olive oil and lemon juice together in a pitcher and season to taste with salt and pepper. Pour the lemon mixture over the wheat and let marinate for 1 hour.

3 Using a sharp knife, finely chop the scallions, then add to the bowl with the green bell pepper, tomatoes, parsley, and mint and toss lightly to mix. Top the salad with the olives and serve.

Spaghetti Bolognese

Serves 4

ingredients

- 3 tbsp olive oil
- 2 garlic cloves, crushed
- 1 large onion, finely chopped
- 1 carrot, diced
- 8 oz/225 g fresh lean ground beef or chicken
- 3 oz/85 g chicken livers, finely chopped
- 3½ oz/100 g lean Parma ham, diced
- ⅔ cup Marsala wine
- 10 oz/280 g canned chopped plum tomatoes
- 1 tbsp chopped fresh basil leaves
- 2 tbsp tomato paste
- 1 lb/450 g dried spaghetti
- salt and pepper
- shavings of fresh Parmesan cheese, to garnish

1 Heat 2 tablespoons of the oil in a large saucepan. Add the garlic, onion, and carrot and fry for 6 minutes.

2 Add the ground meat, chicken livers, and Parma ham to the saucepan and cook over medium heat for 12 minutes, or until well browned.

3 Stir in the Marsala, tomatoes, basil, and tomato paste and cook for 4 minutes. Season to taste with salt and pepper. Cover and let simmer for 30 minutes.

4 Remove the lid from the saucepan, stir, and let simmer for an additional 15 minutes.

5 Meanwhile, bring a large saucepan of lightly salted water to a boil. Add the spaghetti and the remaining oil, return to a boil and cook according to the package directions, or until tender but still firm to the bite. Drain and transfer to a serving dish. Pour the sauce over the pasta, scatter with some fresh Parmesan shavings, and serve hot.

Golden Polenta

Serves 4

ingredients
- 6 cups water
- 1½ tsp salt
- heaping 2 cups polenta
  or coarse cornmeal
- vegetable oil, for frying and oiling
- 2 beaten eggs (optional)
- 2¾ cups fresh fine white
  breadcrumbs (optional)

for the tomato sauce
- 2 tbsp olive oil
- 1 small onion, chopped
- 1 garlic clove, chopped
- 14 oz/400 g canned chopped
  tomatoes
- 2 tbsp chopped fresh parsley
- 1 tsp dried oregano
- 2 bay leaves
- 2 tbsp tomato paste
- 1 tsp sugar
- salt and pepper

1 Thoroughly oil a 11 x 7-inch/28 x 18-cm shallow pan. Bring the water and salt to a boil in a large saucepan and gradually sprinkle in the polenta, stirring continuously to prevent lumps from forming. Simmer gently, stirring frequently, for 30 minutes, or until the polenta becomes thick and begins to draw away from the sides of the pan.

2 Spoon in the polenta into the prepared pan. Spread out evenly, using a wet wooden spoon or spatula. Let cool, then let stand for 2 hours at room temperature, if possible.

3 Cut the polenta into 30–36 squares. Heat the oil in a skillet. Add the pieces and fry until golden brown all over, turning several times, for about 5 minutes. Alternatively, dip each piece of polenta in beaten egg and coat in breadcrumbs before frying in the hot oil. Keep warm.

4 For the tomato sauce, heat the oil in a pan over medium heat. Add the onion and fry for 2 minutes, until translucent. Add the garlic and fry for 1 minute. Stir in the chopped tomatoes, herbs, tomato paste, sugar, and salt and pepper to taste. Bring to a boil, then simmer, uncovered, for 20 minutes, or until the sauce has reduced by half. Remove and discard the bay leaves.

5 Serve the polenta pieces with the hot tomato sauce.

Penne with Mixed Beans

Serves 4

ingredients

- 1 tbsp olive oil
- 1 onion, chopped
- 1 garlic clove, finely chopped
- 1 carrot, finely chopped
- 1 celery stalk, finely chopped
- 15 oz/425 g canned mixed beans, drained and rinsed
- 1 cup tomato puree
- 1 tbsp chopped fresh chervil, plus extra leaves to garnish
- 12 oz/350 g dried penne
- salt and pepper

1 Heat the oil in a large heavy-bottom skillet. Add the onion, garlic, carrot, and celery and cook over low heat, stirring occasionally, for 5 minutes, or until the onion has softened.

2 Add the mixed beans, tomato puree, and chopped chervil to the skillet and season the mixture to taste with salt and pepper. Cover and simmer gently for 15 minutes.

3 Meanwhile, bring a large heavy-bottom saucepan of lightly salted water to a boil. Add the pasta, return to a boil, and cook for 8–10 minutes, or according to the package directions, until tender but still firm to the bite. Drain the pasta and transfer to a warm serving dish. Add the mixed bean sauce, toss well, and serve immediately, garnished with extra chervil.

Vegetable Lasagne

Serves 4

ingredients

- 1 eggplant, sliced
- 3 tbsp olive oil
- 2 garlic cloves, crushed
- 1 red onion, halved and sliced
- 3 mixed bell peppers, seeded and diced
- 8 oz/225 g mixed mushrooms, sliced
- 2 celery stalks, sliced
- 1 zucchini, diced
- ½ tsp chili powder
- ½ tsp ground cumin
- 2 tomatoes, chopped
- 1¼ cups tomato puree
- 2 tbsp chopped fresh basil
- 8 oven-ready lasagna verde noodles
- salt and pepper

for the cheese sauce

- 2 tbsp butter or margarine
- 1 tbsp flour
- ⅔ cup vegetable stock
- 1¼ cups milk
- ⅔ cup grated cheddar cheese
- 1 tsp Dijon-style mustard
- 1 tbsp chopped fresh basil
- 1 egg, beaten

1 Place the eggplant slices in a colander, sprinkle with salt, and let stand for 20 minutes. Rinse under cold water, drain, and reserve.

2 Preheat the oven to 350°F/180°C. Heat the oil in a saucepan. Add the garlic and onion and sauté for 1–2 minutes. Add the bell peppers, mushrooms, celery, and zucchini and cook, stirring continuously, for 3–4 minutes.

3 Stir in the chili powder and cumin and cook for 1 minute. Mix in the chopped tomatoes, tomato puree, and basil and season to taste with salt and pepper.

4 For the sauce, melt the butter in a saucepan. Stir in the flour and cook for 1 minute. Remove from the heat, gradually stir in the stock and milk, return to the heat, then add half of the cheese and all the mustard. Boil, stirring, until thickened. Stir in the basil. Remove from the heat and stir in the egg.

5 Place half of the lasagna noodles in an ovenproof dish. Top with half of the vegetables, half of the tomato sauce, then half of the eggplants. Repeat and then spoon the cheese sauce on top. Sprinkle with the remaining cheese and bake for 40 minutes, or until golden and bubbling.

Rice Pudding

Serves 4–6

ingredients
- 1 tbsp melted butter
- heaping ½ cup glutinous rice
- ¼ cup superfine sugar
- 3½ cups milk
- ½ tsp vanilla extract
- 3 tbsp unsalted butter
- whole nutmeg, for grating
- cream, preserve, fruit puree, stewed fruit, or ice cream, to serve (optional)

1 Preheat the oven to 300ºF/150ºC. Grease a 5-cup ovenproof dish (a gratin dish is good) with the melted butter. Place the rice in the dish and sprinkle with the sugar.

2 Heat the milk in a saucepan until almost boiling, then pour over the rice. Add the vanilla extract and stir well to dissolve the sugar.

3 Cut the butter into small pieces and scatter over the surface of the pudding.

4 Grate the whole nutmeg over the top, using as much as you like to give a good covering.

5 Place the dish on a baking sheet and bake in the center of the oven for 1½–2 hours, until the pudding is well browned on the top. You can stir it after the first half hour to disperse the rice.

6 Serve hot and, if desired, with some cream, preserve, fresh fruit puree, stewed fruit, or ice cream. It is also good cold with fresh fruit or honey.

Chapter 8
Fruit

Introduction

Fruit is a healthy choice because it is full of vitamins and very low in fat. It is also very versatile—delicious in savory dishes and chutneys, and delightful in a wide range of desserts and cakes.

Orchard fruits

Orchard fruits, such as apples, pears, and peaches, are delicious and very versatile. They can be eaten raw on their own and in fruit salads, or in cooked dishes such as fruit tarts and pies.

Apple

Pear

Nectarine

Apricot

Plum

Buying and storing fruit

Some fruit, such as apples and pears, are available fresh all year round, whereas others, such as cherries, have a limited season. Always buy your fruit as fresh as possible from a reputable supplier. Avoid any fruit that is bruised or damaged, or that is showing signs of mold. Choose fruit that are plump and free from blemishes; they should feel firm to the touch and not too soft. Many fruit, such as apples, pears, and oranges, can be stored for around a week at room temperature, or even longer in the refrigerator. Other fruit, such as blueberries, have a short shelf life and should be kept in the refrigerator and eaten by the expiration date, but usually within a couple of days. You can also freeze a wide range of fruit, such as bananas and mangoes (peel and slice them first)—even grapes are excellent frozen whole and used instead of ice cubes in drinks.

Apples

There are countless different varieties of apple in existence, in a range of colors from pale yellow to deep red. Some have a sweet flavor, while others are more acidic. Some apples, such as Golden Delicious and McIntosh, are excellent eaten raw as a snack or in salads. They also pair very well with cheese. Other varieties of apple are excellent for cooking, such as Braeburn, Gravenstein, and Rome Beauty. They make excellent desserts, and are delicious stuffed and baked, or made into pie fillings. They can also be used in some savory dishes, such as curries, and make very good sauces and purees.

Pears

Like apples, there are thousands of different types of pears, although we see only a selection of these in our stores. Pears bruise easily, so buy them while they are still hard and let them ripen at home. Many varieties, such as Comice or Anjou pears, are delicious eaten as a snack, and they are excellent in salads and with cheese. Some types, such as Bartlett, are also very good for cooking. They can be stuffed and baked like apples, and are excellent peeled and poached in red wine.

Peaches

This fruit is similar to nectarines except that peaches have downy skin instead of smooth skin. Store and use them in the same way as nectarines.

Nectarines

This fruit is usually available in summer and fall. Nectarines have smooth skins that should be yellow with patches of red, with no green areas and no bruises. They will keep in the refrigerator for 5–6 days. You can eat nectarines raw as a snack or sliced in desserts. You can also poach or bake them. If they need additional ripening, let them stand at room temperature for 1–2 days. If they do not soften during this time, they will not be suitable for eating raw, so cook them instead.

Orange

Lime

Lemon

Citrus fruit

The fragrance and juicy tang of a ripe citrus fruit is irresistible, and wonderful in a whole host of chilled and cooked desserts. These fruits are also rich sources of vitamin C.

Oranges

This citrus fruit is available all through the year and comes in many different varieties, such as the sweet oranges that can be eaten as a snack and sliced in salads and desserts. A variation of these is the blood orange, which is just as sweet and juicy, but which has redder flesh. Some oranges are seedless, while others have many seeds. You can also buy bitter oranges, such as Seville oranges; they are too sour to eat but they make excellent marmalade. Oranges will keep at room temperature for up to a week, but are better stored in the refrigerator to preserve their vitamin C content. They will keep in the refrigerator for up to 2 weeks. Oranges make excellent garnishes or decorations, and are popular in a wide range of savory and sweet dishes.

Cherries

There are two main types of cherry: the larger sweet cherries, which are delicious eaten raw, and the smaller sour cherries, which are too tart to eat raw but can be cooked and made into excellent desserts and preserves. Cherries are usually available during late spring and in early summer, and should be stored in the refrigerator before use.

Apricots

This fruit is usually yellow or orange and has a large pit. Some apricot varieties are sweet enough to eat raw as a snack, while others need to be cooked. Cooked apricots make excellent desserts and preserves, and can also be used in some savory dishes. Dried apricots are also popular. The deep orange varieties have been treated with sulfur dioxide in order to preserve their color. Untreated dried apricots are dark brown; some people may find them less attractive, but they have just as much, if not more, flavor and goodness.

Plums

There are many plum varieties, and all have a large, central pit. Their color varies from yellow or green to red or purple, and they can grow to up to 3 inches/7.5 cm in diameter. They are in season from summer until early fall, and will keep at room temperature for several days, or a little longer in the refrigerator. Ripe plums are sweet and juicy and can be eaten raw as a snack or in a salad. They can also be cooked. Plum crumble is a baked dessert that consists of a dish of plums covered with a crunchy topping. Plums also make excellent preserves.

Grapefruits

Grapefruits can be seeded or seedless, and vary in color from yellow to pink to red. They are available all year round, and are usually eaten raw. However, they can also be sprinkled with brown sugar and lightly broiled.

Lemons

This oval, yellow fruit has a tart flavor but a wide range of uses. Lemons are available all year round and will keep at room temperature for a week, and in the refrigerator for up to 3 weeks (but less time if cut). Lemons make an excellent flavoring and a good garnish or decoration for savory and sweet dishes. You can use the juice, grated zest, or the flesh.

Limes

This green citrus fruit is smaller than a lemon and has a milder flavor, but can replace lemons in many savory and sweet dishes. Limes will keep whole in the refrigerator for up to 10 days.

Mandarin orange family

This family of small, round, orange fruits includes mandarins, clementines, satsumas, and tangerines. They are generally available in the winter months. Mandarins and tangerines have thick skins that are easy to peel. Clementines have thinner skins and no seeds. Satsumas are also easy to peel and are seedless. They are delicious eaten raw as a snack and in salads, and they all pair well with cream cheese.

Berries

Juicy berries are delicious in desserts, such as sorbets, ice creams, puddings, fruit crumbles, and pies, but they can also be used in a variety of savory dishes, such as chicken with blackberries.

Strawberries

These juicy red berries are available all year round, but peak season for strawberries is spring and early summer. Fresh strawberries will keep for up to 3 days in the refrigerator, and are delicious eaten raw, perhaps with whipped cream or marinated in balsamic vinegar. They also make excellent preserves and syrups, and are popular in a range of desserts. Dried strawberries have a deliciously tangy flavor and are wonderful in granola.

Gooseberries

These large berries are usually green, but can also come in white and yellow. They are available in the summer months and are usually cooked before eating. Gooseberries make excellent preserves and fillings for sweet pies. They will keep in the refrigerator for up to 4 days.

Blackberries

Blackberries come into season in the summer months. Use them right away, or refrigerate them for up to 2 days. You can eat blackberries raw or cooked in sweet pies and desserts. They are often paired with apples. Blackberries also make good jellies and preserves.

Raspberries

The most common color of the raspberry is red. This fruit is popular with dieters, because raspberries are low in calories and fat, and yet have a delicious flavor. They will keep in the refrigerator for up to 3 days, and are delicious raw in a wide range of desserts. They can also be cooked, and make good coulis and fillings for desserts, as well as excellent jellies and preserves.

Blueberries

These small, round, dark blue berries are sweet and can be eaten raw or cooked in sweet pies and other desserts. Like most berries, they make excellent jellies and preserves. They are available during the summer and early fall, and will keep in the refrigerator for 4–5 days.

Cranberries

These small, shiny, red berries are available in late fall and will keep in the refrigerator for 6–8 weeks and in the freezer for around 9 months. They have a tart flavor and, therefore, are usually mixed with sweeter fruit, such as apple—cranberry and apple juice is a very popular combination. Cranberries can also be cooked and make an excellent sauce. They can be used in sweet pies and other cooked desserts.

Currants

Fresh currants are tiny berries that can be white, red, or black. White currants and red currants can be eaten raw and make excellent decorations for sweet dishes. Black currants are tart and are better cooked and made into syrup or preserves. Fresh currants are available in some markets during summer and will keep in the refrigerator for 3–4 days, or you can use frozen currants. They should not be confused with dried currants, which are like dark raisins.

Strawberries

Raspberries

Grapes

Litchis

Star fruit

Fig

Pineapple

Other common fruit

Other well-known fruit, such as bananas, grapes, and melons, are widely available. They are very popular as snacks in their own right, and are also used in a wide range of desserts and cakes.

Grapes

The small oval fruit of grapes range in color from yellowish green to purplish black, and can be seeded or seedless. The eating varieties are sweet and juicy, and are delicious eaten raw as a snack or added to salads. They also make excellent decorations and are wonderful paired with cheese. Other varieties of grapes are made into grape juice, wine, jelly, or raisins.

Bananas

This long fruit starts off green, but turns yellow when it has ripened. Contrary to popular opinion, very fresh bananas can be stored in the refrigerator; the skins will turn brown but the flesh will be unaffected. If you prefer your bananas to stay yellow, store them at room temperature for a day or two. Bananas are delicious peeled and eaten as they are or added to desserts and cakes. They can also be lightly broiled or baked.

Rhubarb

Rhubarb has edible red stalks, and comes into season in spring. The stalks will keep in the refrigerator for up to 3 days. Rhubarb has a tart flavor but, once cooked and sweetened, will make a good sweet pie filling or other dessert. It also pairs well with ginger.

Melons

The members of the melon family come in many sizes and colors. The popular edible types include crenshaw, honeydew, watermelon, and cantaloupe. They are delicious eaten fresh on their own, or as an appetizer, perhaps combined with figs and ham, or with port wine. They are also good in fruit salads.

Pineapples

This golden oval fruit has a tough, prickly exterior and spearlike leaves. Large pineapples are the most common, but baby pineapples are also available. The flesh is juicy with a tangy flavor, and is delicious sliced and eaten on its own or added to fruit salads or other desserts. It is also good when cooked. It can be lightly broiled, or baked in a cake. Fresh pineapple will keep in the refrigerator for up to 3 days. You can also buy canned pineapple chunks or rings.

Tropical fruit

There is a wonderful range of tropical fruit available nowadays, from kiwi to litchis. Here is just a small selection of some of the popular ones you may find in your local supermarket—there are many more.

Mangoes

This large oval fruit varies in color from yellow to red. Eat mangoes raw, perhaps in a fruit salad, or frozen in a sorbet.

Star fruit

These star-shaped yellow fruit, also known as carambola, make beautiful decorations when cut across in slices.

Dates

This oval fruit is available fresh or dried. Chopped dried dates are delicious in granola and desserts.

Kiwi

This oval fruit has brown "hairy" skin and soft green flesh. Eat the flesh with a teaspoon. Alternatively, peel and slice kiwis and add them to fruit salads and other desserts.

Litchis

This small fruit, sometimes spelled lychee, is available fresh or canned. Litchis have a rough, pink, inedible skin, but the flesh inside is juicy and fragrant. You can eat them raw or lightly poached.

Figs

This soft, pear-shape fruit is delicious eaten either raw or poached. Dried figs are also good.

Passion fruit

Cut this brown-skinned, wrinkly fruit in half and eat the pulp by scooping it out with a teaspoon.

Papaya

This large, pear-shape fruit is cooked when green and unripe, or eaten raw when ripe and golden yellow. Papayas are good in salads. The are sometimes called pawpaws—but don't confuse them with papaws from the cherimoya family, which look like bananas.

Couscous with Nuts & Dried Fruit

Serves 6

ingredients

- 1¼ cups couscous
- 2½ cups water
- ½ cup plumped dried apricots
- ⅓ cup blanched almonds
- 2½ cups vegetable stock, chicken stock, or water
- 1 tsp extra virgin olive oil
- 2 tbsp chopped fresh cilantro
- salt and pepper

1 Put the couscous into a bowl and pour in the water. Let soak, stirring frequently with a fork to separate the grains, for 30 minutes, until almost all the liquid has been absorbed.

2 Meanwhile, using a sharp knife, cut the apricots into thin strips and set aside. Heat a heavy-bottom skillet, add the almonds, and cook over low heat, shaking the pan frequently, for 1–2 minutes, until lightly toasted. Remove the pan from the heat.

3 Pour the stock into a saucepan and bring to a boil. Line a steamer with cheesecloth. Stir the apricots into the soaked couscous, season with salt and pepper, and spoon into the steamer. Cover with a tight-fitting lid, set the steamer over the pan, and steam for 20 minutes.

4 Transfer the couscous mixture to a warm serving dish and stir in the olive oil, cilantro, and almonds. Serve immediately.

Smoked Chicken & Cranberry Salad

Serves 4

ingredients
- 3 lb/1.3 kg smoked chicken
- 1½ cups dried cranberries
- 2 tbsp apple juice or water
- 2 cups sugar snap peas
- 2 ripe avocados
- juice of ½ lemon
- 4 lettuce hearts
- 1 bunch watercress, trimmed
- 3 cups arugula
- ½ cup chopped walnuts, to garnish (optional)

for the dressing
- 2 tbsp olive oil
- 1 tbsp walnut oil
- 2 tbsp lemon juice
- 1 tbsp chopped fresh mixed herbs, such as parsley and lemon thyme
- salt and pepper

1 Carve the chicken carefully, slicing the white meat. Divide the legs into thighs and drumsticks and trim the wings. Cover with plastic wrap and refrigerate.

2 Put the cranberries in a bowl. Stir in the apple juice, cover with plastic wrap, and let soak for 30 minutes.

3 Meanwhile, blanch the sugar snap peas in a saucepan of boiling water for 2 minutes, refresh under cold running water, and drain.

4 Peel, pit, and slice the avocados, then toss in the lemon juice to prevent them from browning.

5 Separate the lettuce hearts and arrange on a large serving platter with the avocados, sugar snap peas, watercress, arugula, and chicken.

6 Put all the dressing ingredients, with salt and pepper to taste, in a screw-top jar, screw on the lid, and shake until well blended.

7 Drain the cranberries and mix them with the dressing, then pour over the salad.

8 Serve immediately, scattered with walnuts, if you are using them.

Pear & Roquefort Open Sandwiches

Serves 4–6

ingredients

- 4 slices walnut bread or sourdough bread, about ½ inch/1 cm thick
- 2 ripe pears, such as Bartlett, peeled, halved, cored, and thinly sliced lengthwise
- 3½ oz/100 g Roquefort cheese, very thinly sliced

1 Preheat the broiler to medium–high. Toast the bread slices on the rack in the broiler pan until crisp, but not brown, on both sides. Do not turn off the broiler.

2 Divide the pear slices equally among the breads. Lay the cheese slices on top.

3 Return the breads to the broiler until the cheese melts and bubbles. Serve.

Warm Salmon & Mango Salad

Serves 4

ingredients

- 4 oz/115 g sungold or red cherry tomatoes
- 3 oz/85 g salmon fillets, skinned and cut into small cubes
- 1 large ripe mango, peeled and cut into small chunks
- 2 tbsp orange juice
- 1 tbsp soy sauce
- 4 large handfuls assorted salad greens
- ½ cucumber, trimmed and sliced into sticks
- 6 scallions, trimmed and chopped

for the dressing

- ¼ cup low-fat plain yogurt
- 1 tsp soy sauce
- 1 tbsp finely grated orange rind

1 Soak 4 wooden skewers in a bowl of cold water for 30 minutes to prevent them from burning during cooking. Cut half of the tomatoes in half and set aside.

2 Thread the salmon with the whole tomatoes and half of the mango chunks onto 4 kebab sticks. Mix the orange juice and soy sauce together in a small bowl and brush over the kebabs. Let marinate for 15 minutes, brushing with the remaining orange juice mixture at least once more.

3 Arrange the salad greens on a serving platter with the reserved halved tomatoes, mango chunks, cucumber sticks, and scallions.

4 Preheat the broiler to high and line the broiler rack with foil. To make the dressing, mix the yogurt, soy sauce, and grated orange rind together in a small bowl and reserve.

5 Place the salmon kebabs on the broiler rack, brush again with the marinade, and broil for 5–7 minutes, or until the salmon is cooked. Turn the kebabs over halfway through cooking and brush with any remaining marinade.

6 Divide the prepared salad among 4 plates, top each with a kebab, then drizzle with the dressing.

Cherry with Brandy Jam

Makes about 7 cups

ingredients

- 4 lb/1.8 kg dark cherries, such as Morello, rinsed and pitted
- ½ cup freshly squeezed lemon juice or 1½ tsp citric or tartaric acid
- ⅔ cup water (optional)
- 6¼ cups granulated sugar
- 1 tsp butter
- 4 tbsp brandy
- 1 cup liquid pectin

1 Coarsely chop the cherries and place in a large preserving pan with the lemon juice. If using citric or tartaric acid, add to the pan with the water. Place the pan over gentle heat, cover, and simmer gently for 20 minutes, or until the cherries have collapsed and are very soft.

2 Add the sugar and heat, stirring frequently, until the sugar has completely dissolved. Add the butter and brandy, bring to a boil, and boil rapidly for 3 minutes. Remove from the heat and stir in the pectin.

3 Let cool for 10 minutes, then put into warmed sterilized jars and cover the tops with wax disks. When completely cold, cover with cellophane or lids, label, and store in a cool place.

Fruity Apple Chutney

Makes about 15 cups

ingredients

- 8 cups peeled, cored, and chopped cooking apples (about 2 lb/900 g)
- 3 cups chopped onions
- 2¾ cups rinsed, pitted, and chopped ripe plums
- rind and juice of 2 lemons (preferably unwaxed and organic), scrubbed
- 2¼ cups fresh cranberries (if fresh are unavailable, use dried)
- 2¼ cups brown sugar
- 4 kiwis, peeled and sliced
- 2 cups malt vinegar
- 2 tbsp balsamic vinegar

1 Place the apples, onions, and plums in a preserving pan with the lemon rind and juice and the cranberries. Cook over gentle heat, stirring frequently, for 12 minutes, or until the cranberries are beginning to "pop."

2 Stir in all the remaining ingredients and heat gently, stirring occasionally, until the sugar has completely dissolved. Bring to a boil, then reduce the heat and simmer for 35–40 minutes, or until a thick consistency is reached.

3 Remove from the heat, let cool slightly, then put into warmed sterilized jars. Cover with nonmetallic lids, label, and store in a cool place.

Spiced Tea-Soaked Dried Fruit Salad

Serves 8

ingredients
- 1⅓ cups dried apricots
- ½ cup chopped dried apples
- ½ cup dried pears
- ⅔ cup golden raisins
- ⅔ cup dried cherries
- 5 lemon-ginger tea bags
- several strips freshly pared lemon peel
- 2 cinnamon sticks
- 2 star anise

to serve
- Greek yogurt
- sliced banana (optional)
- honey (optional)

1 Put the dried fruit and the tea bags in a heatproof bowl and pour in enough boiling water to cover the fruit by 1 inch/2.5 cm. Set aside and let the fruit stew in the water for at least 2 hours, but ideally overnight, stirring occasionally.

2 Put the fruit and any remaining soaking liquid, the lemon peel, cinnamon stick, and star anise into a saucepan over medium heat. If necessary, add extra water so the fruit is just covered and simmer for 10–20 minutes, until the fruit is plump and soft.

3 Remove the pan from the heat and let the fruit and liquid cool. Transfer to an airtight container, seal, and store in the refrigerator for up to 2 weeks.

4 To serve, spoon the fruit into a bowl and top with yogurt. Add some sliced banana and honey, if using.

Summer Fruit Slush

Serves 2

ingredients
- 4 tbsp orange juice
- 1 tbsp lime juice
- ½ cup sparkling water
- 3 cups frozen berries (such as blueberries, raspberries, blackberries, and strawberries)
- 4 ice cubes

1 Pour the orange juice, lime juice, and sparkling water into a blender and blend gently until combined.

2 Add the berries and ice cubes and blend until a slushy consistency has been reached.

3 Pour the mixture into glasses and serve.

Fruit Crudités with Chocolate Sauce

Serves 4

ingredients

- 7 oz/200 g good-quality semisweet dark chocolate, at least 60% cocoa solids
- 12 fresh strawberries
- 2 fresh pineapple rings
- 1 orange
- 1 large banana
- 4 tbsp low-fat milk, at room temperature

1 Break the chocolate into a heatproof bowl that fits snugly over a small saucepan, put ¾ inch/2 cm of water in the saucepan, and set the bowl over the saucepan—make sure the bottom of the bowl does not touch the water. Heat the water to a slow simmer and let the chocolate melt slowly, undisturbed—this will take about 10 minutes.

2 Meanwhile, prepare the fruit. Hull the strawberries and, if large, halve. Remove the central core from the pineapple rings and cut the flesh into chunks. Peel the orange and remove all the pith. Cut the flesh into segments. Peel the banana and cut into 1½-inch/4-cm chunks. Arrange the fruit on a platter.

3 When the chocolate has melted, remove the bowl from the saucepan and stir in the milk. Pour the sauce into a serving bowl and serve with the fruit for dipping.

Lemon Tart

Serves 6–8

ingredients
- grated rind of 2–3 large lemons
- ⅔ cup lemon juice
- ½ cup superfine sugar
- ½ cup heavy cream or crème fraîche, plus extra to serve
- 3 extra-large eggs
- 3 extra-large egg yolks
- confectioners' sugar, for dusting
- fresh whole raspberries, to serve

for the pie dough
- heaping 1⅓ cups all-purpose flour, plus extra for dusting
- ½ tsp salt
- ½ cup cold unsalted butter, diced
- 1 egg yolk beaten with 2 tbsp ice-cold water

1 To make the pie dough, sift the flour and salt into a large bowl. Add the butter and rub it in with your fingertips until the mixture resembles fine breadcrumbs. Add the egg yolk and water and stir to mix to a dough.

2 Gather the dough into a ball, wrap in plastic wrap, and let chill for at least 1 hour.

3 Preheat the oven to 400°F/200°C. Roll the dough out on a lightly floured work surface and use to line a fluted tart pan measuring 9–10 inches/23–25 cm in diameter with a removable bottom. Prick the bottom of the pastry all over with a fork and line with parchment paper and pie weights or dried beans.

4 Bake for 15 minutes until the pastry looks set. Remove the paper and weights. Reduce the oven temperature to 375°F/190°C.

5 Beat the lemon rind, lemon juice, and sugar together until blended. Slowly beat in the cream, then beat in the eggs and yolks, one by one.

6 Set the pastry shell on a baking sheet and pour in the filling. Transfer to the preheated oven and bake for 20 minutes, until the filling is set.

7 Let cool completely on a wire rack. Dust with confectioners' sugar and serve with whole raspberries.

Berry Yogurt Ice Cream

Serves 4

ingredients
- 1 cup raspberries
- 1 cup blackberries
- 4½ oz/125 g strawberries
- 1 extra-large egg
- ¾ cup Greek yogurt
- ½ cup red wine
- 2¼ tsp gelatin
- fresh berries, to decorate

1 Place the raspberries, blackberries, and strawberries in a blender or food processor and process until a smooth puree forms. Rub the puree through a strainer into a bowl to remove the seeds.

2 Break the egg and separate the yolk and white into separate bowls. Stir the egg yolk and yogurt into the berry puree and set the egg white aside.

3 Pour the wine into a heatproof bowl set over a saucepan of water. Sprinkle the gelatin on the surface of the wine and let stand for 5 minutes to soften. Heat the pan of water and simmer until the gelatin has dissolved. Pour the mixture into the berry puree in a steady stream, whisking continuously. Transfer the mixture to a freezerproof container and freeze for 2 hours, or until slushy.

4 Whisk the egg white in a spotlessly clean, grease-free bowl until very stiff. Remove the berry mixture from the freezer and fold in the egg white. Return to the freezer and freeze for 2 hours, or until firm. To serve, scoop the berry yogurt ice into glass dishes and decorate with fresh berries of your choice.

Orange Sorbet

Serves 4

ingredients
- 2¼ cups water
- 1 cup superfine sugar
- 4 large oranges
- 2 tbsp orange liqueur, such as Cointreau

1 Heat the water and sugar in a saucepan over low heat, stirring, until dissolved. Boil without stirring for 2 minutes. Pour into a heatproof bowl. Let cool to room temperature.

2 Grate the rind from 2 oranges and extract the juice. Extract the juice from 2 more oranges. Mix the juice and rind in a bowl, cover with plastic wrap, and reserve. Discard all the squeezed oranges. Stir the orange juice, grated rind, and orange liqueur into the cooled syrup. Cover with plastic wrap and let chill for 1 hour. Transfer to an ice cream machine and churn for 15 minutes.

3 If you do not have an ice cream machine, place the mixture in a freezerproof container. Freeze for 1 hour, then transfer to a bowl. Beat to break up the crystals, then return it to the freezerproof container and freeze for 30 minutes. Repeat twice more, freezing for 30 minutes and whisking each time.

4 Divide the frozen sorbet between 4 bowls and serve immediately.

Fruit & Nut Squares

Makes 9

ingredients

- ½ cup unsalted butter, plus extra for greasing
- 2 tbsp honey
- 1 egg, beaten
- scant 1 cup ground almonds
- scant 1 cup finely chopped plumped dried apricots
- ⅓ cup dried cherries
- ½ cup toasted chopped hazelnuts
- 2½ tbsp sesame seeds
- scant 1 cup rolled oats

1 Preheat the oven to 350°F/180°C. Lightly grease a shallow 7-inch/18-cm square baking pan with butter.

2 Beat the butter with the honey in a bowl until creamy, then beat in the egg with the almonds. Add the remaining ingredients and mix together.

3 Press into the prepared pan, making sure that the mixture is firmly packed. Smooth over the top. Bake in the preheated oven for 20–25 minutes, or until firm to the touch and golden brown.

4 Remove from the oven and let cool for 10 minutes before marking into squares. Cool completely before removing from the pan. Store in an airtight container.

Rhubarb & Orange Crumble

Serves 6

ingredients
- 1 lb 2 oz/500 g rhubarb
- 1 lb 2 oz/ 500 g cooking apples
- grated rind and juice of 1 orange
- ½–1 tsp ground cinnamon
- scant ½ cup light brown sugar

for the topping
- 1¾ cups all-purpose flour
- ½ cup unsalted butter or margarine
- ⅔ cup light brown sugar
- ½ cup toasted chopped hazelnuts
- 2 tbsp Demerara sugar or raw brown sugar (optional)

1 Preheat the oven to 400°F/200°C. Cut the rhubarb into 1-inch/2.5-cm lengths and place in a large saucepan.

2 Peel, core, and slice the apples and add to the rhubarb, together with the grated orange rind and juice. Bring to a boil, lower the heat, and simmer for 2–3 minutes, until the fruit softens.

3 Add the cinnamon and sugar to taste and turn the mixture into an ovenproof dish, so it is not more than two-thirds full.

4 Sift the flour into a bowl and rub in the unsalted butter or margarine until the mixture resembles fine breadcrumbs (this can be done by hand or in a food processor). Stir in the sugar, followed by the nuts.

5 Spoon the crumble mixture evenly over the fruit in the dish and lightly smooth the top. Sprinkle with Demerara sugar, if liked.

6 Cook in the preheated oven for 30–40 minutes, until the topping is browned. Serve hot or cold.

Chapter 9
Baking

Introduction

There is nothing like the aroma of freshly baked bread, pastry, cakes, and cookies to stimulate the appetite. Baking these items for yourself is very satisfying, and the mouthwatering aromas will prove to be an irresistible temptation for your family and friends.

Making bread at home

Making your own bread does not have to be difficult, and anyone can make delicious loaves and rolls with the minimum of effort. The key to making perfect bread is to use the right ingredients at the right temperature. Always use bread flour instead of ordinary flour: bread flour has a higher gluten content than ordinary flour, which increases the elasticity of the dough. You can use any of the different kinds of yeast, but it may need a different method for making bread. You will also need to use the correct quantities: one ½ oz/15 g compressed cake of fresh yeast or scant 1 tablespoon (1 envelope) of active dry yeast is enough to make 5½ cups of bread flour rise. When you add water, make sure it is lukewarm, because if it is too hot it will kill the yeast.

Fresh yeast
Crush this in a pitcher with a little lukewarm water, then cover and let stand until the surface starts to bubble.

Active dry yeast
Sprinkle active dry yeast over a little lukewarm water in a pitcher, then stir in a pinch of sugar. Cover and let stand until it froths.

Instant yeast
Also called rapid-rise dry yeast and quick yeast, mix this yeast straight into the flour before the warm water is added.

Yeast

Key techniques for making dough

Making the perfect dough can be straightforward, but it is important to follow a certain procedure to achieve good results every time.

Punching down

After letting the dough rise for the first time for about an hour, simply punch your fist into the risen dough so that it collapses and releases the air. Then turn the dough out onto a floured work surface (some of it may need scraping out) and knead it for about 1 minute, until it has lost its cold feel and has an even temperature.

Rising

This stage literally involves letting the yeast rise. To do this, after punching down the dough, divide and shape it as required (see below). Cover and let rise for a second (but shorter) time, until the dough has doubled in size.

Baking and storing bread

The dough will keep, covered, in the refrigerator for up to a day before baking. To bake the bread, you will need a hot oven, so make sure you preheat it beforehand. Underbaked bread has a moist, doughlike consistency and flavor, so it is always better to overbake if necessary. To test if the bread is properly baked, remove it from the oven, turn it out of its pan, and use your knuckles to give it a sharp tap on the bottom. If it sounds hollow, the bread is done. If it does not, return it to the oven and bake for another 5 minutes, or until the bread is properly baked. When it is done, remove from the oven and let cool on a wire rack. If you want a soft crust, cover the loaf with a clean dish towel while it is cooling. Freshly baked bread will keep, covered, for 2–3 days at room temperature, but no longer because it has no added preservatives. You can also keep it wrapped in the refrigerator for up to a week, or wrap it in a freezer bag and freeze it for up to a month.

Mixing

To mix the dough, sift the flour and salt into a mixing bowl. Make a well in the center, then add the yeast. Pour in lukewarm, or tepid, water, then gradually pull in the flour from the edges and mix together, adding more lukewarm water as necessary in order to form a soft dough.

Kneading

This process is necessary to make the dough smooth and increase its elasticity. To knead the dough, push your hand into it, then stretch it away from you. Pick up the farthest end of the dough and pull it back to the top, then turn the dough 45 degreees and repeat the kneading action away from you. Keep turning the dough 45 degrees and repeating the kneading action. The kneading process usually takes about 5 minutes. To save time and effort, you could use a standing mixer or food processor with a dough hook to mix and knead the dough for you. Kneading will take about 3 minutes if you knead the dough this way.

Rising

After the dough has been kneaded, place it in an oiled bowl, cover it with plastic wrap, and put it in a warm place. Let it rise to about double its original size.

Shaping

To shape the dough correctly for a loaf pan, use your hands to form the dough into an oval, then bring over the two short sides to the center, turn the dough over, and transfer, seam-side down, to a greased loaf pan. To make rolls, simply use your hands to roll even pieces of the dough into balls, and then place them on a greased baking sheet.

Making pastry

Pastry is very versatile and lends a professional finish to a wide range of savory and sweet dishes. Choose your pastry to match the occasion: flaky pastry for savory or sweet pies, quiches, and tartlets; choux pastry for cream puffs and eclairs; paper-thin phyllo pastry for savory turnovers or sweet apple strudel; or puff pastry for canapés and a range of desserts.

Flaky pie dough

This recipe will make enough pie dough to line an 8-inch/20-cm tart pan.

heaping 1⅓ cups all-purpose flour, plus extra for dusting
6½ tbsp butter, diced
2–3 tbsp cold water

1. To make the pie dough, sift the flour.
2. Use your fingertips to rub in the butter until the mixture resembles fine breadcrumbs. Gradually mix in enough water to make a soft dough.
3. Use your hands to shape the dough into a ball. Cover with plastic wrap and refrigerate before use. When you are ready to use it, turn it out onto a lightly floured work surface.
4. Use a rolling pin to roll it out to the desired thickness.

Variation: To make a sweet pastry, stir 1 tablespoon of superfine sugar into the flour after sifting, and replace half of the water with 2 beaten egg yolks.

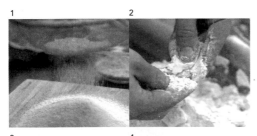

Choux pastry

This quantity will make about 24 round choux buns.

generous ¾ cup water
5½ tbsp butter
scant 1 cup all-purpose flour
½ tsp salt
½ tsp confectioners' sugar
3 eggs

1. Preheat the oven to 400°F/200°C. Pour the water into a saucepan and add the butter. Gently bring to a boil. Sift the flour and salt into a bowl, then mix in the sugar. In a separate bowl, beat the eggs.
2. When the butter is just beginning to boil, remove from the heat and stir in the flour mixture. Continue to stir until smooth, then return to the heat and stir until the mixture begins to pull away from the sides of the saucepan. Remove from the heat and gradually beat in the eggs until the mixture forms a thick, glossy paste.
3. Put 24 rounded spoonfuls of the mixture onto greased baking sheets and brush the tops with a little beaten egg. Bake in the preheated oven for 20 minutes, or until golden. Remove from the oven and let cool.

Serving suggestion: Split the cooled buns in half horizontally and sandwich with whipped cream. You can also brush melted chocolate over the tops and let cool, or serve with a chocolate sauce.

Making cakes and cookies

For cakes and cookies, there are four basic methods of mixing, as follows:

Creaming

This is a good method for making light yellow cakes. Simply beat the butter and sugar together until light, then beat in the eggs and fold in the flour. Use softened butter or margarine for this method.

All-in-one

This method saves time and effort when making light yellow cakes, and can be done manually or in a machine. Put all the ingredients into a mixing bowl and beat well until smooth. Alternatively, put the ingredients into a free-standing mixer or food processor and beat on slow speed for 2–3 minutes, until the batter is smooth.

Rubbing in
This method is ideal for biscuits and quick breads. Use your fingertips to rub the butter into the flour until it resembles fine breadcrumbs. Then mix in the sugar, egg, and any other liquid ingredients. Stir in the flour from the sides of the bowl.

Melting
Use this method for moist cakes and cookies. Melt the butter in a saucepan along with the sugar and any other dissolvable ingredients. Remove from the heat and let cool slightly. Meanwhile, sift the flour into a bowl and make a well in the center. Beat together the eggs and milk and pour into the well, then add the egg mixture. Stir in the flour from the sides of the bowl.

Basic cake batter
This recipe will make enough for two 8-inch/20-cm greased and lined cake pans to make a yellow layer cake.

1 cup unsalted butter, softened,
  or soft margarine suitable for baking
heaping 1 cup superfine sugar
4 eggs
heaping 1¾ cups self-rising flour, sifted
2 tsp baking powder
pinch of salt

1. Preheat the oven to 375°F/190°C. Grease and line two 8-inch/20-cm round cake pans. Put the butter or margarine in a large bowl, then add the sugar and use a wooden spoon to beat together until the mixture is smooth and light. Gradually beat in the eggs, making sure that the mixture stays smooth throughout.
2. In a separate bowl, sift together the flour, baking powder, and salt, then fold into the egg mixture in a figure-eight movement. Divide the batter between the cake pans and bake for about 25 minutes, until golden and risen. Remove from the oven and let cool in the pans for about 5 minutes before turning out onto a wire rack to cool completely.

Variation: To make a chocolate-flavored version of this cake, replace 1 tablespoon of the self-rising flour with 1 tablespoon of unsweetened cocoa.

Butter shortbread
This recipe makes 8 large pieces of shortbread or 16 smaller pieces.

generous ½ cup unsalted butter,
  softened, plus extra for greasing
heaping 1⅓ cups all-purpose flour
¼ cup rice flour
¼ cup superfine sugar, plus extra
  for sprinkling

1. Preheat the oven to 325°F/160°C. Grease an 8-inch/20-cm loose-bottom tart pan. Sift the all-purpose flour and rice flour into a large mixing bowl.
2. In a separate bowl, cream together the butter and superfine sugar, then stir in the sifted flours. Put the dough into the prepared tart pan and smooth the surface. Lightly sprinkle with some superfine sugar, then prick all over the surface using a fork. Using a sharp knife, score the surface into 8 wedges (or 16 smaller wedges, if preferred), then bake in the preheated oven for 30 minutes, or until lightly golden.
3. Remove the baked shortbread from the oven and let cool in the pan for 5 minutes. Carefully slide the shortbread out of the pan, then use a sharp knife to cut along the score marks and divide the shortbread into wedges. Let cool on a wire rack, then serve immediately or store in an airtight container for up to a week.

Mixed Seed Bread

Makes 1 medium loaf

ingredients

- 2¾ cups white bread flour, plus extra for dusting
- 1¼ cups rye flour
- 1½ tbsp dry skim milk
- 1½ tsp salt
- 1 tbsp light brown sugar
- 1 tsp active dry yeast
- 1½ tbsp sunflower oil, plus extra for greasing
- 2 tsp lemon juice
- 1¼ cups lukewarm water
- 1 tsp caraway seeds
- ½ tsp poppy seeds
- ½ tsp sesame seeds

for the topping

- 1 egg white
- 1 tbsp water
- 1 tbsp sunflower seeds or pumpkin seeds

1 Place the flours, milk, salt, sugar, and yeast in a large bowl. Pour in the oil and add the lemon juice and water. Stir in the seeds and mix well to make a smooth dough.

2 Turn the dough out onto a lightly floured work surface and knead for 10 minutes, or until the dough is smooth and elastic. Place the dough in an oiled bowl, cover with plastic wrap, and let stand in a warm place to rise for 1 hour, or until it has doubled in size.

3 Oil a 9 x 5 x 3-inch/23 x 13 x 8-cm loaf pan. Turn the dough out onto a lightly floured work surface and knead for 1 minute, until smooth. Shape the dough the length of the pan and three times the width. Fold the dough into three lengthwise and place it in the pan with the seam underneath. Cover and let stand in a warm place for 30 minutes, until it has risen above the pan.

4 Preheat the oven to 425°F/220°C. For the topping, lightly beat the egg white with the water to make a glaze. Just before baking, brush the glaze over the loaf, then gently press the sunflower seeds or pumpkin seeds all over the top.

5 Bake in the oven for 30 minutes, or until firm and golden brown. Test that the loaf is baked by tapping it on the bottom—it should sound hollow. Transfer the loaf to a wire rack to cool completely before serving.

Bagels

Makes 12

ingredients

- 1 tbsp active dry yeast
- 2 tbsp sugar
- 3½ tbsp vegetable oil, plus extra for oiling
- 1 tsp salt
- 1 cup lukewarm water
- 3⅓ cups all-purpose flour, plus extra for dusting
- 1 egg, beaten
- 1 egg, beaten with ¼ tsp salt, for glazing
- poppy and sesame seeds, for sprinkling

for the filling

- smoked salmon
- cream cheese

1 Combine the yeast and half of the sugar in a small bowl. Heat the remaining sugar, oil, salt, and water in a small saucepan for 1–2 minutes, or until warm and the sugar has dissolved. Pour into the yeast mixture, cover with a dish towel, and let stand for 5–7 minutes, or until the mixture begins to froth. Put the flour into a food processor and, with the machine running, pour in the yeast mixture, then add the egg and process until a ball of dough forms. Add a little more flour if the dough is sticky—it should be smooth and elastic.

2 Lightly oil a large bowl and add the ball of dough, turning to coat on all sides to prevent a crust from forming. Cover with the dish towel and let rise in a warm place for 1½–2 hours, or until doubled in size. Turn out onto a lightly floured work surface. Knead lightly to deflate.

3 Divide the dough into 12 equal pieces. Roll each into a rope about 7 inches/18 cm long and shape into a ring. Wet one end and press firmly to seal. Arrange on a floured baking sheet, cover with the dish towel, and let rise for 25 minutes, or until doubled in size.

4 Meanwhile, preheat the oven to 400°F/200°C. Lightly oil 2 large baking sheets. Bring a large saucepan of water to a boil. Working in batches, slide a few bagels into the water. When they rise to the top of the water, turn over and let cook for 1 minute. Remove with a slotted spoon and drain on paper towels. Arrange the bagels on the baking sheets and carefully brush with the egg mixture. Sprinkle half with sesame seeds and the remainder with poppy seeds. Bake for 12–15 minutes, or until golden and shiny. Remove and place on a wire rack to cool slightly. Serve warm with smoked salmon and cream cheese.

Sourdough Bread

Makes 2 loaves

ingredients
- 3¾ cups whole wheat flour
- 4 tsp salt
- 1½ cups lukewarm water
- 2 tbsp molasses
- 1 tbsp vegetable oil, plus extra for brushing
- all-purpose flour, for dusting

for the sourdough starter
- scant ¾ cup whole wheat flour
- scant ⅔ cup white bread flour
- ¼ cup superfine sugar
- 1 cup milk

1 First, make the starter. Put the flours, sugar, and milk into a nonmetallic bowl and beat well with a fork. Cover with a damp dish towel and let stand at room temperature for 4–5 days, until the mixture is frothy and smells sour.

2 Sift the flour and half of the salt together into a bowl and add the lukewarm water, molasses, vegetable oil, and sourdough starter. Mix well with a wooden spoon until a dough begins to form, then knead with your hands until it leaves the side of the bowl. Turn out onto a lightly floured surface and knead for 10 minutes, until smooth and elastic.

3 Brush a bowl with oil. Form the dough into a ball, put it in the bowl, and put the bowl into a plastic bag or cover with a damp dish towel. Let rise in a warm place for 2 hours, until the dough has doubled in volume.

4 Dust 2 baking sheets with flour. Mix the remaining salt with 4 tablespoons of water in a bowl. Turn out the dough on to a lightly floured surface and punch down with your fist, then knead for an additional 10 minutes. Halve the dough, shape each piece into an oval, and place the loaves on the prepared baking sheets. Brush with the salt water glaze and let stand in a warm place, brushing frequently with the glaze, for 30 minutes.

5 Preheat the oven to 425°F/220°C. Brush the loaves with the remaining glaze and bake for 30 minutes, until the crust is golden brown and they sound hollow when tapped on the bottom with your knuckles. If it is necessary to bake them for longer, lower the oven temperature to 375°F/190°C. Transfer to wire racks to cool.

Crusty White Bread

Serves 4

ingredients
- 1 egg
- 1 egg yolk
- ¾–1 cup lukewarm water
- 3⅔ cups white bread flour, plus extra for dusting
- 1½ tsp salt
- 2 tsp sugar
- 1 tsp active dry yeast
- 2 tbsp butter, diced
- sunflower oil, for greasing

1 Place the egg and egg yolk in a pitcher and beat lightly to mix. Add enough lukewarm water to make up to 1¼ cups. Stir well.

2 Place the flour, salt, sugar, and yeast in a large bowl. Add the butter and rub it in with your fingertips until the mixture resembles breadcrumbs. Make a well in the center, add the egg mixture, and work to a smooth dough.

3 Turn the dough out onto a lightly floured work surface and knead for 10 minutes, or until the dough is smooth and elastic. Place the dough in an oiled bowl, cover with plastic wrap, and let stand in a warm place to rise for 1 hour, or until it has doubled in size.

4 Oil a loaf pan. Turn the dough out onto a lightly floured surface and knead for 1 minute, until smooth. Shape the dough the length of the pan and three times the width. Fold the dough into three lengthwise and place it in the pan with the seam underneath. Cover and let stand in a warm place for 30 minutes, until it has risen above the pan.

5 Preheat the oven to 425°F/220°C. Bake in the oven for 30 minutes, or until firm and golden brown. Test that the loaf is cooked by tapping it on the bottom—it should sound hollow. Transfer to a wire rack to cool completely before serving.

Whole Wheat
Harvest Bread

Makes 1 small loaf

ingredients
- 1⅔ cups whole wheat bread flour, plus extra for dusting
- 1 tbsp dry skim milk
- 1 tsp salt
- 2 tbsp brown sugar
- 1 tsp active dry yeast
- 1½ tbsp sunflower oil, plus extra for greasing
- ¾ cup lukewarm water

1 Place the flour, milk, salt, sugar, and yeast in a large bowl. Pour in the oil and add the water, then mix well to make a smooth dough.

2 Turn the dough out onto a lightly floured work surface and knead for 10 minutes, or until the dough is smooth. Place the dough in an oiled bowl, cover with plastic wrap, and let stand in a warm place to rise for 1 hour, or until it has doubled in size.

3 Oil a 9 x 5 x 3-inch/23 x 13 x 8-cm loaf pan. Turn the dough out onto a lightly floured surface and knead for 1 minute, until smooth. Shape the loaf the width of the pan and three times the length. Fold the dough into three lengthwise and place it in the pan with the seam underneath. Cover and let stand in a warm place for 30 minutes, until it has risen above the pan.

4 Preheat the oven to 425°F/220°C. Bake in the oven for 30 minutes, or until firm and golden brown. Test that the loaf is baked by tapping it on the bottom—it should sound hollow. Transfer to a wire rack to cool completely before serving.

Tomato & Cheese Tart

Serves 8–10

ingredients
- scant 1 cup white bread flour
- 1 cup self-rising flour
- heaping ½ cup chilled butter
- 1 egg yolk
- 4 tbsp cold water
- oil, for greasing
- salt
- arugula salad, to serve

for the filling
- 8–9 tomatoes, peeled, seeded, and cut into eighths
- 1⅓ cups coarsely grated Emmenthal cheese
- 4 eggs
- scant ½ cup heavy cream
- 2 tbsp chopped fresh oregano or marjoram
- 1 tbsp chopped fresh chives
- salt and pepper

1 Sift the flours and salt into a bowl, then sift again to mix thoroughly. Dice the butter and work it into the flours, rubbing between your finger tips and thumb until the mixture resembles breadcrumbs. Beat together the egg yolk and water, and stir into the flour mixture with a fork. Once the dough starts to clump, knead lightly to form a compact ball. Wrap in plastic wrap and let rest in the refrigerator for at least 30 minutes.

2 Preheat the oven to 325°F/160°C. Lightly grease an 11-inch/28-cm loose-bottom tart pan. Roll out the dough thinly and use to line the pan. Pass a rolling pin over the top of the pan to trim off surplus dough. Using the side of your index finger, press the dough into the corner of the pan to raise it slightly above the rim. Line the pastry shell with parchment paper and weigh down with pie weights or dried beans, making sure they go all the way to the edge. Bake in the preheated oven for 15 minutes.

3 Arrange the tomato segments in the pastry shell in concentric circles. Sprinkle the grated cheese evenly over the top. Beat the eggs lightly, then stir in the cream, oregano, chives, and salt and pepper. Mix well, then pour into the pastry shell. Return to the oven and bake for 20–25 minutes, until puffy and golden. Serve hot or warm with an arugula salad.

Leek & Onion Tartlets

Serves 6

ingredients
- butter, for greasing
- 8 oz/225 g prepared flaky pastry
- all-purpose flour, for dusting

for the filling
- 2 tbsp unsalted butter
- 1 onion, thinly sliced
- 5 cups thinly sliced leeks
- 2 tsp chopped fresh thyme
- ½ cup grated Gruyère cheese
- 3 eggs
- 1¼ cups heavy cream
- salt and pepper

1 Lightly grease six 4-inch/10-cm tartlet pans with butter. Roll out the dough on a lightly floured work surface and stamp out 6 rounds with a 5-inch/13-cm cutter. Ease the dough into the pans, prick the bottoms, and let chill for 30 minutes.

2 Preheat the oven to 375°F/190°C. Line the pastry shells with parchment paper and pie weights or dried beans, then place on a baking sheet and bake for 8 minutes. Remove the lining paper and weights and bake for an additional 2 minutes. Transfer the pans to a wire rack to cool. Reduce the oven temperature to 350°F/ 180°C.

3 Meanwhile, make the filling. Melt the butter in a large, heavy-bottom skillet. Add the onion and cook, stirring continuously, for 5 minutes, or until softened. Add the leeks and thyme and cook, stirring, for 10 minutes, or until softened. Divide the leek mixture among the tartlet shells, then sprinkle with the Gruyère cheese.

4 Lightly beat the eggs with the cream and season to taste with salt and pepper. Place the tartlet pans on a baking sheet and divide the egg mixture among them. Bake in the preheated oven for 15 minutes, or until the filling is set and golden brown. Transfer to a wire rack to cool slightly before removing from the pans and serving.

Mushroom & Spinach Puff Pastry

serves 4

ingredients
- 2 tbsp butter
- 1 red onion, halved and sliced
- 2 garlic cloves, crushed
- 8 oz/225 g open-cap mushrooms, sliced
- 6 oz/175 g baby spinach
- pinch of nutmeg
- 4 tbsp heavy cream
- 8 oz/225 g prepared puff pastry
- all-purpose flour, for dusting
- 1 egg, beaten
- 2 tsp poppy seeds
- salt and pepper

1 Preheat the oven to 400ºF/200ºC. Melt the butter in a skillet. Add the onion and garlic and sauté for 3–4 minutes, until the onion has softened.

2 Add the mushrooms, spinach, and nutmeg and cook for an additional 2–3 minutes. Stir in the cream, mixing well. Season to taste with salt and pepper and remove the skillet from the heat.

3 Roll the pastry out on a lightly floured surface and cut into four 6-inch/15-cm rounds. Spoon one-quarter of the filling onto one-half of each round and fold the pastry over to encase the filling. Press down to seal the edges of the pastry and brush with the beaten egg. Sprinkle with the poppy seeds.

4 Place the turnovers onto a dampened baking sheet and cook in the preheated oven for 20 minutes, until they are risen and golden brown.

5 Transfer the turnovers to serving plates and serve immediately.

Frosted Carrot Cake

Serves 16

ingredients
- ¾ cup sunflower oil,
  plus extra for greasing
- scant 1 cup light brown sugar
- 3 eggs, beaten
- 1½ cups grated carrots
- ½ cup golden raisins
- ½ cup walnut pieces
- grated rind of 1 orange
- 1⅓ cups self-rising flour
- 1 tsp baking soda
- 1 tsp ground cinnamon
- ½ tsp grated nutmeg
- strips of orange zest, to decorate

for the frosting
- 1 cup cream cheese
- ¾ cup confectioners' sugar
- 2 tsp orange juice

1 Preheat the oven to 350°F/180°C. Grease and line the bottom of a 9-inch 23-cm square cake pan.

2 In a large bowl, beat together the oil, brown sugar, and eggs. Stir in the grated carrots, golden raisins, walnuts, and orange rind.

3 Sift together the flour, baking soda, cinnamon, and nutmeg, then stir evenly into the carrot mixture.

4 Spoon the batter into the prepared cake pan and bake in the preheated oven for 40–45 minutes, until well risen and firm to the touch.

5 Remove the cake from the oven and set on a wire rack for 5 minutes. Turn out onto the wire rack to cool completely.

6 For the frosting, combine the cream cheese, confectioners' sugar, and orange juice in a bowl and beat until smooth. Spread over the top of the cake and swirl with a palette knife. Decorate with strips of orange zest and serve cut into squares.

Orange Oat Bar Fingers

Makes 18

ingredients
- ¾ cup butter, plus extra for greasing
- ⅔ cup light corn syrup
- ⅓ cup Demerara sugar or raw brown sugar
- scant 2¼ cups rolled oats
- scant ⅔ cup cup whole wheat flour
- ½ cup raisins or golden raisins
- finely grated rind of 1 large orange

1 Preheat the oven to 350°F/180°C. Grease a shallow 10 x 8-inch/25 x 20-cm baking pan, then line the botom and sides with parchment paper.

2 Put the butter, corn syrup, and sugar into a saucepan over high heat and stir until the butter and syrup have melted and the sugar has dissolved, then bring to a boil without stirring.

3 Put the oats, flour, raisins, and orange rind into a large, heatproof mixing bowl. Pour in the butter mixture and mix all the ingredients together. Turn the mixture into the pan and use the back of a wooden spoon to spread it evenly over the bottom of the pan and into the corners.

4 Put the pan in the oven and bake for 25–30 minutes, until the oat batter has set. Remove from the oven, place on a wire rack, and let cool completely.

5 When cool, invert the pan onto a cutting board. Lift off the pan and peel off the paper. Using a serrated knife, cut the slab in half lengthwise, then cut each half into 1-inch/2.5-cm thick fingers. These oat bar fingers will remain fresh for up to a week wrapped in plastic wrap or stored in an airtight container.

Traditional Apple Pie

Serves 6

ingredients

- 1 lb 10 oz–2 lb4 oz/750 g–1 kg cooking apples
- ⅔ cup brown or white sugar, plus extra for sprinkling
- ½–1 tsp ground cinnamon
- 1–2 tbsp water
- custard or vanilla ice cream, to serve (optional)

for the pie dough

- heaping 2¾ cups all-purpose flour, plus extra for dusting
- pinch of salt
- 6 tbsp butter
- scant ⅔ cup vegetable shortening
- about ⅔ cup cold water
- milk or beaten egg, to glaze

1 To make the pie dough, sift the flour and salt into a large bowl. Add the butter and shortening and rub it in with your fingertips until the mixture resembles fine breadcrumbs. Add enough water to mix to a dough. Wrap the dough in plastic wrap and let chill for 30 minutes.

2 Preheat the oven to 425°F/220°C. Roll out almost two-thirds of the pie dough thinly on a lightly floured surface and use to line a deep pie plate or shallow pie pan measuring 8–9 inches/20–23 cm in diameter.

3 Peel, core, and slice the apples, then mix them with the sugar and spice and pack into the pastry shell; the filling can come up above the rim. If the apples are a dry variety, add a little water to moisten.

4 Roll out the remaining dough to form a lid. Dampen the edges of the pie rim with water and position the lid, pressing the edges together firmly. Trim and crimp the edges. Use the pastry trimmings to cut out leaves or other shapes to decorate the top of the pie. Dampen the shapes and attach. Glaze the top of the pie with milk or beaten egg, make 1–2 slits in the top to let the steam escape, and put the pie on a baking sheet.

5 Bake in the oven for 20 minutes, then reduce the oven temperature to 350°F/180°C and cook for 30 minutes, or until the pastry is a light golden brown. Serve hot, sprinkled with sugar and served with custard or vanilla ice cream, if desired.

Chocolate Chip Muffins

Makes 12

ingredients

- 7 tbsp soft margarine
- heaping 1 cup superfine sugar
- 2 extra-large eggs
- ⅔ cup plain yogurt
- 5 tbsp milk
- scant 2¼ cups all-purpose flour
- 1 tsp baking soda
- 6 oz/175 g semisweet dark
  chocolate chips

1 Preheat the oven to 375°F/190°C. Line a 12-hole muffin pan with baking cups.

2 Place the margarine and sugar in a mixing bowl and beat with a wooden spoon until light and fluffy. Beat in the eggs, yogurt, and milk until combined.

3 Sift the flour and baking soda together and add to the mixture. Stir until just blended.

4 Stir in the chocolate chips, then spoon the batter into the baking cups and bake in the preheated oven for 25 minutes, or until a fine skewer inserted into the center comes out clean. Let cool in the pan for 5 minutes, then turn out onto a wire rack to cool completely before serving.

Crunchy Peanut Cookies

Makes 20

ingredients

- heaping ½ cup butter, softened, plus extra for greasing
- ½ cup chunky peanut butter
- heaping 1 cup granulated sugar
- 1 egg, lightly beaten
- scant 1¼ cups all-purpose flour
- ½ tsp baking powder
- pinch of salt
- ½ cup chopped unsalted, natural peanuts

1 Lightly grease 2 baking sheets. Beat the butter and peanut butter together in a large mixing bowl.

2 Gradually add the granulated sugar and beat together well. Add the egg to the mixture, a little at a time, until it is thoroughly combined.

3 Sift the flour, baking powder, and salt into the peanut butter mixture. Add the peanuts and bring all of the ingredients together to form a soft dough.

4 Wrap the dough in plastic wrap and chill in the refrigerator for 30 minutes.

5 Preheat the oven to 375°F/190°C. Form the dough into 20 balls and place them onto the prepared baking sheets about 2 inches/5 cm apart to allow for spreading. Flatten them slightly with your hand.

6 Bake in the preheated oven for 15 minutes, or until golden brown. Transfer the cookies to a wire rack and let cool.

Strawberry Mousse Choux

Makes 12

ingredients

for the filling and topping
- 2 tsp gelatin
- 2 tbsp water
- 12 oz/350 g strawberries
- 8 oz/225 g ricotta cheese
- 1 tbsp superfine sugar
- 2 tsp crème de fraises de bois (strawberry liqueur)
- confectioners' sugar, for dusting

for the choux
- heaping ¾ cup all-purpose flour
- 2 tbsp unsweetened cocoa
- pinch of salt
- 6 tbsp unsalted butter
- 1 cup water
- 2 eggs, plus 1 egg white, beaten

1 Sprinkle the gelatin over the water in a heatproof bowl. Let it soften for 2 minutes. Place the bowl over a saucepan of simmering water and stir until the gelatin dissolves. Remove from the heat.

2 Place two-thirds of the strawberries in a blender with the ricotta, sugar, and liqueur. Process until blended. Add the gelatin and process briefly. Transfer the mousse to a bowl, cover with plastic wrap, and chill for 1–1½ hours, until set.

3 Meanwhile, make the choux. Line a baking sheet with parchment paper. Sift together the flour, cocoa, and salt. Put the butter and water into a heavy-bottom saucepan and heat gently until the butter has melted.

4 Preheat the oven to 425°F/220°C. Remove the saucepan from the heat and add the flour, cocoa, and salt all at once, stirring well until the mixture leaves the sides of the saucepan. Let cool slightly.

5 Gradually beat the eggs into the flour paste and continue beating until it is smooth and glossy. Drop 12 rounded tablespoonfuls of the batter onto the prepared baking sheet and bake for 20–25 minutes, until puffed up and crisp.

6 Remove from the oven and make a slit in the side of each chou. Return to the oven for 5 minutes. Transfer to a wire rack.

7 Slice the remaining strawberries. Cut the choux in half, divide the mousse and strawberry slices among them, then replace the tops. Dust lightly with confectioners' sugar and place in the refrigerator. Serve within 1½ hours.

Chocolate Brownies

Makes 12

ingredients
- butter, for greasing
- ⅓ cup chopped unsweetened pitted dates
- ⅓ cup chopped plumped dried plums (prunes)
- 6 tbsp unsweetened apple juice
- 4 eggs, beaten
- 1½ cups dark brown sugar
- 1 tsp vanilla extract
- ¼ cup low-fat hot cocoa mix, plus extra for dusting
- 2 tbsp unsweetened cocoa
- 1⅓ cups all-purpose flour
- ⅓ cup semisweet dark chocolate chips

for the icing
- 1 cup confectioners' sugar
- 1–2 tsp water
- 1 tsp vanilla extract

1 Preheat the oven to 350°F/180°C. Grease and line a 7 x 11-inch/18 x 28-cm cake pan with parchment paper. Place the dates and dried plums in a small saucepan and add the apple juice. Bring to a boil, cover, and simmer for 10 minutes, until soft. Beat to form a smooth paste, then let stand to cool.

2 Place the cooled fruit in a mixing bowl and stir in the eggs, sugar, and vanilla extract. Sift in the hot cocoa mix, and flour, and fold in along with the chocolate chips until well incorporated.

3 Spoon the batter into the prepared pan and smooth over the top. Bake in the preheated oven for 25–30 minutes, until firm to the touch or until a skewer inserted into the center comes out clean. Cut into 12 bars and let cool in the pan for 10 minutes. Transfer to a wire rack to cool completely.

4 To make the icing, sift the sugar into a bowl and mix with enough water and the vanilla extract to form a soft, but not too runny, icing.

5 Drizzle the icing over the chocolate brownies and let set. Dust with the extra hot cocoa mix before serving.

GLOSSARY

THIS GLOSSARY IS NOT INTENDED TO BE EXHAUSTIVE BUT TO PROVIDE A CONCISE GUIDE TO KEY TERMS THAT MAY BE UNFAMILIAR TO A BEGINNER. SOME OF THE BASIC COOKING TECHNIQUES AND INGREDIENTS, INCLUDING SEVERAL OUTLINED EARLIER IN THIS BOOK, ARE LISTED HERE FOR EASE OF REFERENCE.

A

Agar (Also agar agar); thickening and setting agent made from seaweed. A vegetarian alternative to gelatin.

Al dente Italian term, literally meaning "at the teeth," indicating desired texture of cooked pasta, soft on the outside but still firm and not overcooked inside.

Antipasto Italian term, literally meaning "before pasta," denoting a hot or cold appetizer or "hors d'oeuvre."

Arborio rice Medium- to long-grain type of rice, from Northern Italy, that is ideal for risotto because it absorbs liquid while retaining a firm texture.

Arrowroot Starch extract of maranta root used to thicken sauces.

Aspic Clear jelly made from clarified meat, fish, or vegetable stock mixed with gelatin. It is used to glaze or protect meat, fish, and other foods or for savory dishes set in a mold.

B

Bain-marie Method of cooking ingredients where they are placed in a dish, which is in turn placed in a shallow container of water and is gently heated in an oven or on a stove. This is used to melt ingredients, such as chocolate, without burning them.

Baking powder Leavening agent used in baking cakes, cookies, and breads. It usually contains baking soda, tartaric acid, and dried starch or flour for absorbing moisture.

Balsamic vinegar Dark brown vinegar from Italy, made from fermented, reduced white grape juice and aged in wooden barrels.

Basmati rice Small but long-grain type of rice grown in the Himalayan foothills. It is a creamy yellow with a nutty flavor and aroma.

Basting Spooning or brushing food with melted fat or stock during cooking to add flavor and color and to prevent the food from drying out.

Bay leaf Aromatic herb used for flavoring meat, casseroles, and soups, often in a bouquet garni.

Béarnaise sauce French sauce made from reduced vinegar, white wine, tarragon, black peppercorns, and shallots, finished with egg yolks and butter.

Béchamel sauce Basic French, smooth white sauce made from flour stirred into a mixture of milk and butter.

Beurre manié French term meaning "kneaded butter," a mixture of flour and softened butter, used to thicken sauces.

Bisque Thick, rich soup, made with cream and usually shellfish.

Black butter Butter cooked over low heat until dark brown and usually flavored with vinegar or lemon juice, capers, and parsley.

Black pepper Dried whole peppercorn, which is often crushed or ground to add flavor to food.

Blanching Technique of plunging food into boiling water, then placing in cold water to stop the cooking process. This is used to loosen skins, or preserve color and flavor.

Blind baking Partially baking a pastry shell before the filling is added. This involves baking the pastry with a foil or paper lining and weighing down with pie weights or dried beans. It avoids overbaking the pastry or making its bottom too moist when the filling is added.

Borscht Eastern European soup made with beet, cabbage, and/or other vegetables and served hot or cold with sour cream.

Bouillabaisse Fish stew from southern France.

Bouquet garni Small group of herbs, usually parsley, bay leaf, and thyme, tied together and used to flavor soups, casseroles, and stocks in cooking, but removed before serving.

Brochette Cubes of meat or fish, and vegetables, cooked on a skewer.

Buttermilk Sour-tasting liquid remaining when milk has been churned to butter. It is often used in biscuits and soda breads.

C

Calvados Northern French dry liqueur made from distilled hard cider and used to flavor meat dishes.

Canapés Small appetizers, often served with drinks.

Capers Sun-dried flower buds of a shrub from the Mediterranean and parts of Asia. They need to be rinsed to remove excess salt or brine, and are used to provide a piquant flavor to sauces or condiments, or as a garnish.

Caramelizing Heating sugar until it melts and turns brown, resetting as a hard glaze, or cooking chopped fruit or vegetables in water and sugar until they brown and glaze.

Cayenne pepper Ground spice with a hot flavor, made from the flesh and seeds of chile pepper.

Chantilly cream Sweetened whipped heavy cream, often flavored with vanilla, used as a topping for desserts, or folded into custards or cream for fillings.

Chiffonade Thin strips of shredded vegetables (usually sorrel or lettuce), used raw or lightly sautéed, often as a garnish.

Chile Chile peppers are small, come in many varieties, and are characterized by their extremely hot seeds and flesh. Their potency can be reduced by removing their seeds, but this must be done carefully. It is important to avoid touching sensitive skin or eyes when handling chiles and to wash your hands thoroughly immediately afterward.

Chinois Conical, fine-meshed strainer used to strain soups and sauces.

Choux pastry Light, double-cooked pastry used to make cakes and buns. It has a hard, crisp exterior and a hollow inside.

Clarified butter Unsalted butter heated slowly to evaporate the water content, and then strained to separate the milk solids. The clarified butter can then be used for cooking at higher temperatures than normal butter without burning.

Compote Dish of fruit, slowly cooked whole or in sugar.

Cornstarch Fine, white, powdered starch extract of corn, used to thicken sauces. To stop it from forming lumps, the cornstarch should be mixed with twice its weight in cold liquid before being added to the sauce, which should be continuously stirred until it boils.

Coulis Thick, smooth vegetable or fruit sauce served hot or cold.

Court-bouillon Spiced stock commonly used for cooking fish, seafood, or vegetables.

Crème anglaise French term for rich custard cream, made with sugar, egg yolks, and milk and flavored with vanilla; it is served hot or cold with dessert.

Crème fraîche French term for a thickened, tangy-flavor cream made from pasteurized cow's milk.

Croutons Small cubes of broiled, toasted, or fried bread, which are then drained and cooled. Used to garnish salads or soups.

Crudités Raw seasonal vegetables, sometimes sliced or grated, usually served as an appetizer with a dipping sauce.

Custard A smooth mixture of eggs and milk that can be used as the basis for a savory or sweet sauce or dish.

D

Dariole Small, steep-side cylindrical mold for shaping pastry, or the pastry cooked in it.

Daube French dish of red meat, vegetables, and seasoning, slowly braised in a red wine stock, or meat, vegetables, or fish cooked in a similar way.

Dauphinoise (à la) French term referring to the method of slowly baking in an oven with cream and garlic (such as potatoes).

Dropping consistency Required consistency of cake batter, where it reluctantly falls from the spoon.

E

Emulsifying Combining fats (for instance, butter or oil) and vinegar or citric juices together with a binding agent, such as egg yolk.

Entrecôte French term, meaning "between the ribs," referring to a tender section of beef cut from the sirloin.

Escalope French term for scallop, a thin slice of meat or fish, often flattened for quick cooking.

Extract or Essence Concentrated extract or oil from foods, such as fish, almonds, vanilla, coffee beans, or various plants, used to flavor foods.

F

Fines herbes French term referring to a mixture of chopped aromatic herbs, usually chervil, tarragon, parsley, and chives, used to flavor dishes.

Flaky pastry Crumbly pastry usually used for sweet or savory pies and tarts.

Florentine In the style of a dish from Florence, usually referring to dishes served on a bed of cooked spinach. It is also a small cookie of dried fruit and nuts, usually coated in chocolate on one side.

French dressing Cold sauce, made from olive oil and wine vinegar, seasoned with herbs and salt and pepper, and used to dress salads.

Fricassee Stew made from lightly frying white meat, such as chicken, and then cooking it in a white sauce with vegetables.

Fritter Piece of meat, fish, or vegetable coated in batter and deep-fried until crisp and cooked.

Fromage frais Fresh, soft, low-fat cheese made from cow's milk.

G

Galangal Spice related to ginger and used in Southeast Asian cooking for flavor.

Garam masala Mixture of dry-roasted, ground spices, including cumin, coriander, and turmeric, mixed to form a paste, or added to a dish for flavor just before the end of cooking.

Gelatin Setting agent derived from the protein of animal bones, used to set sweet or savory jellies or thicken soups. Agar is a vegetarian alternative, derived from red algae.

Ghee Type of clarified butter with a nutty, caramel-like flavor, created by simmering until the milk solids turn brown. It can be used for sautéing or frying at higher temperatures than normal butter without burning.

Gluten Flour protein that gives dough its elasticity and strength when mixed with water.

Granita Italian sorbet made from sweetened syrup flavored with coffee or liqueur and often served as a refreshment.

Gratin Any dish topped with cheese or breadcrumbs, mixed with pieces of butter, and heated until crisp and brown.

Gravy Sauce made from meat juices, mixed with a stock, wine, or milk and thickened with flour. Also refers to the juices remaining in the pan after meat, fish, or poultry has been cooked.

Griddle Flat, shallow, cast-iron pan for cooking food, such as pancakes, on a stove.

Grill pan Similar to a griddle but with ridges; used for grilling meats, often creating a striped pattern.

H

Harissa North African paste with a very hot flavor, made from chiles, garlic, cumin, coriander, mint, and oil. It is usually served with couscous, and is used to flavor soups and stews.

Herbes de Provence Mixture of herbs traditionally used in the Provence region of southern France, usually consisting of basil, bay, marjoram, oregano, parsley, rosemary, tarragon, and thyme.

Hoisin sauce Thick, reddish brown, sweet, spicy Chinese sauce, made from a mixture of soybeans, garlic, chile peppers, and spices, commonly used as a table condiment or flavoring.

Hollandaise Rich, creamy, and smooth sauce made from egg yolks, butter, and lemon juice, and usually served on vegetables, fish, or egg dishes.

Horseradish Herb grown for its leaves (for salads) and root. The pungent, spicy root is peeled and grated, and used to flavor sauces.

I

Infusing Imbuing a liquid (usually hot or boiling) with the flavors of herbs, spices, tea, or coffee, by leaving them to steep in the liquid.

J

Jambalaya Spicy Creole rice dish traditionally including ham, sausage, chiles, and tomatoes, but can also consist of any kind of meat, poultry, or shellfish.

Julienne Shredded or thinly cut vegetables or citrus zest, commonly used as a garnish.

Jus French term for "juice," referring to fruit or vegetable extract, or juice from meat.

K

Kedgeree Traditional British breakfast dish, originally deriving from India, consisting of rice, flaked fish (usually smoked haddock), and hard-cooked eggs.

Kneading Stretching and mixing dough by hand or mechanically, to make it smoother, softer, more elastic, and pliable. The movement helps the gluten strands in the dough to stretch and enables the dough to retain gas bubbles and rise when cooked.

L

Lardons Small chunks of fatty bacon or pork fat used to flavor dishes.

Lemongrass Root used in Southeast Asian (especially Thai) cooking to impart a lemon flavor to sweet or savory dishes.

Lyonnaise (à la) French term describing dishes including chopped onions. Lyonnaise sauce is made with sautéed onions and white wine and is then strained. It is usually served with meat or poultry dishes.

M

Mace Pungent spice made from the outer membrane of nutmeg, used to flavor various sweet and savory dishes.

Macerating Soaking fruit in a liquid, such as brandy, to soften and add flavor.

Madeleine Small, buttery yellow cake, made with sugar, flour, butter, and eggs, usually flavored with lemon or almonds.

Marinating Soaking food in a seasoned liquid mixture, or marinade (usually containing oil, lemon or wine, herbs, and spices), to tenderize and add flavor.

Marinière (à la) French term meaning "in the style of a mariner," referring to cooking shellfish, or

other seafood, in white wine and herbs. It can also refer to a dish garnished with mussels.

Mascarpone Thick, creamy, and soft Italian cheese used in savory and sweet dishes.

Mayonnaise Thick, creamy dressing made from oil, egg yolks, vinegar or lemon juice, and seasoning.

Meringue Light, sweet dessert made by beating egg whites and sugar together stiffly and baking.

Meunière (à la) French term meaning "in the style of a miller's wife," referring to the method of cooking where the food (usually fish) is coated in flour, then shallow-fried in butter.

Mille-feuille French term for "a thousand leaves," referring to a dessert made from puff pastry, whipped cream, jam, and fruit.

Miso Paste made from soybeans and used as a flavoring in Japanese cookery, including soups, sauces, and dressings.

Molasses By-product of refining sugar, molasses is a thick, dark syrup with a slightly bitter flavor.

Mornay sauce Béchamel sauce with grated cheese (usually Gruyère or Parmesan) added, often served with fish, egg, or vegetable dishes.

Mustard Plant that has seeds with a piquant taste; used in whole, ground, or powdered form as a flavoring for seasonings, dressings, sauces, and accompaniments.

N

Navarin French stew made from lamb or mutton, potatoes, and other vegetables.

Noodles Thin pasta strips, made with flour and water, and egg or egg yolk.

O

Olive oil Rich oil extracted from pressed olives, used for shallow-frying, dressings, marinades, and baking. Extra virgin olive oil is the purest form of the oil, which is taken from the first pressing of the olives.

P

Pancetta Italian bacon cured with salt and spices and used to flavor pasta, rice, soup, or salad dishes.

Panna cotta Italian term meaning "cooked cream," referring to a cold dessert made from a set custard of cream and gelatin, often flavored with vanilla or caramel.

Papillote (en) French term meaning "in a parcel," referring to a method of cooking food in a folded parcel of wax paper to protect it from the high heat of the oven and help it retain moisture and flavor.

Parboiling Boiling food until halfway cooked, in preparation for adding to other ingredients with shorter cooking times or to tenderize the food before roasting (as with potatoes).

Parmesan Hard, dry cheese, made from skim cow's milk, with a rich, sharp taste and used grated, usually after cooking, to flavor a dish, especially pasta and sauces.

Passata Smooth Italian-style tomato sauce, similar to a prepared tomato puree.

Pasta Italian for "paste," referring to the dough made from durum-wheat semolina, water, and sometimes egg. Pasta comes in a variety of shapes and sizes and is served with sauces or soups.

Pectin Natural gelling agent extracted from ripe fruit and vegetables, and used in making jams and jellies.

Pesto Italian term meaning "pounded," referring to a green sauce made from a blend of pine nuts, fresh basil, Parmesan cheese, garlic, and olive oil. It is most commonly served with pasta or as a dressing.

Phyllo pastry Sometimes called filo pastry, thin layers of pastry dough, often used in Greek or Middle Eastern dishes, which dry out and cook quickly.

Pita Middle Eastern flat, hollow bread made from white flour or whole wheat flour. It is usually served with fillings or to accompany spicy dishes and various dips.

Polenta An Italian cornmeal porridge, which can be eaten either hot or, when cooled and firm, fried.

Prosciutto Italian term for a ham that has been seasoned, salt-cured, and air dried, and served thinly sliced, traditionally as an appetizer.

Pureeing Grinding or mashing fruit or vegetables to form a smooth paste; this is done manually by pressing the food through a strainer, or mechanically in a food processor or blender.

Q

Quenelle Small dumpling made from seasoned, ground meat, fish, or vegetables, bound with eggs and usually poached in stock.

Quiche Open pastry tart, usually filled with an egg and milk custard and savory ingredients.

Quinoa Small, beadlike grain, very rich in protein and mild in taste, which is cooked and served like rice.

R

Ragoût Thick, well-seasoned French stew consisting of meat, poultry, fish, or vegetables, flavored with wine.

Ratatouille French vegetable stew consisting of eggplants, zucchini, tomatoes, onions, bell peppers, and garlic simmered in olive oil.

Reducing Boiling an uncovered liquid, such as stock, wine, or sauce, quickly to reduce its volume by evaporation, thicken it, and concentrate the flavors.

Relaxing Leaving pastry to "rest" after rolling in order to prevent it from shrinking.

Ricotta Rich, creamy, smooth Italian cheese made from ewe's milk curd, used in many Italian dishes and as a stuffing for pasta.

Rissole Sweet or savory round pastry, filled with chopped meat or fish, and breadcrumbs, and cooked by frying or baking.

Risotto Italian rice dish, made by gradually mixing hot stock and rice during cooking so that the rice absorbs the liquid. Traditionally, Arborio rice, a type of risotto rice, is used because of its capacity to absorb liquid and retain a firm texture.

Rösti Swiss term meaning "crisp and golden," referring to a flat, round pancake of shredded potato, shallow-fried on both sides until crisp and brown.

Rouille French term meaning "rust," referring to a hot, chile-flavored red sauce usually served as a garnish with fish or fish stews.

Roulade French term, referring to a sweet or savory rolled dish. The savory dish may be a slice of meat, poultry, or fish rolled around a stuffing, while the sweet dish is usually a filled and rolled cake.

Roux Mixture of flour and fat, slowly cooked over low heat, and used as a base for soups and sauces to thicken them.

S

Saffron Pungent and aromatic spice, yellow in color, and available in whole or powdered form, which is used for coloring and flavoring dishes. The spice is derived from the stigmas of the saffron crocus and is very expensive.

Salsa Spanish and Mexican term meaning "sauce," and specifically referring to a spicy, hot-flavored, thick relish made from chiles and fruit, and served cold.

Salt Sodium chloride crystals, used for seasoning and preserving food. It is available in various forms, including sea salt and rock salt, from which cooking and table salt are derived.

Samosa Indian triangle-shape pastry, filled with spiced meat or vegetables, and deep-fried.

Satay Indonesian specialty, consisting of meat, fish, or poultry cubes, broiled on a skewer, and usually served with a spicy sauce.

Scaling Removing the scales from a fish by scraping the back of a knife along its surface, from the tail to the head.

Shucking To remove the edible part of food from its outer casing, such as corn from its husk, or removing an oyster from its shell, using a small knife with a thick blade.

Sirloin Premium cut of tender beef, from the back, available as a steak.

Smoothie Thick, smooth and cold drink made from blending fruit or vegetables, often with liquids, such as water, milk, or ice cream.

Sorbet Smooth, semifrozen water ice mixed with fruit juice or liqueur, and sometimes egg white or gelatin, and commonly served as a dessert.

Soy sauce Sauce commonly used in Chinese and Japanese cooking, made from fermented and boiled soybeans. It is used to flavor sauces, soups, marinades, meat, fish, and vegetables.

Stock Flavored, strained liquid made by cooking meat, fish, poultry, and vegetables, with seasoning, in water, used for flavoring sauces, soups, stews, or braised dishes.

Sweating Method of cooking ingredients, usually vegetables, in a little fat, slowly over low heat so that they cook in their own steam without browning.

T

Tabasco sauce Hot-flavored, spicy sauce made from Tabasco chile peppers, vinegar, and salt, and used to add flavor to sauces, meat, or cocktails.

Tapenade Thick French paste made from black olives, capers, anchovies, lemon juice, olive oil, and herbs, used to flavor sauces, marinades, stews, pasta, or meat.

Tarte Tatin French apple tart made in a shallow dish by covering butter, sugar, and apples with a pastry topping and baking until the ingredients caramelize. The tart is served upside down.

Terrine Pâté cooked in a small, fat-lined, deep-sided dish (also called terrine), and usually made from pieces of fish or meat.

Timbale Dish cooked in a mold (also called timbale), consisting of layers, usually of rice and vegetables.

Tisane Infusion of herbs in boiling water, drunk hot.

Tofu This is made from the curd of the soybean, pressed into firm, cheeselike blocks. It is bland in flavor but rich in iron and protein.

Commonly used in Asian dishes, it can be cooked in soups, stir-fries, casseroles, or sauces. The flavor is improved by marinating.

Turmeric Spice derived from the root of a ginger-related plant, with a yellow color and bitter taste, used in Asian cooking to add color and flavor.

V

Vanilla Sweet and fragrant flavoring extracted from the dried beans and seeds of the vanilla orchid, and used to flavor sweet and savory foods.

Vichyssoise Rich and creamy soup, served cold, made from potatoes, leeks, and cream, and garnished with chopped chives.

Vinaigrette Cold sauce made from a mixture of vinegar, oil, and seasoning, normally used as a dressing for green salads or other cold dishes.

W

White sauce Basic smooth sauce, also known as Béchamel, made from flour stirred into a mixture of milk and butter.

Y

Yeast Microscopic, live fungus that converts its food, through fermentation, into carbon dioxide and alcohol, so is used in making bread to make dough rise, or in brewing to make alcohol.

Z

Zabaglione Italian frothy dessert made by whisking egg yolks, wine, and sugar together, while heating gently, and is served slightly warm.

Zest Fragrant outer rind of citrus fruit, grated or shredded and used to add flavor or as a garnish or decoration for a dish.

INDEX